TWICE OVER LIGHTLY

Twice Over Lightly
NEW YORK THEN AND NOW

HELEN HAYES
&
ANITA LOOS

HARCOURT BRACE JOVANOVICH, INC., NEW YORK

ISBN 0-15-192150-4
Library of Congress Catalog Card Number: 72-75417
Printed in the United States of America

E

ONTENTS

$\mathscr{I}$LLUSTRATIONS

(Following page 184)

Helen Hayes in *Happy Birthday*

At the South Street Seaport Museum

In the Children's Ward of Bellevue Hospital
with Nurse Betty Kauffman

The tugboat *Martha Moran* with garbage scows

The Atlas Barber School

Ophelia de Vore's Charm School

Christmas at Rockefeller Center

Inspecting the armor at the Metropolitan Museum with Leo Lerman

The United Nations Gardens

Luncheon of the Friends of George Spelvin

Puerto Rican Market in Spanish Harlem

TWICE OVER LIGHTLY

"GOOD LORD,"

SAID AL HIRSCHFELD

$\mathcal{G}$ood Lord," said Al Hirschfeld, "what have you two got in common?"

Al was speaking about us—Helen Hayes and me—for he had just heard we were writing a book together. Al has known us individually for years and, being the foremost caricaturist of show business, he has always revealed an almost uncanny understanding of personality. But Al's question may have been prompted by the fact that he had seldom seen us together. Al, like Helen, is hypnotized by the theatre. She adores every phase of stagecraft, from a first rehearsal to a closing night. When she's not at work, she spends a great deal of time seeing plays or going to theatrical parties. She sparkles in the camaraderie, persiflage, and small talk that sweeten those events. She doesn't even dodge Judas kisses or balk at the backlash kind that accompany greetings between show folks who mostly can't stand each other.

On the other hand I, who have made much of my living in show business, am rather like a violinist who hates music. I wish I were more like Helen, but the bright gloss of people I meet at parties is frequently tarnished by the skulduggery I happen to know about them—and in show business skulduggery reaches a high perfection. So, while Helen is holding forth brilliantly at parties, I stay at home in company with some honest old cynic like Anthony Trollope.

My first connection with Helen is one she remembers well but I had almost forgotten until she nudged my memory. It occurred in 1927, at a time when I was caught up in the brouhaha of putting my book, *Gentlemen Prefer Blondes*, on stage as a play. (In later

3

years it became a movie, a musical movie, and a musical comedy.) The play had been acquired by a Broadway producer, Edgar Selwyn, and he was having his problems trying to cast the heroine. There were any number of real live prototypes of her on Broadway, but a high order of acting is required to play a dumb blonde without being monotonous.

Now Selwyn had been approached by two youthful stage stars who had recently been married and they brought him the news that they'd found exactly the right actress for the role . . . little Helen Hayes. She had just been raised to stardom playing a tragic young Southern belle in *Coquette,* but Mr. and Mrs. Alfred Lunt assured Selwyn that she was also a comedienne of rare talent.

As author, I wasn't consulted about the casting of my play, but Selwyn and my husband, who, following the tradition of Broadway husbands, was managing my affairs, rejected Helen hands down. I vaguely remember Selwyn saying, "Little Helen Hayes couldn't even approach that character. Why, she's a virgin!"

So Helen's connection with me began with heartbreak. And she had the chagrin of seeing a role she coveted go to a young actress who was anything but a virgin. There was a bitchy story about her current around Broadway. When she was about to be married, she had approached Tallulah Bankhead in wide-eyed innocence and asked, "When a girl marries, what can she do to prevent getting pregnant?" And Tallulah had answered, throatily, "Just what you're doing now, my dear!"

Many years later I came to realize that Helen could play anything, even the most hilarious comedy. I saw her take the stage at the Théâtre Sarah Bernhardt in Paris and deliver a comic monologue in *The Skin of Our Teeth* as well as Jack Benny, Bob Hope, or any great stand-up comedian could. And only recently she won an Academy Award for the outrageous scalawag she played in the movie *Airport.*

The girl chosen to play Lorelei Lee in *Gentlemen Prefer Blondes* was a competent actress and she got away with the part.

4

But I now realize that had it gone to Helen, she would have given it that extra dimension which separates art from adequacy.

The early encounters Helen and I had in New York in the Twenties centered about the Algonquin Hotel, and here again our paths diverged. Helen was steered into that group of self-styled wits which called itself "The Round Table." They met at lunch every day and, from my point of view, were a boring set of exhibitionists. I avoided The Round Table as if it were a swamp, for in those days I was a devotee of H. L. Mencken, George Jean Nathan, Joe Hergesheimer, and Theodore Dreiser, from whom I took my prejudice against The Round Table. There were three people close to that clique, however, who disarmed even me. They were the Broadway wits and playboys Charlie MacArthur, Bob Benchley, and Ben Hecht, Musketeers of the Twenties who free-wheeled about town dipping into everything. And, as they were much too amiable to withstand the advances of The Round Table group, they sometimes joined it.

When Charlie fell in love with Helen, a recurrent question went the rounds of Broadway: "How could a sophisticate like Charlie MacArthur ever have been attracted to that naïve little Hayes girl?" It was a question which, in due time, I managed to answer. Helen has two qualities that have always been overshadowed by her acting talent. She was as graceful a ballroom dancer as the great Irene Castle herself—an accomplishment that made her vastly popular with the collegiate set.

Charlie, however, was no dancing man. In the process of wooing Helen, he had even flunked a course at Arthur Murray's. But he was a very special connoisseur of a certain something that Helen had in common with Jean Harlow: an exceptional fitness to wear décolleté. On reminding Helen of this, she modestly disclaimed it as a reason for Charlie's devotion. "No, Anita, more than anything else, he needed me to listen while he talked big. That Algonquin crowd was as hard on each other as they were on everybody else. It was dangerous to expose anyone's dream to the

5

death rays of their 'sophistication.' A fellow needed a starry-eyed listener like me."

At any rate, Charlie introduced his shy little fiancée to The Round Table, and Helen, who lacked my sour viewpoint, accepted such phony intellectuals as Alec Woollcott at their own valuation. In those days, I felt that Helen could be hypnotized by fourflushers and made to see them as they see themselves. In one word, adorable. So Helen's allegiance to The Round Table lengthened the distance between us, which was rather long in the first place.

While very few of Helen's favorite friends are friends of mine, without exception any friend I have is cherished by Helen. It is the plain, astonishing truth that in Helen's eyes most of humanity is lovable.

I admired Charlie's outrageous wit and we were good pals from our very first meeting. So after he married Helen, I became a regular visitor at their home. It was then I really came to know Helen, to realize that underneath her sentimental, homespun exterior she had a rollicking Irish sense of humor. How else could she have held on to Charlie, when even the world-renowned cleverness of Dorothy Parker had failed?

The event that really cemented our friendship took place one day in 1940. Charlie had taken the two of us to lunch at Twenty-One, during which Helen began to complain about two eminent ladies she had been portraying: Queen Victoria and Harriet Beecher Stowe. "I'm afraid of getting to be grandiose," she said and turning to me asked, "Why don't you write me a really rowdy part, where I can kick up my heels?"

As a matter of fact, I had had a play in mind for some time that concerned just such a character. I'd never before connected her with Helen, but now I did.

"How would you like to play a drunk?" I inquired.

Charlie pricked up his ears at once, but Helen looked a trace bewildered.

"Did you say a . . . drunk?" she asked.

"How about a frustrated old maid," I went on, "a teetotaler who is against anyone ever having fun? But she gets gloriously tight one evening and during a twelve-hour bender becomes an understanding and sympathetic human being?"

"That would be fine!" said Helen. "Go ahead and write it."

I was under contract at M-G-M at the time, writing movies, but while waiting for a conference with Irving Thalberg I had plenty of time to write *Happy Birthday*.

Before it went into rehearsal, friends warned Helen and me that doing a play together was hazardous; even Charlie felt it might end our beautiful friendship. When anyone suggested that he write a play for his bride Charlie's answer was, "Marriage is strewn with enough land mines as it is." So while Charlie desisted, I rushed in where angels fear to tread. But it turned out that Charlie was wrong; people who know their jobs seldom fight. We had both been pros since the age of seven.

What I admire most in life is an expert; *any* expert. An expert is a complete human being, at the top of his form. I believe I have as great respect for a master piano tuner as I feel for a genius like Duke Ellington. Helen's rating as an expert came to full flower at a time when Rodgers and Hammerstein, who produced *Happy Birthday*, ordered changes in the script which I felt were wrong. I consulted Helen, who agreed with me, but she decided the only way to prove we were right was to go ahead and make those changes. They were disastrous and lasted for only one performance. As an expert who not only knew *her* job, but could understand mine even better than our eminent producers, Helen became pretty special in my eyes.

But even a superlative actress like Helen has her faults, the most common being a tendency to lose important and unimportant items. (When Noël Coward wrote "Don't Put Your Daughter on the Stage, Mrs. Worthington," all he needed to know about *Miss* Worthington was that she could return from posting a letter without losing her gloves.)

An actress friend of ours who is a different type of loser from Helen is Paulette Goddard. While Paulette can hold on to a vast fortune in jewels, furs, art objects, real estate, stocks and bonds, she invariably loses a pencil. This prompted one of her admirers to give her a gold one set with a ten-carat diamond. Had that pencil been Helen's, she could have lost it in quick order, but Paulette hangs on to it with a firm grip.

Helen's sense of values generally towers above material loss. Losing things distresses Helen no more than I resent helping to look for them because, during the search, we can always chatter.

I recall a day in London when Helen was scheduled to take off for Moscow the next morning. She had just finished a movie in which she played the Russian Dowager Empress who took umbrage at the Communists for murdering her family, so it would be tough enough for Helen to get into Russia even *with* a passport. A circumstance of this type gave Helen such a chance to lose something really important that she simply couldn't resist. She lost her passport.

Well, the two of us spent a long day scurrying about London in taxis until, at His Majesty's Bureau for Lost Articles, we finally tracked down her passport. But by that time, Helen figured it had caused as much inconvenience and frustration as she could get from a trip to the U.S.S.R. itself, so the two of us bounced off to Paris instead.

In addition to our work together, our fun, and the many holiday trips we've taken, Helen and I have been through some pretty rugged times. Yet even these difficult periods are, at least in recall, punctuated with unexpected humor.

During the several years when Charlie was desperately ill, Helen trusted me to watch over him when she had to be in the theatre. Shortly before he died, she was acting at the Palm Beach Playhouse and I was their house guest. One night, when I was left alone with Charlie, he suddenly lapsed into a coma and became so inert that I actually thought it was going to be the end. In a panic, I phoned for a doctor. He arrived at the house and, never having met Charlie, was tremendously in awe of his distinguished patient.

After examining Charlie, the doctor beckoned me into the adjoining room to tell me of a problem. The hospital he was affiliated with was allied to a church and he didn't want to take Charlie there if his religious precepts might conflict. "What is Mr. Mac-Arthur's faith?" the doctor asked. I was somewhat reluctant to report that Charlie didn't have any faith at all, so I suggested that he try to rouse Charlie and ask him.

The doctor gently shook Charlie and asked, "Mr. MacArthur, what is your religious faith?"

Charlie opened one weak eyelid and answered, "I am a phallic worshiper." At which he slipped back into his coma and, for all I know, that square old doctor may still be in a state of shock.

Even the extremes of grief seem colored by a sort of black humor that no one but Charlie could have achieved. Many times during his long illness, Charlie admonished Helen to spare him the "barbaric ordeal" of a funeral. "If you do that to me," he threatened, "I'll haunt you!"

But the day after Charlie left us, Helen called me in great distress. "I may be doing something terrible to Charlie," she said, "but I just can't deny the plea of all those friends who want a chance to say good-by to him." Helen had consulted Ben Hecht, who agreed with her, so she asked if he would read a farewell message to his old friend.

Those last rites were held at Campbell's, that genteel institution on Madison Avenue and 81st Street, where tears have been shed for so many colorful New Yorkers. In deference to his pal, Ben's eulogy was anything but sad. However, in the midst of it, a large floral piece that hung on a curtain behind Ben started for some uncanny reason to sway back and forth. Helen and I watched it aghast, each of us thinking it might be Charlie expressing his disapproval.

So, in spite of Helen's ever ready sentiment and my tough cynicism, we have been brought together at even the worst of times by the saving grace of humor.

Have I answered your question, Al Hirschfeld?

KEEPING UP WITH HELEN

*T*here's a big difference between an idea and a notion. An idea can lead to something; a notion gets you nowhere. When Helen suggested taking a close look at New York, I felt it was a notion and would have let it blow over. Not Helen! She figuratively grabbed me by the nose and led me off on a trip that lasted eighteen months and never took us away from home.

After the more than forty years we've spent in gossip, Helen and I do most of it over the phone these days. The pressures of modern life have squeezed out the leisure we used to spend together, so we may talk every day without having looked at each other for weeks, which has become typical of life in New York. Sometimes, having just hung up the receiver on an old friend, one may fail to recognize her on the street because she has gotten fat or thin, had her face lifted or been rejuvenated by K.H.3, or, having been a brunette, is now a blonde—an embarrassment that could disappear if the Bell Company would come across with that see-through invention it keeps promising. Even the hazard of having to dash from the bathtub to answer a phone no longer holds good now that nudity has invaded public life.

One day during our nonstop chatter, Helen said, "Tell me, darling, where are you going to spend next summer?" Her question mystified me because, as a creature of habit, I've spent every summer for over thirty years in the same place.

"I'll be in Montecatini, as usual, for my cure."

"Cure for *what*?"

This was a stumper.

"Oh . . . well, arthritis. . . ."

"You've no more arthritis than a lizard! You're just looking for an excuse to get to Italy."

10

Helen was right so I tried to laugh that off, but she wouldn't let me. "So you're running away as if New York were a sinking ship."

I didn't mention the fact that years ago, when Manhattan was safe, clean, and shipshape, she herself had run away to Nyack, where she and Charlie settled after their honeymoon, and Helen hasn't deserted that haven to this day.

"I'm not leaving town for keeps," I argued, "but the whole place may be blown up this summer. Why stick around and try to side-step bombs?"

"Then will you tell me why all our European friends still rave about New York?" she asked.

I suggested that perhaps it was because they see about as much of it as an American tourist sees on a two-week jaunt abroad. "Most of our foreign friends are misled by the sterilized glamour of the Plaza Hotel or the Regency; when they venture into a Broadway theatre or an East Side discotheque, they only see the glitter. What do they really know of this city?" I asked.

"Just about as much as you do!" answered Helen.

I was forced to admit that I knew mighty little. But I couldn't help reminding her that she leaves the theatre after work, gets into a car, and is driven straight to her Nyack hideout, which is about all *she* ever sees of New York.

Guilt caused Helen to change the subject, so now she launched into nostalgia. "I used to think this was the most enthralling place in the world," she said. "I'll bet it still is, and if I were free next summer I could prove it."

There was no opportunity to do that because Helen had set her sights on London for a season of theatregoing. To my mind, this was ill-advised because she desperately needed a rest. She was starring in a revival of *Harvey* with Jimmy Stewart, playing eight performances a week, and at the same time appearing at countless benefits, luncheons, banquets, seminars, and radio and TV interviews. Then as soon as *Harvey* closed, Helen had agreed to make a

11

television documentary that would immortalize her seventieth
birthday the following October.

Helen is that rare type whose vital energy is so great that she
can only be classed as a force of nature. I was certain her TV
stint would drag on interminably. She had had a similar experience in Hollywood, where she'd been talked into playing a cameo
role in the movie *Airport*. The producer had assured Helen she'd
only have to spend two weeks before the cameras. But he was no
fool, and the moment she was hooked to a contract that "cameo"
role began to expand until even Helen felt the physical, mental,
and spiritual exhaustion of five months in Hollywood. In addition
to her job in *Airport*, Helen undertook to fly to Chicago every
weekend to conduct a course in play reading at the University of
Illinois. When film schedules permitted, she went far afield to
accept various awards and honorary degrees—for Helen is to
Academe what Sophia Loren is to sex: catnip.

There had also been private occasions when she flitted off to
Honolulu to play grandma to two young MacArthurs for a weekend. All of which indicates that Helen has never learned how or
when to relax. I assured her she needed Montecatini more than I
did and had better join me at the Hotel Pace, the very name of
which means peace in Italian.

But then it came out that Helen, the eternal do-gooder who likes
nothing more than to lead a troop of Girl Scouts over the Rockies,
had found a new cause. Her fighting Irish spirit had recently been
kindled at a chic luncheon where most of the guests and also the
hostess voiced their detestation of New York. "The filthiest, most
crime-ridden spot in the world," one fashionable New York lady
called it.

Helen instantly blazed out in its defense. "But can't you realize," she demanded, "that our city is so big it's got to have the
most of *everything*? And by the very same token, it's got more
that's good than any place I know!"

At which point, Nella Rubinstein, the beautiful Polish wife of
the great Artur, called out approvingly, "Hear! Hear!" Nella went

on backing Helen up: "Life in Europe is static, confined, and predestined. Here in New York the unexpected happens every day. Whether it's good or bad, it makes you feel alive, young, and involved. And there's no limit to your destiny; here you can be and do anything you're equipped for."

"The only thing that's static in New York," exclaimed Helen, "is the fad of repeating stupid clichés that attack it." She thus closed the topic for that day and succeeded in pooping the party for some very smart members of the jet set.

The next thing I heard about Helen's new cause was when she canceled her trip to London in order to spend the summer at home and take a good, close look at New York. And the mystery of why she had inquired about my plans was solved when she asked, "Why don't you join me?"

As I stalled for time, Helen continued. "The things that used to make our lives here so fascinating haven't disappeared. They're merely buried under a mass of—"

"Garbage," I interrupted, "with the garbage men on strike!"

Helen was not amused. "Do you know any garbage men?" she asked. I didn't. "Neither do I," said Helen. "But if they choose to spend their lives coping with garbage, they must be men of character. Why not meet some of them and find out?" Helen's idea began to have possibilities. "These days you and I never get really to know any new people," she went on. "Why not give this glorious opportunity a grab?"

Thinking of my rendezvous with Montecatini, I reminded Helen of a recent article in the *New York Times* headed: "Fun City, Slob City." Now, I, myself, never read a newspaper that's too heavy to lift, but I have a friend who keeps me supplied with clippings from the *Times* and phones me Grand Guignol tales of our town's horrors. For instance, a friend of hers, age eighty-two, was mugged on Lexington Avenue at 9:00 P.M. and not a single passer-by came to his aid until he was stretched out on the sidewalk with a concussion. Then there was a friend who was attacked in the self-service elevator of her own building. "And crimes like

13

those are so prevalent," she exclaimed, "that the *Times* only gave them a paragraph!"

Now it so happened that I was one up on my doleful friend, for I had just been present at an atrocity that blazed forth in a *front page headline of the Times*. I had been at lunch with Paulette Goddard in the Palm Court at the Plaza Hotel, having gone there because it's quiet and cozy. But, just as we were starting lunch, the son of Chiang Kai-shek entered through the revolving door and a political guerrilla took a shot at him. Paulette and I were sitting right in the line of the bullet, but it skimmed the Palm Court and lodged in the wall behind us without hitting anybody.

My friend who reads the *Times* reminded me that our particular atrocity took place in glamorous surroundings. And that the superb behavior of Chiang Ching-kuo, who looked through his would-be assassins as if they were empty space, gave the episode an Oriental grandeur. "But if you and Helen go into the back streets and alleys of New York," she said, "you're only asking for calamity."

I began to relay those timorous pleas to Helen; said we might be trudging streets that were littered with trash, some of which might be alive and human. We'd probably have to skirt riots, run into muggers, purse snatchers, and dope fiends. But as she airily waved me off I finally felt defeat closing in.

It couldn't have been solely the result of her unquenchable optimism, for even I began to think of arguments for living dangerously. I remembered that in World War II Adèle Astaire had preferred London and the heroic anguish of the Battle of Britain to the shelter of her Irish castle.

Any newspaper photo of a disaster shows the participants grinning as if to say, "I was here! I seen it!" And from our Plaza experience Paulette and I had learned that Nature comes to one's aid in time of peril with a shot of adrenaline that's pretty much like champagne. Paulette's first animated comment after our escape was, "To think we lunched here because it was cozy and then darn near got shot!" For weeks afterward, we had dined out

14

on our adventure and felt pretty smug over our participation in world affairs. Suppose that Stanley and Livingstone had sat at their firesides instead of braving the jungle and creating one of history's most durable wisecracks?

I then began to compare the shocks of our city with the languor of Montecatini, where it takes no effort to survive, while to go through twenty-four hours in New York and still be breathing is a triumph that makes the risk well worth while. So I gave in to Helen.

At the same time I reported, as I always do, to my household manager, guide, and religious consultant, Gladys, to find out if I'd made the right decision. Gladys allowed that New York in the summer might be less fun than Disneyland, but added, "You two gadabouts didn't get shot that day at the Plaza. Don't you think it's about time you had a little Faith?" So, I put my faith in Gladys and prayed that Helen and I might come through the New York summer unscathed.

ABROAD AT HOME

With the farsightedness Helen applies to all her ventures she began collecting guidebooks. Although I find it hard to keep up with her physically, I do my feeble best to go along with her mentally. We read *The City* by Mayor Lindsay, which explains our outdated tax structure. Most city taxes are grabbed by State and Federal governments that never earned them and then spent on rural projects city dwellers never use. "Why is it," Helen asked, "that we Americans are so smart at inventing new things and so stubborn about changing the old things that are bad? I'm sorry for every big city in the nation!"

"I'm sorry for John Lindsay," I ventured. "Operating New York is like running the Waldorf Astoria with a part-time maid."

"And the old place keeps growing all the time," sighed Helen.

"You're lucky to have a hideaway," I told her. "I'd rather be here than not, but it's the same as staying home while your apartment's being painted."

"Right!" Helen said and added with her most disarming grin, "So aren't I smart to sneak out to Nyack?"

We decided to meet before our first venture to make plans. It seemed best to start with lunch, but where? All the exclusive restaurants are jammed by Texans and might be mere extensions of Dallas. "Why not go back to the stamping grounds of our past?" Helen suggested. "Don't you remember some old tavern you haven't seen for ages?"

"Yes, I do!" I exclaimed. "In the old days when Henry Mencken used to come to town, he'd take me down to Whyte's, where they make a specialty of sea food from the Fulton Street fish markets." Even in Mencken's day, Whyte's was a time-honored institution. Moreover, Menck was a native of Baltimore, which is one of the gourmet centers of our nation. So when he invaded Manhattan, he was well-practiced in finding the best.

In most cases, the best was unfashionable or even downright shabby. During prohibition Menck used to take us on a breezy ferry ride to Hoboken, where we drank beer that had never been "needled." (For the young who are unfamiliar with "needled" beer, may I close the generation gap by explaining that it began as a legal, nonalcoholic brew which could be bought openly in a grocery store. But then a jot of alcohol was inserted. With luck, the alcohol was potable, made from grain; but if it had a wood basis, one was left blind or otherwise disabled.) Unfortunately, Menck, although seldom tight, was an opportune drinker who carelessly took his liquor where he found it. So did his pals Joe Hergesheimer, Ernest Boyd, and Theodore Dreiser, all of whom left this life much too young. I wonder how many lusty intellects were destroyed while prohibition was making the likes of Carrie Nation happy?

While reminiscing about the past, Helen suddenly remembered a rumor that the Fulton Market was soon to be moved and said dramatically, "This might be the last time we'll see the historic old place."

"Don't forget it's also our *first* time!" I admonished. By then I began to worry about whether Whyte's was still in existence. A look in the phone book proved that it was. So then and there we picked out a starting date for our adventures.

It was early in March and bitterly cold. Being a realist, I dressed for the weather like an Eskimo. Helen, the eternal dreamer, glanced at her calendar in Nyack and conjured up an airy notion that spring was here. If her lightweight clothes hadn't been stashed away in the attic, she might have put on an organdy frock, topped by a straw hat trimmed in field flowers. However, she did wear a turban that might have kept her ears warm if it hadn't ended three inches short of them. So she showed up at my apartment with frosty ears and her teeth chattering. Never mind, enthusiasm was enough to keep Helen warm. We were going to be

17

late for our one o'clock reservation at Whyte's, so we rushed out, miraculously found a taxi on Seventh Avenue, scrambled into it, and started down Broadway.

As our cab approached Howard Street at downtown Broadway, Helen spotted a brand-new red brick octagonal building that was evidently inspired by Philadelphia Federal or New England colonial or just plain Howard Johnson. At any rate, it nestled on a bright green lawn, as it would have done in colonial days. "And," said Helen, "it houses, of all things, a bank! That should silence a few enemies of the Establishment who claim that big business lacks a soul."

From there on for several blocks Broadway flaunted the window displays of wholesale fabric houses. We were on the edge of springtime, and that year's colors looked to me as if they'd been diluted with skimmed milk. But those chalky materials brought forth "oohs" and "ahs" from Helen, the pastel type of blonde. One of her favorite expressions, "yummy," now came into full play.

I had just learned from an eleven-year-old associate a word which is a favorite in the Rabelaisian circles of the fifth grade. This word, the opposite of *yummy*, is *yucky* and should be accompanied by a grimace indicating oncoming nausea. Those fabrics which were yummy to Helen could only be yucky to me, with my preference for navy, Balenciaga brown, and black.

And yet, I know I'm wrong. The great Florenz Ziegfeld himself once told me that diluted shades have a much greater impact on men than basic colors. A girl might just as well go into a nunnery as be chic, which patrons of *haute couture*, like me, never seem to learn. Nothing could better point up the difference between Helen and me than our taste in clothes. She can go into ecstasies over the wholesale product of Seventh Avenue, while my taste runs to the *couture* houses of Mainbocher and Balenciaga.

The area we were entering is a fascinating one—the hub of the community that was once New Amsterdam, the early and still financial capital of the country, the original part—some of the streets here are even now called "slips."

As we came to the neighborhood of Whyte's, we were attracted by an old church on lower Broadway, its yard dotted with aging headstones. Helen was all for investigating at once, but I got her to postpone it until after lunch. Then, turning into Fulton Street, we began to have an eerie feeling that some sort of Spectral Being was guiding us. It first manifested itself when the cab veered away from our destination by mistake. The driver apologized, saying, "I'm sorry, ladies. This here is Theatre Alley."

Any reference to show business makes Helen light up like a flare. She clutched my arm and gasped, *"Theatre Alley! Why, this is Fate!"* She was all for finding some evidence of the show business of long ago, but since food came first with me, she restrained herself. The driver deposited us at the rear of Whyte's.

We went in through the kitchen entrance, recklessly crossed the bar (peopled, of course, by men), and climbed the back stairs into an enormous Ladies' Dining Room on the second floor. Funny that women, the weaker sex, are almost always shunted upstairs. "Let's contribute this thought to the Women's Lib movement," said Helen, "in case it runs out of things to grouse about." I sardonically said, "It won't!" I would more cheerfully back the girls in their move for liberation if it weren't for the fact that women have frequently done me more dirt than men. And the sort of dirt that any woman can contrive makes a man's evildoing seem like a snowdrift.

I had taken the precaution of reserving our table in the name of Helen Hayes, so the maître d'hôtel greeted us heartily and may still be using Helen as a conversation piece. He treated us to a table beside a window looking down on a typical New York jumble of the old and the new. Across Fulton Street is an ancient delicatessen, looking as smoke-cured as a salami, while lording over it is a snack joint of spanking avant-garde décor.

Studying menus that were notable for their length, Helen was tempted by a fattening item of creamed oysters on toast. She is on a "permanent" diet to take off an extra five pounds, so she hesitated, but not for long. And then gave in with one of her favorite clichés: "Oh dear, why can't I have more character?"

I chose crabmeat under a blanket of Russian dressing, which required no character, because it is permitted by the Drinking Man's Diet, to which I am devoted although not the drinking type. Since it includes items generally considered fattening, I can be greedy and, at the same time, keep my normal weight of 92.

We'd no sooner made our choices than Helen had to find a phone (an all-too-frequent habit).

"Oh, Helen! Can't it wait?"

"No!"

"But what's the rush?"

"You'll find out later!" And she whisked away. Looking about, I began to get used to the dim lighting of the great oak-lined room and was able to make out the restaurant art that adorned the walls. Helen, who is a member of the National Arts Council, adores the Hudson River landscapes. Her home is on the banks of the Hudson and she is so obsessed with that river she thinks she owns it. Now Helen returned, her face glowing with satisfaction.

"Well? What about your phone call?"

"That's a surprise. I'll tell you later." She took a pencil from her pocketbook. "Now let's concentrate on our future line of action."

While we were waiting for lunch we discussed an over-all procedure for exploring our town. "Wherever possible, let's walk," said Helen. Some of our happiest memories are of walks we've taken in the past. We've walked for miles around the Chelsea district in London, the ancient Place des Vosges in Paris, long stretches of waterfront in Palm Beach, Nyack on the Hudson, and Santa Monica on the Pacific. Together we discovered some Etruscan tombs in Florence and trudged through the world's fair in Montreal. "And just think," Helen exclaimed, "New York is an unending world's fair at any time or season."

20

Prompted by memory, Helen started to make a list on the back of a menu. But even that lengthy menu was too short for all the things that tempted us.

"We'll just have to pick out the most prominent places," said Helen.

"Better still," I argued, "the *least* prominent places might be more interesting."

"What sort of places?"

I then confessed that while she was studying guidebooks, I was putting a little time in on the Yellow Pages of the phonebook. So I gingerly made a suggestion. "For instance, how about the . . . Atlas Barber School?"

For a moment Helen was stunned and then her whole face lit up. "Really, Anita," she exclaimed, "you never fail me!"

But then she got to thinking. "Wait a minute," she said, "we only have one year.* If we spend time at a barber school it might mean we'd have to neglect places like the Metropolitan Museum." And then Helen added rather suspiciously, "Are you sure you're not really interested in getting to meet a few barbers?"

This might have been true, for barbers rate high on my list of preferences. But just the same I put up an argument. "Think how few people ever visit a barber school," said I, "while there's really nothing new to learn about the Metropolitan Museum."

This gave Helen pause. "Don't you think we might discover a few things there that people don't know about?" she suggested.

"Like what?"

"Well, let's prowl around and see what we can find," said Helen. And then, for my benefit, she added, enticingly, "I'm told they've got some fakes hidden away in the cellar."

Now *my* face lit up. "Really, Helen," I said, "*you* never fail *me!*"

We proceeded to add those two items to our list along with a few others I'd spotted in the Yellow Pages. Helen endorsed all of

* This is where we made our mistake. It took us eighteen months, and even they weren't half enough.

21

them with continuing delight. Then, trying further to be helpful, I asked, "Shouldn't we find ourselves a guide?"

"No," Helen replied, "the best guide in any neighborhood is somebody who lives there. Just trust me to make a few pickups as we go along." This was an excellent idea, for Helen is such an extrovert that she can pick up strangers even when she didn't speak their language.

We agreed to let the weather decide our course, be it outdoors or in. Then, too, we figured that special occasions would always be cropping up: a parade or an impromptu happening such as a riot.

"And let's use the common carriers, Anita—the commoner the better. Subways and buses when possible and taxis for special occasions." Both Helen and my housekeeper Gladys own cars which, in themselves, are pretty common, being heavy-duty station wagons. But we seldom use them because of the difficulty of parking and our Mayor's tow-away policy.

So our plan would simply be to have no plan at all. "Have you noticed, Anita, that the best things always happen in a way you least expect? Like me getting to be an actress."

This led us quite naturally to the New York of our youth. As we looked back, it seemed that even in our teens we had known everyone worth knowing and mixed in every exciting event from the Twenties on.

"Let's not curb our memories," said Helen. "Those old days were so gay, so undisturbed by world chaos, why not tell about them? And, in the meantime, let's feel free to take on New York, as it is today, hit or miss; follow a hunch or a sudden notion and then carry through. The great charm of New York is that it's still unpredictable. Any sidewalk might lead us to something unexpected, something that could exist nowhere else in the world."

She gestured out the window toward Fulton Street and the East River beyond. "Do you realize that one can't look in any direction in Manhattan without seeing water at the end of the street: the Harbor, the Hudson and East Rivers, the Narrows, and even the

Atlantic. Here we are entering the age of Aquarius, the age of water, with New York the wateriest city in the entire world. Yet we, who could be beachcombers on a dozen exciting waterfronts, live here as if we were in the middle of the Sahara!"

At this moment the headwaiter arrived with a couple of assistants to assist in the honor of serving Helen, and we were back where we began.

We quizzed our new friend about the customers who in this ladies' sanctuary were predominantly male. "That's right," said the headwaiter, "most of the working women in this district are too young to appreciate our cuisine." Then he added, with disdain, "They're quite content to eat in lunchrooms."

But there was one couple that deserved consideration. A pink-faced, jolly, and balding man with a pretty girl who had brought along a notebook in which, from time to time, she took a word or two of dictation.

"That notebook is a ruse and an alibi," I stated.

Helen, who dearly loves romance, said, "Let's hope it is!"

The headwaiter informed us that the gentleman was a big shot executive from Westinghouse. "A lot of our patrons work there and at the Telephone Company and the insurance firms in the neighborhood."

Studying the room, Helen remarked that nobody seemed to fit the old cliché of "the tired businessman." They were beaming, relaxed, and completely at home.

"They're probably more at home here than they'll be when they get back to their families," I remarked.

"That may well be, just as an actor's more at home on stage than in the bosom of his family. I think we malign the American businessman. Money isn't his obsession, but the making of it is. The idea that his obsession with work is venal is completely false," said she. "These men can't possibly love money for material reasons. They work so hard they don't have time to spend it. I'm convinced that their devotion to business is unworldly, fanciful, and pure; that they venerate their deals, their advertising campaigns.

23

They expand creatively in their TV commercials, their shiny brochures with fascinating pictures, in color, of the Chairman of the Board."

Helen's encomium was now interrupted, for news had filtered into the kitchen that the lady who had passed through there and looked like Helen Hayes actually *was* Helen Hayes. Whyte's chef appeared to ask for an autograph. He was soon joined by a dozen guests who most unselfishly wanted autographs for some child, grandmother, or arthritic aunt. I always suspect these characters of trying to prove they're above such trivia and thus the peers of the celebrities they badger.

Leaving by the front entrance, Helen grabbed my arm and steered me around toward the rear. "Now I'm going to explain the phone call you were so curious about. I rang up The New-York Historical Society to learn something about Theatre Alley!"

"And so . . ." I inquired, trying to duplicate her interest.

As Helen gestured off toward a row of trash barrels, she might have been declaiming "The Battle Hymn of the Republic": "This is the exact location of the famous old Park Theatre. Folks used to drive here from as far away as the Battery, so an elegant approach was constructed and they called it Theatre Alley!"

Smiling wryly, she added, "The one theatre alley in the U.S.A. I never got to trod." At that, I pulled Helen out of her acute attack of nostalgia and we proceeded west to Broadway, where we had first spotted that old church. We then learned it was St. Paul's Chapel. Prowling through its ancient cemetery, we found some weather-beaten headstones with the inscriptions still legible. One marker read, "Died of the pestilence that struck in 1795." What pestilence? Plague, smallpox, or merely influenza? Why did I say "merely"? If flu is fatal, why are plague and small-pox more so? But even more dramatic was the fact that the poor young victim's name was *Mary Sword*. Today's names are pretty anemic in comparison with those of the eighteenth century. The only one I could think of that might stand up to Mary Sword's is Rip Torn. "How intriguing it would be," I said, "to couple Miss

24

Sword with a man named Rip in the four-poster bed of a sexy historical novel!"

"You and your sex-bitten mind!" chided Helen.

Presently, a blast of icy wind chilled our curiosity and blew us right into the Chapel. Anyone who looks on the religion of colonial times as gloomy would be astonished by the cheery interior of St. Paul's. Sunlight was streaming through enormous window-panes of clear glass; none of those Biblical scenes designed to inspire awe. The Waterford chandeliers, huge though they are, manage to seem dainty. The altar and pulpit are painted ivory, picked out with gold; the walls are pink, the ceiling sky blue. "A perfect color scheme for a young girl's debut party!" said Helen.

She must have been thinking back to the party she and Charlie gave for their own deb daughter, Mary, who outlived it by so short a time. I can always tell when Helen is thinking of Mary because she looks so happy.

She called my attention to the pews. "Look at the fragile woodwork of these partitions, Anita! And these upholstered chairs might belong in a colonial parlor." We inspected George Washington's own pew, where he and Martha knelt in worship on April 30, 1789, following his Inauguration.

Near their pew a small case displays a tiny Bible that once belonged to Sara Pingle. Another early-American name! "I can see Miss Pingle vividly," mused Helen, then forgetting me and our sanctified surroundings, she launched into a series of faces and a prim, period prance up and down the aisle. I felt pretty sure that Helen would one day play some girl very much like Sara Pingle.

By that time we felt warm enough to brave the icy winds of Broadway again. Near the exit we stopped at a stand to pick up post cards and drop coins to pay for them in a slot: evidence of an old-fashioned trust in Christian honesty. As we braced ourselves to step into the cold, Helen stopped for a last glance around the church, where two lone men, seated far apart, seemed to be in moody contemplation. "It always heartens me," she whispered, "that I've never been in a church anywhere in the world, to find it empty of worshipers!" Perhaps they just came in to get warm, I suggested. "Well, I did once see a man in St. Malachy's, the actors' church on 49th Street, reading the *Racing Form*," she confessed as she followed me into Broadway.

Crossing over to Fulton Street, we passed Whyte's and, from then on, seemed to be entering another century. The riverfront was almost deserted; the long row of sheds that houses the fish markets and had been a hotbed of activity at 4:00 A.M. was empty and slicked up as if by some early-American housewife. We noticed only one smidgen of oyster shells in a gutter, but of the odor of fish there was nothing.

We passed Rolfe's Chop House with a window full of time-dulled silver and pewter, and, crossing Gold Street, noticed a battered sign over a grubby storefront, reading "The Brokers Restaurant." There were even brokers in that early day! We decided to investigate, expecting to find an American version of London's Cheshire Cheese, and were peering through the dim glass of the front door when it was jerked open by a young man who asked suspiciously, "Are you ladies looking for something?"

Harking back to the slang of her girlhood, Helen answered brightly, "No, we're just rubbernecking." At which the young man beamed and said, "Help yourself, Ma'am." When caught on the snoop, that term of Helen's is invaluable; people who "rubberneck" are curious in only the most innocent way. Had I said, "We're just casing the joint," I might have wrecked our public relations at "The Brokers."

We entered and found our first summation was right: it actually is an American version of the Cheshire Cheese. But the brokers had all departed, so we thanked the young man and stepped back into the cold. Helen again started to shiver and, accustomed though I am to her monumental vitality, I suggested we look for a cab and call the expedition quits.

But Helen had suddenly spotted a sign on a small building that read "South Street Seaport Museum." "If you think the threat of pneumonia's going to stop me now," said Helen staunchly, "you're only an amateur thinker." At which she barged into the Museum. Not having her fortitude to cope with big museums, I harbor no ill will toward small ones, and here in a museum no larger than Helen's double parlor in Nyack we found records of two centuries of waterfront activity. The lady in charge was working at her desk but, recognizing Helen, offered to be our guide. "Don't let us interfere," said Helen. "We'd adore to wander about on our own."

We found numberless engravings of the clipper ships which brought many of our forefathers to the new world. "My ancestors certainly boarded one of these out of Cobh or Belfast," said Helen. And my own great-great-grandpa even left a description of the clipper that brought him over from England.

Presently, we came upon an exhibit spread out on a large table. It was the scale model of an early colonial settlement, complete with old Dutch houses and cobblestone streets, dotted with horse-drawn vehicles. But the main thoroughfare rose in an arc above ground level, and its traffic consisted of tiny automobiles. "What are those motorcars doing in this eighteenth-century scene?" I asked. Helen agreed that it was a "puzzlement" (a word she filched from *The King and I*). We were about to inquire from the lady in charge, when our Spirit Guide provided us with a corporeal one. The Museum's historian himself, Mr. Val Wenzel, just happened to drop in, and now he introduced himself and took us on.

Val Wenzel turned out to be a man with an obsession. I've heard Helen remark, "It's all very well to have a hobby, but there's nothing so precious as a good, strong, healthy obsession." Val's obsession is the South Street waterfront.

Explaining the scale model, Val said, "This illustrates a project now afoot to reconstruct the entire South Street waterfront as an enormous out-of-door museum. It will include the fine old Dutch houses which still exist on what was once called Schermerhorn Row. Actually, you're standing in one famous old landmark right now.

"Of course, some of those old homes have disappeared but we'll be able to reproduce them from engravings of New York when it was Nieuw Amsterdam."

Val then explained the automobile traffic which had puzzled us. "We intend to raise Water Street above ground level as a bridge, so that automobiles can pass overhead without spoiling the ambiance of an ancient time."

And there now came an electric moment when Val's obsession for the waterfront met up with Helen's for the theatre. Indicating a tiny building in the center of the project, he announced, "This is a model of the first theatre ever built in the new world."

"A theatre!" Helen exclaimed in a voice that was practically a caress. "Oh, what was it called?"

"It didn't need a name," Val answered, "because it was the only theatre Nieuw Amsterdam had."

Val now produced a playbill which was merely headed "Theatre" and announced a grand opening on March 11, 1779.

"1779!" Helen exclaimed. "That means it opened while the Revolution was still on. And it must have helped people forget the agonies of those awful days for an hour or so."

She proceeded to read the program aloud; it stated that the manager, a certain Mr. Grant, was honored to present a comedy titled *Ye Old Beggarman and His Termagant Landlady.*

"That title role sounds as if it had been written for Helen," I told Val.

Her face lit up and she turned to him. "I'll tell you what I'll do," she said. "When your theatre's ready for its next grand opening, I'll come down and play that termagant landlady as a benefit for the Museum." Then, addressing me, she asked, "Do you suppose you could reconstruct that old play?"

"Why not?" said I. "I've lifted many a plot in my day."

Although Val laughed, I'm sure he was obsessively counting up the box office receipts on Helen's benefit.

We were now to learn that a part of the South Street reconstruction had already been completed. Val was anxious to show it to us and, while steering us down toward the river, he explained how he came to be connected with the Museum. "I had retired from my career as an architect," said Val, "and was free to haunt the river-front, which had always fascinated me. Then one day I happened to drop in at the Museum. That visit gave me a new career. For the first time since I quit work, I found something to fill my entire life."

His story thrilled Helen. "Sometimes," she exclaimed, "I think our whole city is the product of these magnificent obsessions."

We reached the river where the city's first pier still exists, restored as in colonial days. Anchored there are two ancient vessels which had also been put into shipshape condition: the original Ambrose Lightship and a fishing boat called *The Caviare*.

"What a presumption of elegance!" I exclaimed.

"Not at all," said Helen. "I think we make an error about our pioneer days when we overlook their elegance."

As Val showed us about the innards of the old lightship, I was forced to admit that in those days the people really did themselves very well on the high seas. The cabins were less cramped than many of those on a modern ocean liner. "Look at those bunks," said Helen. "They were certainly built to fit some very portly married couples."

In the spacious lounge of the *Ambrose* is a long center table with a classic green baize cover and it accommodates a dozen or more easy chairs where voyagers could while away the hours, spinning tall tales of the sea. "Nobody tells stories any more," Helen remarked. "We watch television and all our tall tales are TV commercials."

When Val took us up to the forecastle, we were introduced to three exceedingly handsome young men. We learned that they worked as ship custodians and guides for sightseers, even serving them with a hospitable cup of coffee. They work for the same salary that Val earns as a historian—nothing. Their recompense is contact with the sea, for which they, too, have an obsession.

The young custodians told us about a forthcoming event when

the ancient cargo schooner, *Wavertree*, which sailed from that
selfsame pier in 1895, will soon return to anchor there for good.
There it will be joined by the schooner *Pioneer* (1885), the
steam tug *Matilda* (1889), and the last of the old Fulton Ferry
boats, *John Lynch* (1925). Those young men had no difficulty
getting Helen and me to donate to their cause; Helen is a compulsive joiner, and I am an equally compulsive fancier of virile
males. But I can warn any girls in the lives of those young men
that they'll always be competing with ships and had better learn
to be satisfied with second place.

Leaving the pier, Val guided us along the riverfront, where he
pointed out Meyer's Hotel, a four-story wooden structure with a
sign that gives its date as 1778. "It was built at a time when it
looked as if New York was going to need a hotel," Val explained.
"Today, Meyer's still operates as a sailors' lodginghouse."

"From the look of it," I concluded, "the rates have got to be
dirt cheap!"

Across from Meyer's Hotel is New York's first skyscraper, a
clapboard building *five stories tall* which is fully tenanted today.
A tavern occupies its ground floor, with a sign that reads "The
Brightwood Bar." The tavern looked so lusty that it crossed my
mind its patrons must be a far cry from those we meet in the
cocktail lounges of mid-Manhattan. I often regret that there are so
few square-shooting males around these days. Feeling that the
Brightwood Bar might fill that deficiency in my life, I suggested
dropping in there for a coke. "Not now, darling," said Helen, "it's
too late." Thinking she was referring to my age, I wilted. But
Helen only meant that she had to get to her theatre, so I cheered
up.

Our new and, by now, permanent friend Val succeeded in cap-
turing a taxi to take us back to our own effete territory. Uplifted
both physically and emotionally, we felt sure that our discoveries
were over for that afternoon. But as the cab turned west on 61st
Street, Helen's eagle eye spotted an early colonial clapboard house

between Lexington and Third Avenues which is labeled as the home of Abigail Adams.

Abigail has always been an idol of Helen's; she had only recently read a volume of her love letters to John Adams. "Wives don't write such things to husbands any more," sighed Helen.

At which our taxi driver spoke up in manly protest. "I hate to contradict you, lady," said he, "but you oughtta see a greetin' card the missus sent me onct! It's as hot as a firecracker, and I ain't kiddin'."

I glowed with satisfaction. One more canard against our city had just been squashed: that the taxi drivers of New York lack sex appeal.

POTS OF GOLD AT
BOTH ENDS OF THE RAINBOW

We had made plans that required a sunny day, but now we were in for bad weather. Early in the morning Helen called me and said, "Never mind the rain. I've got a long list of fascinating things to do indoors."

"Like what?" I asked resentfully because, rain or shine, my heart was set on the Bronx Zoo.

"How about the Stock Exchange?" Helen suggested. "The Federal Reserve Bank is just around the corner. We can knock off all New York's finances in one short session."

"We could never get in on such short notice," I argued.

"Let's try," Helen persisted. "Why don't we phone Ed Scott?" This was indeed an inspiration; Ed, Jr., is my broker and Edgar, Sr., once wrote a book especially for females who are rich in dollars and poor in sense, called *How to Lay a Nest Egg*. Furthermore, both Helen and I have been friends with the entire delectable Scott family since girlhood and to call one of them up, even on business, is a pleasure. Ed listened to my plea and asked for half an hour to set some wheels in motion. But in less time than that, he phoned back with all the details for a guided tour to both places.

By the time Helen arrived to pick me up, the rain had turned into the kind of snow that's awfully wet. The outlook was grim, but down we went into the subway. Sitting next to me was a man with a newspaper that had a big black headline. Peering over at it, I nudged Helen. "We picked a fine time to go to Wall Street! The bottom's falling out of the stock market!"

"Well," said Helen, the optimist, "it won't be dull, at any rate."

We reached our destination and got out on Broad Street. Sticking to schedule, we pushed on to the Exchange. Its lobby is smallish and unimpressive, rather like the entrance to an ordinary office building. But waiting there for us were two charmers. A young man, Charles Storer, introduced himself as Assistant to the Director of Public Relations. And an attractive girl, Jean Geiger, turned out to be the Manager of the Reception Staff.

They were to be our guides, and it appeared that we were first to be taken to meet the President of the New York Stock Exchange, Mr. Robert Haack.

"Oh dear!" Helen fretted. "It's embarrassing to interrupt him while the market's taking such a tumble!"

"That's just why he may appreciate a change of pace," said Charlie Storer. "Come along!"

First thing we knew, we were right in the heart of the Establishment. The President's suite of offices is like no other business place we'd ever seen. "This might be the parlor of a lovely eighteenth-century home!" exclaimed Helen. The furniture is all pure Federal; a delicate mahogany desk dominates the reception room; upholstery and drapes are in striped brocade of pastel shades; the over-all atmosphere is opulent but at the same time very cheerful.

Mr. Haack entered and greeted us as Charlie said he would, delighted to get his mind off the sliding market.

In appearance, Robert Haack is the same type as Mayor Lindsay—lean, fit, and, said Helen, "handsome enough to be a leading man." That period when the financial big shots of our city were bloated and wheezy characters like Charlie Schwab and J. P. Morgan belongs only to the self-indulgent past. "What a source of civic pride," Helen remarked later, "that men like Robert Haack are so typical of New York City."

Helen and I made our intrusion as brief as possible and shortly Mr. Haack handed us over to Charlie Storer. "See that the ladies are taken right onto the floor." This seemed to shock Charlie and he ventured that the rules of the Exchange didn't allow our sex on the floor. "But why do we have rules except to break them?" replied Mr. Haack, who made the old cliché sound fresh.

On our way down, we passed through a large hall where there is an exhibition of animated displays that dramatize the industries in which shareholders can invest.

"You see," explained Charlie, "the stock market, after all, is just made up of people. The Exchange itself doesn't buy, sell, or even set prices. It merely provides a market place for the public at large. When you buy or sell stock, your bid is phoned or cabled to the New York Exchange from branches all over the world; even such faraway spots as Kuwait and Lebanon. The market is regulated only by the personal opinions of investors. And they're reflected, minute by minute, onto the floor of the New York Exchange."

Trying to make light of the fact that I understood very little of all this, I asked Charlie if he had a good tip we might gamble on.

Charlie laughed. "Never connect gambling with investing," he said. "A gambler bets on chance and has no control over his wager. A speculator has to have a sound knowledge of what he's doing or he'll very soon be wiped out."

"The Exchange has nothing but contempt for amateurs who buy on a hunch," spoke up Jean Geiger.

And I, without thinking that she might be "liberated" and touchy, asked, "Is that a hint for us females to keep out of the market?"

"If it is," she chuckled, "we don't seem to take the hint because the ratio of stockholders favors women by fifty-one per cent." At which moment we were ushered onto the floor.

There, in Helen's words, "we clung together like orphans of the storm." She admitted to being frightened by the crowd of milling men. "I'm a born puss in the corner," said she, "who's always being pushed into the middle of the action."

"But this is a very sluggish day," Charlie assured her. And it

was true that, once we got accustomed to the floor, it was not quite
the bedlam that we had been led to expect by movies and TV.
Although messengers were darting about, helter-skelter, and the
floor was littered with scraps of paper, members were going about
their business with no visible hurry or pressure.

A steady drone of offers and bids went on. The prices and sales
quotations circulated on the big board above us, like the news on
the Times Building. "But today," said Charlie, "the usual exhilaration is missing."

(Several weeks later when Helen was off at her hacienda in
Cuernavaca, she wrote me some comments on our day at the Exchange which were typical of her theatre-oriented slant on everything. "I wonder," she wrote, "if those dealers in dollars don't
become as sensitive as actors toward a foreboding of disaster. I
can feel it myself as soon as I walk onto a stage: the sure instinct
that whatever audience is there has left half its heart at home. I
had the same feeling that day on the floor of the Exchange; an
uneasy suspicion in the air that before long things would be much
worse.")

But the fact which impressed us most that day on Wall Street
was that a broker's life is the hardest kind of mental and physical
work. Helen, with her vivid social sense, was more aware of the
labor than of its rewards. "It's obvious," she reflected, "that
whether a member of the Exchange inherited his seat or had it
bought for him by a brokerage house, he hasn't fallen onto a bed
of roses. They may go home to posh Park Avenue apartments or
Tudor mansions in Westchester, but their place of business is no
more comfortable than a lot of the one-night stands I've played in
my time."

That truth was brought home to us more starkly in the matter of
the Exchange's wooden floor. That area, which is two thirds the
size of a football field, frequently has to be renewed because of the
constant treading of those wealthy feet. When Helen asked
Charlie why they didn't install a marble or cement floor which
would stand up to the traffic, his answer actually touched our

hearts. "The poor fellows need the resilience of wood to keep from developing fallen arches."

We observed that some of those money jugglers were belting down sandwiches and gulping coffee from cardboard cups right where they stood. Jean explained that no broker dares go out for a proper lunch. He has to be on the spot at every moment. "Those steady calls of buying and selling make my throat ache in sympathy," said Helen. "Why, it's like a perpetual opening night five times a week!"

After we'd been dignified by our visit to the floor itself, our guides wanted us to view it from the visitors' gallery. So we climbed the stairs to join a group of sightseers looking down on the activities through wide panels of extremely thick glass. "That glass," said Jean, "is shatterproof. About a year ago," she went on to explain, "the Exchange was forced to provide some sort of protection for brokers on the floor, because filth and even missiles were being thrown at them by a few of the high school kids who were brought here on group tours."

At which Helen flared forth: "Those kids haven't the stamina for hard work, and in my opinion, that's the cause of their resentment."

We ended our visit at the Exchange by watching the Bond Room from the visitors' window. There, the cast is older and the transactions are carried on coolly, by Men of Distinction types. But still nobody sits down, and five hours of calculating on your feet is tough. We left the Exchange, feeling a greater regard for our brokers. Helen hoped their wives paid an occasional visit to the Exchange. Surely then they'd let their poor husbands off those dinner parties and theatregoings (David Merrick, forgive us) in mercy for those aching feet.

But speaking honestly, we were still quite mystified by the world of finance. However, we collected a raft of pamphlets—two of which, "Understanding the New York Stock Exchange" and "The Language of Investing," Helen means to study the next time she's not learning a new part. As for me, I prefer to view the Stock Exchange through a heavy veil of mystery.

Charlie and Jean bid us Godspeed on our next exploration and steered us off in the direction of the Federal Reserve Bank. It turned out to be a massive stone pile on the order of a Florentine palace of the Renaissance. "I take comfort in all this solidity," Helen observed. "These days, banks are getting altogether too airy-fairy with their souvenirs, gifts, afternoon tea, and offers of friendship by way of TV commercials. I don't ask for friendship from my bank, just good, stout walls, like these."

We entered a palatial lobby so vast that I felt our footsteps should have made an echo, but they were muffled by the marble floor. A tall, black, and handsome receptionist paced the area, in peril of contracting fallen arches, as we now realized. When he approached us, Helen explained our appointment, and he ushered us to an anteroom to wait.

There we found several racks full of brochures, on which Helen eagerly pounced, and I, out of duty, followed suit. Then, having learned all I knew about world finance from an old James Bond movie, I discovered it had misled me on a pretty major fact. Anxious to pass my discovery on to Helen as dramatically as possible, I asked her, "Where do you think the largest store of gold in the world is buried?" And Helen replied, "Why, at Fort Knox, of course!" (She must have seen that same James Bond movie.)

"You're wrong!" said I, and then I sprang my surprise. "It's right where we are at this moment."

"But . . . what about Fort Knox?" she asked. Reading from my brochure, I enlightened her. "The treasure at Fort Knox is confined to that belonging solely to the United States. But the gold bullion of more than seventy foreign countries is buried in the vaults of the Federal Reserve Bank. A large part of it arrived by ship on the eve of World War II, to find a haven from the approaching holocaust on the bedrock of Manhattan Island.

"Do you realize what this means?" I asked. "It's a sure-fire

37

guarantee that more than seventy countries will think twice before they ever drop a bomb on New York City!" I was feeling rather pert over my discovery when our guide arrived.

She turned out to be a pretty girl and was accompanied by another who admitted that she begged permission to join up in order to meet Helen. Both girls wore badges which we found provided open sesame to all the massive steel doors we would pass along our way.

Our awesome trek among the world's greatest treasure began. We were escorted into a wide and stately elevator which descended six stories below ground by impressively slow degrees. Eventually we emerged into a long corridor. It was painted white, which might have seemed rather frivolous had we not felt there was a formidable structure of steel underneath it.

But now, our nostrils were greeted by a strangely pure ozone, and one of our guides spoke up to ask, "Do you notice anything unusual about the air we're breathing?"

"I certainly do," said Helen. "Why, it's as fresh as a mountain breeze." Our guides explained it is especially manufactured for these subterranean depths.

"Let's take some extra gulps as a treat for our lungs," Helen suggested, "after our long years of breathing pollution."

At the far end of the hall we came upon what might have been the imposing main desk of the Waldorf, except that here the clerks stood behind heavy steel bars, wore uniforms, and were handing out some pretty serious-looking guns to a shift of guards just coming on duty. "I approve this," said Helen, "but I can't imagine how a thief could ever get down here undetected in the first place." Our guide explained that since the recent bomb scares, extra guards had been taken on.

Turning a corner, we ventured through a hallway that looked like a giant rabbit warren. It was deserted for a long stretch but at length we came upon some action. Through a row of shatterproof windows we could look into a large room in which numberless, nondescript women sat at little separate tables. They were going through packets of old greenbacks, flipping them rapidly one by one with rubber-tipped thumbs.

Their tables were spaced far apart, so it would be easier to detect anyone slipping a bill up her sleeve. At the same time, it prevented the ladies from indulging in any time-consuming gossip.

They were inspecting greenbacks which were that day's quota sent in by banks. Most of the bills were worn out, but there were also new ones which were counterfeits, and these were set aside for investigation.

As our steel-lined promenade continued, our guide gestured toward a cart that was being trundled off, piled high with bags full of retired money. "They're on their way to the incinerator," she explained, "and every one of those sacks holds a hundred thousand dollars in ten-dollar bills."

I was impressed, but not Helen. "I can be overawed by a hundred thousand dollars written on a contract," she said, "but stuffed into a dirty canvas sack, it sort of looks like trash."

We turned another corner and were faced by another vast area behind glass. A number of men, also spaced beyond the possibility of small talk, seemed to be playing separate games of roulette. Each man stood at a large, slowly revolving wheel on which a jumble of coins rattled about and dropped over the edge, one by one, into what resembled a large trash can. They were inspectors who stand there all day long, silent and intent, scrutinizing coins.

This time we were allowed inside for a closer look, and our guides led us to an inspector who was checking nickels. The last of a batch had just dropped off the revolving wheel into his container, and he now poured on a fresh supply from a heavy sackful and resumed his examination. He was searching for Canadian coins, slugs, buttons, or anything else with which a humble malefactor might chisel slot machines and phone boxes.

We trudged dutifully on behind our guides into one more arid hallway. But this time there began to be a difference in the sterile mountain air: a heart-warming fragrance of coffee. As we went along, it became more pungent and was mixed with scents redo-

39

lent of delicatessen: pickles, potato salad, and mustard. Somewhere in these steel-lined premises there must be something like
. . . a *picnic*? We followed our nostrils around another corner and there it was; a large-scale picnic party had been set up at the end of the wide corridor.

On a long table with a fancy paper cover were the remains of a picnic lunch, which included a highly decorated cake and a jumble of used cardboard plates and cups. The attention of a group of middle-aged guests was focusing on a Foxy Grandpa of a man who was beaming as he clutched a paper tote bag full of packages that were gay with plastic ribbon and ready-made, dime-store rosettes. All the lady guests were bunched with orchids that had lots and lots of tulle and plastic ribbon.

Wistful good-bys were being said to Foxy Grandpa, whose eyes were moist in spite of his tote bag full of loot. Our guide explained that he was being retired; this was his farewell party after forty years of service. "What did he do?" I asked.

"He inspected nickels."

Deeply touched over being onlookers at the end of a man's forty years of petty usefulness, Helen apologized for her emotion. "I can't help it when things like this break me up. It isn't *my* fault that we had to come onto a farewell party in the vaults of the Federal Reserve."

Leaving that emotional scene, we went on and at length came to the very heart of the Establishment: the bottommost vault, buried seventy-six feet into the solid rock of Manhattan and fifty feet below the level of the sea, where the major wealth of the entire Free World rests under guard.

Visitors are not allowed inside the vault itself, but as we neared the massive steel door it just happened to start through one of the automatic revolutions with which it slowly, inexorably closes all that gold in and now closed us out. Our guide said it was sheer luck that we arrived just as the door was performing, for it allowed us a precious peek at the ninety-ton cone-shaped steel door in action.

We were allowed to peer through a shatterproof window on stack upon stack of gold bricks. "I get more kick out of looking at candy boxes in a Loft's window," said Helen.

Nor could either of us muster up much awe when our guides explained the *modus operandi* of international economics. It seems that each of those seventy-odd countries owns a separate compartment in the vault. New supplies of gold arrive at the bank in armored cars, after which each bar is weighed to the nearest one hundredth of a troy ounce. The bars are then carefully stacked into their proper compartment and sealed. Every time some country pays a debt or makes a deal, the guards shift the gold, brick by brick, into its new resting place a few feet away. A force of expert marksmen maintains surveillance and, in case of alarm, it can block off all means of escape from the bank within seconds.

Every night that ninety-ton steel door is lowered three eighths of an inch into place, where it remains like a cork in a bottle and the world's most active gold lies idle until the next business day begins.

How silly it all seemed, swapping those heavy gold bricks back and forth from one cubbyhole to another. "We women," said Helen, "could work the whole thing out more sensibly."

We came up into the street, quite content to be leaving the major loot of the world behind.

41

RING AROUND NEW YORK

*C*harlie MacArthur the Second, aged nine, had flown out from California to spend a week with Grandma Helen. One morning the three of us met at my apartment in a gay holiday mood and started off by cab. "This will be the experience of a lifetime," Helen said to little Charlie, "because today Grandma's going to show you all five boroughs of New York City from the railing of a boat!"

She spoke with such authority that it seemed logical when Charlie asked, "Do you do this all the time, Grandma?" which was a stumper.

"Not as often as I should," Helen said evasively, which wasn't a very complete answer. Helen had never done it before. Neither had I. And yet one reason for writing this book was to shame other New Yorkers for not cherishing the city of our dreams.

Helen might have argued that she lived outside New York but, weak as her excuse was, I had none at all. The Circle Line Pier is a five-minute taxi ride from my apartment. Here at my doorstep was an outlook as awe-inspiring as a view of Paris from the *bateaux mouches*. Both Helen and I had availed ourselves of that experience more times than we could count. But we had passed up this opportunity because it was too obvious.

Prompted by our own negligence, Helen told little Charlie to keep his eyes open and take in everything, at which he glanced out the cab window and asked the name of a skyscraper in the distance. "Good boy!" Helen exclaimed, "you're already beginning to take notice." She informed Charlie that it was the Empire State Building, a real old-timer sponsored by Al Smith, back in the Twenties.

The Circle Line Pier at the foot of West 43rd Street is spick-

and-span, having been completed only four years ago. It is also smallish and has somewhat the atmosphere of a yacht basin, which further enhanced our holiday mood. And when we entered the waiting room, Helen and I felt a return to virtue, because we seemed to be the only New Yorkers in the crowd.

Trooping up the gangplank, we boarded a spacious boat which had no name, being merely labeled the "Circle Line XII."

No sooner had our tour started than a voice came over the loud-speaker informing us about the sights along the route. Describing some odd-looking towers that seemed to spring from nowhere, our guide said, "Over there, folks, are the windpipes of Lincoln Tunnel. They're what keep you breathing when you duck underneath the Hudson River."

Helen, as a speech authority, identified the voice and its owner's racy comments as being native to Brooklyn. The next day I called up the Circle Line, got the gentleman's phone number, and asked where he came from. Helen was right. Our guide, philosopher, and friend came from Brooklyn, and his name is Johnny Mason.

Our next landmark, the Port Authority Bus Terminal, fills the entire block between 40th and 41st Streets, and it meets all Helen's requirements for our city's new spare and streamlined look. On its roof there were row after row of buses, lined up like toys.

From the beginning of that ride our views were marked by dramatic contrasts. The Hoboken shipyard spreads far enough along the riverfront to accommodate twenty ocean liners, but at the same time it is dwarfed by the Maxwell House Coffee sign. "The cup on that sign," said Johnny, "is big enough to hold all the tea in China!" Then, correcting himself, he added, "Well, anyhow, a couple million cups."

Madison Square Garden next came into focus. Helen compared it to the Circus Maximus in ancient Rome and commented on the fact that it has the same sleek simplicity. I could only think of the Penn Station within its walls—one of the two major railway passenger terminals in New York City—with its miracles of computerized services and total lack of human aid. I had recently taken a trip and found not a single porter in that huge area. I remembered the indignity of having to juggle a suitcase up the narrow escalator. But I admit to speculating about the damages I might collect if I came to grief. And I wondered why, during the present panic over job shortages, the Penn Central line can't put a thousand men to work as redcaps. I find, however, that the mysteries of our day can generally be solved by either of two answers: taxes or unions. So the answer must be unions. To those who use the Penn Central line I offer a tip: send your luggage on ahead, by freight.

Helen, as usual, had left some important items behind. One was a scarf to keep her hair in control. So, as the Circle XII breezed around the Statue of Liberty, we had to move inside. Looking at Miss Liberty through the protection of the window, I observed, "Have you noticed that one of her arms is too long? And her legs are definitely too short."

Helen admonished me for my lack of patriotic zeal. "Who would you want her to look like?" asked Helen, "Twiggy?" And as a further reprimand, she addressed little Charlie, "I'm going to have Miss Loos take a snapshot of us with that Grand Old Girl in the background!"

"Okay, Grandma!" said Charlie, adding mischievously, "What'll she take it with?"

"Oh, dear!" said Grandma, "I forgot my camera."

Exchanging an eloquent glance with Charlie, I offered to look for someone with a camera who might help out and finally spotted two young priests loaded with photographic equipment. Screwing up courage, I asked if we could engage them to snap a picture.

They turned out to be Berliners, and while polite in a rather heavy Prussian manner, they said they had only one exposure left and were saving it for something "unusual." Naturally, they didn't know how unusual Helen is.

It's amusing to watch the impact Helen sometimes fails to have, on the public at large. One day, while we were strolling down Broadway between a matinee and evening performance, she was busily occupied with an ice-cream cone when a group of ladies came along. They'd evidently just left the Music Hall, where they'd seen Helen as the outrageous scalawag she played in *Airport*. On spotting her, they stopped dead in their tracks to argue whether or not it was she. They finally decided she was behaving too much like an outrageous scalawag to be the eminent Helen Hayes and passed on without asking for autographs.

But there are occasions when Helen *is* approached by the most appreciative fans. One day we were sitting on a bench in Central Park watching the squirrels, when one of them scampered up Helen's skirt, presented her with a nut, and slithered away, leaving a tribute which, in terms of squirreldom, was equal to giving a banquet in Helen's honor.

Presently our need for a camera solved itself when a group from Detroit recognized Helen and *asked* if they might take a picture. In due time she received the snapshot which shows the two of us smiling gratefully into the camera while little Charlie points into the distance at the Empire State Building.

We next passed the floating dormitory for the Stevens Institute of Technology. "It provides every element of seamanship," said our Brooklyn navigator, "except that it hasn't got any engine because it isn't going anywhere." From behind the Stevens Institute, a plume of smoke arose, and Johnny added, "Some guy's house is on fire. When he gets home tonight he's gonna find his dinner overcooked."

A line of barges passed us on their way down the harbor, loaded with processed garbage which we learned would fill in some swamps; a whole new area of homes and gardens would rise on a groundwork of pressurized trash. "Leave us pay a little more respect to New York's garbage," Johnny said. "It may be starting right now to solve one of our woist predicatiments!"

As our boat approached Greenwich Village, I was reminded of one of my favorite bits of general information, which I proceeded to air by asking Helen, "Do you know the reason why Greenwich Village has been able to keep its picturesque low buildings in the midst of all those skyscrapers?" Helen had never given any thought to the matter. "It's because there's an earthquake fault running underneath the Village that frightens off the realtors from putting up any more skyscrapers. Geologists have even traced the fault along 14th Street and, according to the soothsayer Edgar Cayce, a large slice of Manhattan is going to break off someday and slide into the Atlantic."

"Nonsense," declared Helen, "if that were a fact, why would so many foreign nations deposit their gold in our Federal Reserve Bank?"

"You're right!" I agreed, and added with gratitude, "One can always rely on cupidity!"

We passed the ship for training merchant marines. Addressing little Charlie, Helen said, "A school on board a ship! Isn't that terrific?"

"It isn't as tall as the Empire State Building," said Charlie.

Now we were nearing Pier 40 of the Holland-America Line, and here again the world of the present jostled the past. For virtually every other pier in our harbor is a grubby, drafty, hollow, barn-like structure that makes one glad to get away to Europe and equally depressed on coming home. The Holland-America pier, however, is as neat and tidy as a Dutch kitchen. It is so spacious that you can drive onto the dock, park your car at will, take a ship to Europe, and return weeks later to find your car waiting and ready to drive away in.

But we felt, just the same, that there's something to be said for the old docks of the Erie Railroad, not far off, with their fancy façades and gingerbread decorations of the 1880's. "How wonderful it would be to hold a costume party there, Anita! All the ladies could wear bustles and leg-o'-muttons sleeves." But, alas, the old pier is going to be torn down, in order to add acreage to Battery Park. "And that," declared Helen, "is a noble enough reason to cancel any party!"

46

Certainly the most dramatic sight one sees along the entire Harbor front are the towers of the World Trade Center, which will be finished by 1973. And nearby will be the biggest real-estate development since the Egyptian pyramids, according to our guide; the landfill, at the river's edge, will comprise one hundred acres of earth and rock removed in the construction of the Center. "And it's gonna be called Battery Park City."

" 'Battery Park City' has no euphony," I objected.

But then as if in answer to my protest, Johnny added, "It won't be long before everyone'll be calling the place 'Bat City.' "

And I said, "Good! Now there's a name one can have an affection for. Bat City! I adore it!"

At any rate, "Bat City," now rising on 91 acres of what was once wasteland, will provide apartment homes for 55,000 people, most of whom will work in the area. "They'll be able to walk to their jobs," said Helen. "And what a place to walk!" For she'd seen a prospectus that showed broad plazas along the water, restaurants where people can dine and view the activity on the Harbor; promenades, shops, and out-of-door cafés.

"I wish I could be reborn as a New Yorker," Helen said, "so I could see Bat City in full swing. I'd like to see Welfare Island, too, at the end of the century when it's going to be a model city without any cars. So I just better aim at a visit to the Planet Earth as a future New Yorker. Or, failing that, come back here as a visiting ghost."

Both towers of the World Trade Center have already reached their final height, but neither is completed. A first tenant will be the Moran Towing Corporation, which owns the numberless red tugboats that scoot about the Harbor carrying out the most basic and immediate needs of the Port. There are all sorts of accusations directed against those towers, one inspired by an allegation that they affect television reception all over the city. "So much the better," said Helen. "It's time our technicians got down off the moon and put their minds on improving the earth!"

Now we were approaching Governors Island, with the skyline of lower Manhattan in the background. "The island was purchased from the Manhattan Indians in 1626," said our Brooklyn adviser, "and the price tab was three axeheads, a handful of nails, and a string of beads."

Helen began to shake her head and make typical clucking sounds of displeasure. "How reprehensible we Americans have been in our treatment of the Indians!" she said. Then, anxious to change the unpatriotic subject out of deference to Charlie, Helen began to wonder about a large white cross that rises high into the sky from the tip of the Battery. Johnny Mason was right on cue with an answer to her question. "That cross is on the Seamen's Institute," he announced. "It's a hotel for all seagoing men and women whether they're Catholic, Jewish, Hindus, or Jehovah's Witnesses who don't have to travel any farther than their headquarters in Brooklyn. And it's got clubrooms, gymnasiums, and restaurants; naturally, no floor shows but, on the other hand, no cover charge."

Presently, we got a dramatically close look at the giant clock on the Chase Manhattan Bank. "The big hand on that clock has to jump three feet to register one minute," our Brooklyn boy announced. "And it runs by atomic power, which is a lot more constructive than blowing up Hiroshima."

As we sailed past Ellis Island, Johnny informed us that over sixty million would-be Americans had passed through there. "And from what I hear tell," said he, "it wasn't any bowl of roses."

Now Helen began to cluck in disapproval. "How shortsighted it is to harp on the inconveniences that used to be attached to entering our glorious country! Why not give credit to the later achievements of those inspired seekers after freedom and opportunity and . . ." Helen hesitated.

"And *what*, Grandma?"

"Well, dear, I guess they were also interested in our dollars."

At any rate, it was cheering to hear that the old landmark will be turned into a place for celebrations, concerts, and sporting events by the National Park Service. One more project to spruce up a derelict part of our city!

We sailed under Brooklyn Bridge. "Thank heaven, it's a historical monument and there'll be no new, 'sleek' bridge to replace it."

"*Touché*," Helen agreed.

Now the sites became distinctly clinical. Our boat passed the Institute for Crippled and Disabled Children; next, the enormous N. Y. U. Dental Center, which, according to our guide, celebrated its hundredth anniversary in 1965.

Helen now explained to Charlie that anywhere an American in Europe gets a toothache, the first thing he does is to find a dentist who was trained in New York. "My own Parisian dentist, Dr. Vidal," I remarked, "treats most of Europe's royalty, and he not only trained here but frequently comes over to find out what our new dentists are up to!"

"Let's stop talking about teeth," pleaded Charlie. So we dropped that subject, only to be confronted with Hospital Row, the Veterans Administration Hospital and Bellevue Hospital Center. (Thereby hangs a tale which is so traumatic and lengthy that we must devote a lot of time to it later.) Then, for a welcome breather and a change of pace, came the dramatic approach to the United Nations Building—a view which, in itself, is sufficient reason for the entire tour. At this point, our Brooklyn analyst almost waxed enthusiastic. "Thanks to the efforts of the UN, there's gonna be peace in the twenty-first century . . . if we ever make it."

As if to demonstrate that our town's civic concern extends over and beyond human beings, there was the Animal Medical Center, which is so humanitarian that only two dog patients are assigned to a single room, and what a view they have!

The twenty-one buildings of the New York Hospital loomed ahead. "One of those buildings," I informed Helen, "is named for my own beloved Dr. Connie Guion, one of the great New

Yorkers of her century. She was a character such as can only thrive in our city. None of her regular patients called her anything but Connie. She used to wear a nondescript business suit, sensible ground-gripper shoes, and her white hair was pulled back into an uncompromising bun. But she sported a fancy turban sprinkled with field flowers, such as hasn't been in vogue since 1880. As a matter of fact," I announced to Helen, "Connie wore hats that were a lot like yours."

"What courage!" exclaimed Helen. "Hurray for her!"

Connie's clientele was most distinguished. She treated entire families of Vanderbilts, Whitneys, and Astors who were glad to be the victims of her old-fashioned no-nonsense methods. She always gave short shrift to alcoholics. "I haven't time for a patient like you!" she'd declare. "And don't give me any of that guff about alcoholism being a disease. It's nothing more nor less than sheer self-indulgence and disregard of everybody else. If you really want to be cured you can do it yourself. I'm too busy with people who are actually sick to bother with a selfish nonentity like you."

"Did any of Connie's patients ever cure themselves?" Helen inquired.

I had to admit, so far as I knew, not a single one.

One wing of the New York Hospital, the Payne Whitney Clinic, contains the psychiatric ward. From the boat we could see the stout, steel webbing that keeps patients from jumping off the roof. The most eminent kooks of our city have been confined there. Helen and I know two of them personally who, when admitted, were as nutty as squirrels. The treatment must be good because they're out now, leading the lives of normal geniuses (if a genius can ever be called normal).

When we passed the building which houses the Lying-In Hospital, Helen said, "Sometimes I feel like donating a giant statue of a stork for the top of that building because it delivers about one tenth of all the babies born in Manhattan." (Which with time has become a very great many babies, because the hospital dates from 1771, five years before the Declaration of Independence.)

We now looked across the river at Welfare Island, with its hospitals for the indigent, the aged, the criminal, and for drug addicts. A macabre fascination led me to suggest to Helen that we really must do a tour of Welfare Island.

Helen's expression turned grim. "Oh, no, we mustn't!" said she. It appeared that I had touched on a sore spot in her memory. It stemmed from the period when she, Charlie, and Bea Lillie occupied apartments on the sixth floor of 25 East End Avenue.

"Our back windows faced the river," said Helen, "so we had a fine view of Welfare Island, with its hospital for criminal cases and a brood of smaller institutes of correction.

"On Sunday afternoons Bea, Charlie, and I used to walk along the river with little Mary. She was only two and had to be pushed in her stroller. We regularly used to watch a small group of visitors boarding the ferry at 79th Street to go to Welfare Island, and we developed a morbid curiosity about it. Charlie, as an ex-Chicago reporter, was especially obsessed with the hospital where Legs Diamond was cured of a rash of bullet wounds he suffered at the time of his melodramatic escape from Sing Sing. It had also been a refuge for other gangster victims of mob violence. And it was there that Mae West for some mysterious reason was incarcerated briefly when she went too far in that play called *Sex*—and what a nursery story it would seem now!

"One day we succumbed to our mutual whim and, taking Mary back to our apartment (lucky child), went down to the ferry slip and joined the crowd of visitors to Welfare Island. When we arrived there, the other passengers were bent on visiting patients in the wards, so we started to explore.

"The sun was shining and everything looked charming. On close view the architecture, even though vulgar, had that special cozy charm of the turn of the century. Some of the patients were sitting outside on benches; their gray robes made them seem a

51

little like inmates of a monastery. The only indication we were at a jail was that the windows were barred.

"After a couple of hours' prowling, we thought it time to get back, since Bea and I had performances. So we stepped smartly up to the ferry entrance and were just as smartly stopped by a pugnacious-looking guard. 'Where are your visitor's passes?' he demanded. We patiently explained that nobody had offered us any passes when we boarded the ferry. We were big about it, however, and made no complaint. But was he a mean man! Hinting that we were prisoners trying to escape, he refused to let us board the ferry. Charlie told him to keep a civil tongue, at which he summoned an even ruder guard who took us in charge.

"In vain did we tell him who we were. In fact, it seemed to make matters worse when Bea, becoming very grand, declared, 'I am Beatrice Lillie, Lady Peel, and this is Helen Hayes, star of the theatre and screen, and this is Charles MacArthur, the famous playwright.' Our antagonist uttered that ever recurring joke, 'Oh yeah? And I'm Napoleon Bonaparte.'

"Now another element entered the altercation. Charlie was a compulsive slugger, and he began to advance on the guard." Now little Charlie began to pick up interest which spurred his grandma on to new dramatic heights. "I threw myself between the guard and your grandpa, while your Auntie Bea fluttered through the crowd admonishing it to 'Please!'"

"Please do what?" asked little Charlie.

"She didn't say, but don't interrupt Grandma.

"The upshot was we were all hauled off to the *un*friendly neighborhood police station and allowed to tell our story to an *un*-sympathetic sergeant. He grudgingly allowed Charlie to make one phone call. With only one call, we had to use our wits. We conferred. Bea remembered that her doctor, Morton Rodgers, brother of the composer Richard, held a clinic on Welfare Island once a week. Charlie called his office. The answering service said *he had left!*"

"Gee!" gasped little Charlie.

At which Helen's dramatic talent reached a new high. "It was getting on toward evening. Bea grabbed the receiver and explained to the answering service that it was a matter of life and death. The operator finally promised to track down the doctor and tell him to call us at the number Bea read to her off the phone.

"We waited. And we waited." Helen paused for effect.

"And what then, Grandma?"

"Your Grandma just simply panicked. I had no understudy and I was going to miss the show. By this time your grandpop regained his good sense and decided that if we had to spend the night on Welfare Island, Bea and I should be grateful. He was a newspaperman at heart and he visualized front-page publicity for us in the *Mirror* and the *News*.

"Well—after an hour of agony, Morty Rodgers phoned, heard our story, and promised to come to the rescue. But when he arrived he was pretty sore, not at the behavior of the Welfare Island staff, but because he thought we were all too old to be indulging in such childish capers. Moreover, we were going to make him late for a dinner party. And speaking of dinner," Helen concluded, "Bea and I played our shows that night on empty stomachs."

By this time we were nearing Gracie Mansion, and Helen's memories took a turn for the better. Gracie Mansion had been the ancestral home of Alice Duer Miller, who was an idol of Charlie's, both as friend and as a brilliant writer. The house had been built by the Gracie family, it passed into the Duer family, was later presented by them to the city, and was first used as the Museum of the City of New York. "When we were young," Helen recalled, "Charlie and I used to prowl those gracious rooms, studying the memorabilia of old New York. Later, after the city turned Gracie Mansion into a residence for our mayors, we used to dine there with Bill O'Dwyer; just family affairs with a clutch of Bill's relatives, looking a wee bit lace-curtain Irish in the restrained elegance of that Federal décor. I remember Bill O'Dwyer telling me once that the mayor he'd most like to resemble in his administration of our city was Gentleman Jimmy Walker. Imagine! And he was nearly impeached. But, oh, he was colorful, and both he and Bill had the New York spirit!"

Our boat passed the training area for Fire Department rookies; the East End Hotel for Women, where decent lodgings can be had at thirty dollars a week. (Make a note of that if ever you need an economical place to live.) We breezed by a library which houses the largest collection of books in the world dedicated to blacks: the Schomburg Collection. Then came the Harlem Hospital, which gained scant attention from little Charlie. *And* then Yankee Stadium. "It will open tomorrow!" our guide announced dramatically. But as his spiel continued, Helen grew distrait.

"I missed every word," she confessed after we'd passed that hallowed spot. "Memories blotted him out. I thought of my friendship with Eleanor Gehrig, wife of the great Lou. She used to take me to games at Yankee Stadium, where we sat in one of the boxes assigned to players' wives and mothers. The tension was fierce, like an opening night when you find yourself among a few friends and a lot of enemies. A good many wives and mothers were Italian, and they said their Rosaries throughout the game, jumping up and waving them whenever our side scored, closing their eyes and praying out loud when we goofed."

We passed the Polo Grounds and, to the right, Barnett Hill where the solid rock under Manhattan dramatically comes to the surface in boulders, among which one can be in the wilds within twenty minutes of Times Square.

New York University's Hall of Fame is located around here. But who ever visits there or ever even heard of many of the ninety-four famous people whose statues are on deposit? We saw another depository that is not quite so noble—the subway trash pile, where retired subway cars are cut into pieces and sold for scrap.

We headed close to Spuyten Duyvil Creek, which joins the Harlem and Hudson Rivers. The origin of its name is so well related by Washington Irving that anyone who doesn't know it had better read his *Knickerbocker's History of New York*.

We saw the Henry Hudson Bridge choked with traffic, in typical New York contrast to the densely wooded hills of Inwood Hill Park where, as "Professor" Mason now advised us, "sometimes kids that go there on scouting trips can still find Indian arrowheads." Turning to see what sort of effect this had on little Charlie, we found he had dozed off.

And finally we came into view of the George Washington Bridge, the most dramatic in the world. Helen calls it "my bridge" because she crosses it so often. And, too, she remembers her Charlie bundling her and a very small Mary into the family car to drive them across the bridge on the day it opened.

We next sailed past the enormous complex of the Columbia Presbyterian Medical Center, which inspired Helen to call New York the "Sick-Care Center of the World." Anyway, it is a proving ground for experiments in new techniques like heart surgery and transplants of other vital organs. And as if to make us more awesomely conscious of our tendency to be the mostest, our Brooklyn statistician called attention to the interdenominational Riverside Church, the largest in America, and to the Church Center across the way, where headquarters for all Protestant denominations are under one roof.

Nearing the end of the tour, we passed the Tomb of Ulysses S. Grant with his own words graven above the entrance: "Let Us Have Peace." "I hope Ulysses is forgiving us for what we're up to today," said John Mason gravely.

His parting information was to the effect that on and around this small island, only thirteen and a half miles long and two and a quarter miles wide at its widest point, there has grown a population of some eight million people. It is the world's third-largest city, surpassed only by Tokyo and London.

At length, fulfilled by three giddy hours of looking on splendor, affliction, wealth, need, efficiency, waste, historical landmarks, and noble dreams of the future, we finally reached the end of that grandest of all short tours. But, as we roused little Charlie from his nap, he blinked, looked off toward the skyline, and informed us brightly, "There's the Empire State Building!"

Where Charlie MacArthur the Second is concerned, our city planners might have finished the Empire State Building, handed it over to Al Smith, and lain down on their jobs forever.

The next time I saw Helen, she reported that her grandson had taken her to the Empire State Building. It was Charlie's treat and he paid for the tickets. The interminable ride up to the observation walk seemed even longer to Helen because of her vivid memory that, during the blackout of November, 1965, the elevators had stopped and trapped dozens of passengers for hours in the dark.

"At last," said Helen, "we reached that awful height. But Charlie got caught up in the wonders of the souvenir stand and could hardly be dragged outside for a look at the view. Finally he yielded to persuasion, plus a few insults and aspersions, and went out to the observation platform, where he was extremely bored until he caught sight of a Circle Line boat making its way up the Hudson. 'Gee,' he exclaimed, 'we could see the Empire State Building better down there!' That's grandchildren for you!" said Helen.

THE VILLAGES—EAST AND WEST

*T*his particular expedition had an incongruous start at the Spanish Pavilion, an expensive restaurant on Park Avenue frequented by sybarites. Our publisher and host, a man of tremendous dynamism, spoke up briskly. "Of course you'll go to the East Village," said he.

Helen and I had already discussed that idea so she was ready with her answer. "Not under any circumstance." Then she went on to explain, "The only time I ever got to the East Village was when I went to see *You're a Good Man, Charlie Brown.* The night people of the Village were abroad after the show, and on our way to the parking lot it was downright scary.

"We ran into a clutch of Hell's Angels and their chicks. They were clustered among their motorcycles smoking homemade cigarettes, and we knew what those were. Several of them were locked in alarming embraces. Nobody was paying them any mind at all and I was sure the strollers wouldn't even bother to look on when a gray-haired grandma like me got mugged right before their eyes. I walked along bravely with my head up and my shoulders back, but when we got to safety my escort told me that I had been calling rather audibly on Jesus, Mary, and Joseph to save me. So you see," Helen concluded, "I am really too cowardly to be of much use in the East Village."

I had my own objections to going there. "I haven't got anything to wear," I said.

However, our publisher persisted. "The Village is there, and if you're writing about New York City you can't ignore it." He was right, of course.

The next day we acquired a guide in the person of Stefan, an authentic East Villager. He introduced himself over the phone and offered to escort us around the area, since he happened to be living there. Knowing Stefan's parents to be normal, cultured, and rich, Helen decided he must be either a rebel or a nut to live in a slum, when his home life could be so attractive. Helen, who as a rule believes only the best, now began to fear the worst. "This boy could even be an addict," she said, "or if he isn't, he'll steer us into them just to let us know he's 'with it.' "

But Stefan considered our quest so seriously that he took the trouble to brief us in writing, straightening out the complicated structure of the Villages so ably that we wish to share this enlightening introduction with our readers:

"The Village still has the most varied population in New York. It is the one place where you can meet anybody: Puerto Ricans, Italians, Blacks, Hippies, middle-class Whites, and just plain bums. Why it is that these people who are normally at each other's throats have peaceably accepted polychrome integration is the most fascinating thing about the Village.

"Visually, Greenwich Village is an expensive but strangely flat mixture of town houses, new high-rise apartment buildings, residential hotels, chichi antique shops, and deceptively expensive restaurants. It is the testing ground for upper-middle-class children who want to throw bombs without getting into the army. The original architecture still survives; much of it is first-rate, particularly on West 11th Street.

"One section of the Village has developed a kind of ersatz charm all its own. Now specified as West Village, it covers the area west of Sixth Avenue to the Hudson and used to be a warehouse district. On Washington Street one can still see remnants of the New York Central's elevated tracks. In the late nineteenth century, Negroes escaping from the South would just get off the tourist trains and settle right there where they found themselves. Because the neighborhood was also near the docks, Italians, Irish, German, Polish, and all the other European emigrants would do the same. The area became one of the most dense in New York. Since then most of the Blacks have moved off to Harlem, the Italians and Irish to Brooklyn and Queens, leaving middle-class Anglo-Saxons to take over.

"The West Village is today the most tranquil neighborhood in the entire city. There are trees, narrow streets without too much traffic, excellent shops, special delicatessens run by the few Italians who stayed behind, and there are iron railings along the sidewalks. It is a neighborhood where the artistic, who have money, can settle inconspicuously.

"The fringes of the West Village remain what they were fifty years ago—loft industries and warehouses. Recently artists have been moving into the Cast-Iron District to take advantage of low rents and high ceilings. Homosexuals, on the other hand, having a great deal more money, are beginning to edge them out. With them, the similarly styled heterosexuals of advertising, publishing, and even the garment business have moved in; there are shops for bell-bottom pants, trinkets, restaurants with earthenware mugs, and an entirely new variety of pickup joint. Christopher Street is the center of all this depravity and supposed libertinism. It is, however, even by night, a depressingly tame place.

"The parts of the Village that are less tame are the areas around Washington Square and the East Village. The park is the one place where you can always count on finding rock musicians and political radicals exhibiting their wares to crowds on park benches; it is also one of the places where the unwary come to buy drugs, and to which all tourists are brought for a glimpse of the 'real' Greenwich Village.

"The area around Bleecker Street, running erratically south and west of the Square, once was quite real in its own way, but now the famed Figaro coffeehouse, where more talented people wasted their talents talking over caffeine than at any other place in New York, has made way for a Blimpie sandwich shop and Bleecker has become a parody of its former Bohemianism.

"The East Village is the neighborhood most recently populated by the now set. There along St. Marks Place you can see the hippies doing their thing—which mainly consists in asking for handouts. Five blocks south on East Third Street you can see the older generation doing their version of panhandling outside the Men's Shelter. Down there the Bowery and the younger generation co-exist in more ways than one.

"But the East Village is also the center of off-Broadway theatre and the womb of the rock music clubs as well as the hiding place of a surprising number of genuine writers, photographers, and artists. Many of these have taken over storefronts on the side streets off Second Avenue and converted them to live-in studios.

"The Italians and Ukrainians left over from the past remain, stoically tolerating the artists, hippies, Puerto Ricans, and blacks who have moved in with them. They have to be stoics: it's not always a happy mixture. Of all the Greenwich Village area the East Village is where the problems of New York City hit the hardest: crime, poverty, racial antagonism, and just plain garbage. One can get hurt in this neighborhood, especially if he strays east of Second Avenue."

Thus forewarned, we prepared for that trip as if it were a safari. Friends and well-wishers offered tips. No jewelry, no purses, no gaudy colors to catch the eye. Be as inconspicuous as possible. At one point I suggested faded blue jeans, but there was no time to fade them and brand-new ones would be a sure giveaway.

I don't know how it came about, but the day of our rendezvous with Stefan we had stupidly made a lunch date at the Pavillon. And this posed a problem: how to dress for a fashionable restaurant and at the same time look rakish enough for a slumming expedition. At the last moment the weather came to our rescue with a hint of rain; it was only a hint, but it gave us an excuse to cover our respectable dresses with trench coats, those garments that are suitable to a palace or a hovel. We looked anonymous enough, except that Helen insisted on keeping the black bow in her hair. "It helps me to know who I am when I catch a glimpse of myself in a shop window."

We awaited Stefan somewhat nervously, apprehensive of the effect a hippie would have on the Pavillon's very correct maître d'. But when that young neighbor of Hell's Angels arrived, with an old-fashioned short haircut, Brooks Brothers suit, immaculate shirt, and a restrained necktie, he looked, if possible, even squarer than we did.

Letdown number one. The second was the spectacle of a large black town car with chauffeur in livery waiting outside the Pavillon—courtesy of our publisher. It was in this inconspicuous style that we were to find out about life in our city's most Bohemian, not to say low-down, section.

Arriving at St. Marks Place, we drove at a slow pace east to Tompkins Square. "It's rather dangerous here," Stefan said. "I live in that tenement just around the corner." I thought he sounded a little proud, and with reason. It took real courage to venture forth in this area, looking as normal as he did. We peered out of our glass case as we turned west again to Astor Place, then went down the Bowery past Bleecker and across to Washington Square.

Now we were entering the Greenwich Village that was the home of Helen's youth. "I was about nineteen when Mother and I moved into a charming little nineteenth-century house on Charles Street," Helen told us. "The next stop in our staggered move uptown was the ground floor of a house on West 11th with a pretty little front yard. After that, a carriage house on East 19th. Next, up to Gramercy Park for a spell, and finally to 35th and Park Avenue. I was married to Charlie from that apartment," said Helen, "and from that day on I was distinctly Uptown."

As Helen's nostalgia grew, she began to be restless. Finally she blurted out: "I can't stand this another minute! I've got to get out and walk!"

A stroll along 8th Street restored her spirits. "The neighborhood hasn't really changed any more than people change, fundamentally," Helen held forth on her home ground. "It only looks slightly different. Today people are more imaginative and uninhibited in their getups, and, like everyplace else, it's more crowded; there are more mixed couples—black and white—but

the young people look free and self-important, just as I remember
we were, all those years ago. Maybe that's the allure of the Village. It's still a 'neighborhood.' And, one needn't feel unimportant
or invisible here. That's the great thing about the Village: everybody has always thought his bag was just as important as the
other fellow's. The Village is no place for those who enjoy competition and belong out in the thick of things. The Village is Paradise for the insecure."

Helen recalled a darling creature of that type named Julie
Brown who barely eked out a living cutting black paper into sil-
houettes. But she lived only for her art, and why not? She was the
very best silhouette cutter in all Greenwich Village. Of course,
Helen also knew plenty of successful artists who lived down there:
Helen Dryden, who drew covers for *Harper's Bazaar* and occupied
a funny little helter-skelter flat on one of the old streets; James
Reynolds, who did set designs for the *Ziegfeld Follies* and lived
in a third-floor walk-up. And then, of course, we each remembered
Hendrik Van Loon.

I recall sitting in saloons with that charming, nonviolent protes-
tor of the Establishment where I was much more a freak than any
of the Villagers. I came from that magnificent anti-Village called
Hollywood; my dresses were imported from Paris and my hair
was bobbed. In those days, the Village girls wore their hair
long, matted, and unwashed just as they do today.

Hendrik wrote me very literate mash notes. Shall I quote one of
them? Well, why not? The following was written after he felt I
had been neglecting him. It stated: "A reward is hereby offered
for information which will lead to the detection of Anita Loos. She
was last seen in the Brevoort Hotel with a long-nosed stranger who
tried to entertain her by reciting all he knew about Baruch
Spinoza. If contacted, will she please communicate with him and
hear something to her advantage." The letter ends with a self-
portrait in India ink and Hendrik's autograph.

In meandering with Stefan that day we wandered along a block
which provided Helen and me with a mutual recollection. The

Howard Dietzes lived there, on West 11th Street (Number 18, to be exact). They gave very special parties at which one met intellectual and social figures from all over the world. Lucinda designed costumes for the theatre and was responsible for some of Helen's daffiest as well as her loveliest character outfits. Howard, besides being a fine lyricist, was also Vice President of M-G-M when Helen starred in her early movies and Charlie MacArthur and I were at the studio writing scripts. We would have loved to toss a nostalgic look at what Helen referred to as "that darling little house," but, alas, a bevy of young folk had recently bombed it, leaving a crater full of splinters, grit, and shreds of several corpses.

I feel we should be very understanding of today's young derelicts, for now, as always, it is the sacred right of youth to rile their elders. We did it in the Twenties by the simple means of bootleg gin, hip flasks, long cigarette holders, bobbed hair, and skirts that, for the first time in centuries, bared our knees. In those days we had no particular grievance against our elders except that they were our elders. Today the bloody events in Southeast Asia serve not only as an excuse for violence, but they also set an example to do likewise.

It is unnerving, of course, when youthful bombers remain at large, but whether they're caught or not, they're inescapably marching toward a doom they fear more than the death penalty itself. They have got to grow up. Nothing can prevent their maturing like us who are the objects of their deepest scorn. And because of overindulgence in sex, pot, LSD, hard drugs, premature parenthood, and the septic dandruff of unwashed hair, they may suffer more than our generation from venereal disease, arthritis, pernicious anemia, locomotor ataxia, colitis, hardening of the arteries, and tooth decay. Such plagues, however, enforce moderation. Then forbearance may set in in those who do manage to reach middle age. And in future years their own offspring will discover fiendish ways to rile them—such as washing their hair or donning garments that have suitability and proportion.

As we went through the business districts that day, Helen was struck by one minor change. Shops which used to sell cigarettes now had windows full of little pipes. Stefan explained to us that in smoking a marijuana cigarette, one is left with a "roach" (called in the refined old days a "butt"). A pipe allows you to get your money's worth of precious pot, right to the last noxious puff. Well, at least the young rebels are learning to be thrifty.

By that time the afternoon was far advanced and we were back at Greenwich Avenue. It was balmy, and we wandered through a scene that could make the Casbah look like some back lane in New Canaan, Connecticut. Cars were lined up along the curbs, bumper to bumper. And spread out on the hood of every single car was a delectable young boy posing to look his best for the strolling customers who passed by. "Let's hang around that pretty little blond," Helen suggested, "and get some data about his market price."

We tarried long enough to witness a bargaining session and to hear the deal closed for a mere slice of pizza. Nothing about the situation seemed crass, however; it was just a case of teen-age dropouts earning their keep by play instead of work.

As we wandered on, we came to the Salvation Army's tiny one-room rescue mission, with its mad psychedelic décor, there for the purpose of uniting runaway young with their folks back home. Like every job that is launched by the Salvation Army, it deserves enormous respect. The young man in charge obviously came from a well-to-do home, possibly had no need to earn a living, and was working with real dedication.

An inexhaustible supply of disoriented young people drifts into the rescue mission from every point of the compass. One bearded boy was strumming a guitar. A forlorn-looking woman, possibly thirty, was sewing spangles on a blue satin bikini. The guitarist presently began to wail a rock number that bemoaned an economy which requires anyone to work. The bikini-maker spoke up to join in his plaint. I finally couldn't keep my mouth shut. "Look here," I said to that sorrowful young lady, "for years Miss Hayes has

64

been trying to find someone to keep house for her over in Nyack. Her home has every luxury: a garden, a tennis court, and a swimming pool. Moreover, she is away a good deal of the time so the work is light. But she can't find anyone who'll accept the job."

The young lady had her answer and delivered it with pride. "I wasn't brought up to do housework," said she.

Helen, more compassionately minded, questioned the young Salvation Army officer about the damage done by pot to his charges. He felt it too early to know about physical damage, but moral damage was unmistakable. "It's always deteriorating to the character to be forced to break a law every day," he said, "no matter whether it's just or not."

We jumped him on this, reminding him that our generation grew up breaking a stupid, unworkable attempt at prohibition in the Twenties, and what happened to us? The majority weathered the damage to our systems from bathtub gin and the demoralizing results of being chronic lawbreakers, and became the squares the new generation is rebelling against.

It was here that Stefan entered the debate and gave us a hint which might curb the use of marijuana, at least among females. "It makes girls fat," said Stefan, "and it's also bad for the complexion." He had only to point out a few broad-bottomed, mottled maidens in their tight-to-bursting blue jeans to prove his point. So Helen and I might spread Stefan's message and, if there's a grain of vanity left in girls these days, it might wipe out the marijuana traffic in a wink.

But what we shall remember most of 105 MacDougal Street is that charming young man, bearded and, in looks, not unlike the dropouts around him, telling us of nights he's spent sleeping on the floor, sometimes with fifteen or more kids, and of his frequently successful efforts to get them to go back home. His record month was three hundred returns. "Some come back," he said, "but most do not. It all depends on my success in educating parents."

One of the girls made a revealing statement. "I left the Village for a whole year; I got married, then my husband died and I came back." She seemed apologetic about it and, gesturing toward the young Salvation Army man, said, "He didn't want me to come back, but I did."

Helen commented, "I have a feeling that maybe the Village is not a place; it's a state of being. Maybe you become a Villager because anywhere else you're an alien."

When the three of us parted that night, Helen still felt she hadn't seen enough. She had, moreover, summoned up the courage to examine the East Village in depth. So we arranged to meet Stefan for lunch the next day at O'Henry's restaurant on Sixth Avenue and 4th Street, an old stamping ground of hers. This time Stefan provided us with yet another surprise: he arrived on a motorcycle, with helmet and heavy metal chain around his waist, very much in tune with his environment. The chain, we saw later, was for locking his motorcycle while parked.

We realized that his outfit of a bourgeois square had all been for us and felt flattered when he came as himself the next day. After lunch—"Such great hamburgers!" Helen said—we bravely ventured over to the East Village, on foot. Stopping at a street corner, Stefan announced, "Well, here we are, right in the heart of it!"

Helen blinked and looked around. "Oh no! Not here!" She took a long breath before she could speak again. And then she said, "Well, I'll be jiggered!"

It turned out that for several years she had been rehearsing TV and even stage productions in the old Central Plaza Hall on Second Avenue near 7th Street. During lunch breaks Helen had taken to wandering around the neighborhood alone, in and out of the side streets. They were so excessively drab and quiet they made an ideal place for learning lines and speaking them out loud.

And only now did Helen realize that she had been wandering alone and unprotected in one of the most dangerous areas of the city. "Perhaps I was protected by going around spouting that dialogue out loud. I was merely considered a friendly neighborhood junkie on a bad trip."

Later on, when we were checking back, Helen realized she'd been in the same block at about the same hour when a society girl had been brutally cut to pieces by her Hell's Angel lover. But the most astounding fact of all was that, at the time, Helen could find nothing of interest and was glad to get back to rehearsal hall to see a little action.

Under the aegis of Stefan we visited McSorley's famed old saloon, the recent battle ground of Women's Lib which had tried to brace its ground-gripper footwear on the brass rail. It looks as any other saloon might have looked back in the 1880's . . . just great!

The customers who were entering that day (or being thrown out) were nonhippies with old-fashioned haircuts. McSorley's is obviously the sole refuge in that area for truck drivers and other genuine, undiluted males. Helen said to me, "I'll bet you'd like to crash there yourself." I would.

But then Helen remembered a time when she had hankered just as ardently as any liberated woman to enter McSorley's tantalizing portals. "We'd been rehearsing a TV production of *The Royal Family* at the Central Plaza. In the cast were Claudette Colbert, Fredric March, and Charles Coburn, all of us old friends and all of us playing other old friends—the Royal Barrymore Family. Every day we'd been taking lunch together at a very fine kosher restaurant, but the menu of gefilte fish, sour cream, and dill pickles had begun to pall. There wasn't another restaurant in the vicinity except for McSorley's saloon, which boasted a free lunch counter. Charles and Freddy withstood its temptation as long as they could, but they finally deserted Claudette and me and succumbed to McSorley's. I remember how we stood on the street outside, our noses pressed against the window, trying to spoil their appetites by making ugly faces.

"But now that women are about to be fully liberated, I don't want to crash McSorley's. To me there's a sort of virile halo about a place where women aren't allowed. I don't like to admit that such spots no longer exist. What about weak-willed characters who are masochists, like me? Aren't we going to be allowed *our* kind of fun any more?"

Dismissing Helen's oratory, we wandered on to a sidewalk café that was as crowded with weirdos as a Fellini mob scene. And there Stefan began to speak *his* mind.

"I've never understood any of the various mystiques attached to living in the Villages," he said. "People like me live here simply because it's cheap and convenient. We're completely puzzled by foreigners from the upper East Side who declare how much they wish they, too, could live in the Village. Perhaps you can explain this mystery in your book. If you do, there'll be hundreds of puzzled Villagers like me lining up to buy a copy. We'd like to know, once and for all, what it really means to live in the *real* Greenwich Village—really."

At this point I had a revelation. "I know what the answer is," I announced. "Greenwich Village is the only spot in New York where you can go out for the Sunday newspaper in your pajamas and bare feet and nobody pays you any attention."

"You're probably right!" said Stefan.

GO TO BELLEVUE AND LIVE

On the night we visited Bellevue Hospital we were prepared by our guide for its reputation as a hellhole. Leading us through the big sprawling complex, she said, "Did you see what the *Times* said about us last month? The headline read, 'Go to Bellevue and Die.' "

We were seeing Bellevue under the auspices of Mrs. McCloy, wife of John McCloy, U.S. Military Governor and High Commissioner for Germany after World War II. She holds down a non-paying job as head of the Bellevue School of Nursing. Nothing about Mrs. McCloy suggests the lower depths. She's much more Park Avenue. She had chosen to show us around after visiting hours when the hospital is no longer on display. "Then," she said, "the drama begins." So we arrived at 8:30 P.M.

The main building at Bellevue *is* old and shabby. The new one, now in course of construction, won't be ready until 1974. In the meanwhile Bellevue is overcrowded, understaffed, and, like every other such place in this richest city on earth, it suffers from a crushing lack of funds.

After its eighty years of existence, the Bellevue complex does sport a new nurses' dormitory. "It looks rather like a luxury hotel in Atlantic City," Helen observed, "let's say the Traymore."

"I want you to meet our Director of Nurses," said Mrs. McCloy. She proceeded to take us to that lady's office and there introduced us to Miss Betty Kauffman. She turned out to be a wholesome, healthy, serene, and happy-looking young woman. Her hair is hair-colored and its wave, like everything else about her, is natural. Her voice is forthright. Her smile is easy and when she laughs she means it. In today's fashion world Betty Kauffman

69

might be considered a trace too ample, but when Titian was painting Venuses he could have used her for inspiration.

Nurse Kauffman started us on our rounds. As she ushered us into the main corridor, suddenly a scene of picaresque gaiety, for which we were totally unprepared, burst into view. Milling about the elevators was a throng of characters in various bedtime garments: cotton-crash dressing gowns, kimonos, and limp pajamas, and there were a couple of children in nighties. But every last one of them sported around its neck a Hawaiian lei made of colored paper.

"They've been having a fiesta in the assembly hall," Nurse Kauffman explained quite matter-of-factly.

Helen and I politely muttered "Oh," as if a fiesta in nighties were nothing unusual. But then Helen managed to ask, "Are they celebrating some particular occasion?"

Our guide answered no, but added, "You see, life in the convalescent ward gets to be rather dull, so a group of patients organized the party for no particular reason at all. Except if there is any profit from balloon sales it is earmarked for the hospital fund."

It seemed that every patient who could make it out of bed had been invited, and, taking place during visitors' hour, any number of relatives and friends had been able to join the festivity.

"Well," exclaimed Helen, "New York's at it again! Another party—just like at the Federal Reserve."

As we trailed Betty Kauffman on a tour of the various wards, the thing that most fascinated Helen and me was the unusual quality of the patients. We saw many more engrossing alcoholics than you'd ever find in tonier places like the New York Hospital, Harkness Pavilion, or Lenox Hill, all combined. For the prosperous drunk, as a rule, is full of self-pity, but an alcoholic without funds can be justly proud of his achievement. And any good, rowdy hobo will express himself in terms that make your ears perk up.

In the psychiatric wards many of the patients appeared to be doing their own thing just as they did before apprehension. And we learned that because of insufficient guards, they lurk in corridors, stalking nurses like a bevy of Groucho Marxes. They filch drugs out of the lockers; steal everything they can, which includes strips of copper which they rip off the roof of the main building. Any seasoned junkie knows that a strip of copper is as good as a credit card or a traveler's check.

It was not long before we found out that the nurses and interns at Bellevue are as high-spirited as its patients. The young doctors, having just left college, are instantly swamped by cases into which they can really get their teeth: virulent diseases with symptoms which have become acute through neglect. There is a minimum of those tiresome pests of the high-class hospital, the hypochondriacs.

But perhaps the liveliest contribution Bellevue makes toward recuperation and well-being is its color scheme. The tattiness of its corridors and wards is disguised by paint in strong colors, bright red, blue, pink, green, and orange. "They remind me of a theory worked out by Elsie Mendl," Helen observed. "Remember when she was ordered to a hospital in Los Angeles, sick as a cat, but insisted that her room be painted apple green before she'd check in? She simply couldn't stand that stark bathroom white."

As we followed Nurse Kauffman down the hall she suddenly stopped at one of the doors to say, "Why, I believe they're operating in here!" Then, looking at a chart, she exclaimed, "A hemorrhaging ulcer, brought in just a half hour ago. They only operate at night in an extreme emergency. You're in luck, ladies!" Then, opening the door that led to somebody's doom, she added, "Step right in!"

Well . . . Helen wasn't going to be the one to show a yellow streak, so in she went and I followed meekly. We mounted steps leading to a narrow gallery. There were no chairs into which we might have slumped while passing out. We had to stand. We braced ourselves, took deep breaths, and peered through a glass partition onto the goriest event to which either of us had ever been invited.

The amphitheatre below was in shadow, except for the spotlight on a group of doctors and nurses huddled about the operating table, exactly as in the famous painting by Rembrandt. Their modern uniforms glistened in a pulsating tone of blue and Helen whispered to me, "Let's try not to spoil the color scheme by turning green."

Frequently, when revolted, I can look right at something and hypnotize myself into not seeing it. I can almost always do this at a play by Harold Pinter. But on this occasion—not a chance! I saw it all. And so did Helen.

The patient's skin was dark; he might have been Puerto Rican. But his fully exposed insides glistened moistly in the spotlight, red, green, and blue, as if made of plastic. The job was being done calmly and with dexterity by a young surgeon. Assisting him were three nurses, an anesthetist (a black girl pretty enough to be a fashion model), and an assistant surgeon.

I'm sure that the nonpaying patient was getting more prompt attention than if he'd been in an expensive hospital. I can cite the instance of a friend of mine recently suffering a broken nose in a taxi collision and being taken to one of our most respected hospitals (which shall be nameless). She had to find her own way into the Emergency Ward, where she was completely ignored for over three hours. Finally she was able to phone a doctor friend who rushed to the rescue and got her out of the place. Here, a non-affluent Puerto Rican, facing his life-or-death struggle late at night, found himself on an operating table inside half an hour. "Most snob hospitals would have refused even to take him in," Nurse Kauffman remarked with pride.

Leaving the operation only half done, we departed the surgery and on the way out received another invitation—to nothing less than a *real* birthday party. The earnest young obstetrician who invited us said his patient should be dilating properly in about half an hour. "After all," he said, "she's had seven kids in the past six years, so it shouldn't take her too long."

We excused ourselves from that happy event, however, and followed our guide off to the Nursery. Now, any babe born into a

72

legal family may be full of charm, but there was something about those illegitimate little tykes we saw that started the imagination spinning. And I sensed an aura of drama about them which planned parenthood seldom achieves. As a matter of fact, universal planned parenthood might fill the world with a whole population of squares.

But, with all the drama abounding in that ward, we were privileged to get involved with one which was to be spread over all the newspapers in town the next morning.

It seemed that several days previously an East Village patrolman named James Scott, having been sent to a grubby hotel in response to a panic call from a night clerk, came upon a newborn baby girl bleeding to death in the washbasin of a bathroom. "She was only a few hours old," Nurse Kauffman told us. "Scott commandeered a blanket, wrapped the baby up, and brought her here to Bellevue, which luckily isn't too far away. The umbilical cord was tied and the baby's life was saved."

The next day, Patrolman Scott dropped in at the hospital to see how his foundling was making out. She was doing fine. The following day he dropped in again. "By that time the baby had become the darling of our nursery staff. She hadn't any name so we simply called her 'Jim Scott's baby,'" said Nurse Kauffman. "On his third visit, he gave the little girl a name—Eileen."

Scott has a family over in Brooklyn: a wife, Dolores, and their children, Danny, Patricia, and Susan. He talked so much about the foundling that finally Dolores decided to drop in at Bellevue and see her. Dolores fell in love with the baby. Next day she took the kids to see her, and by the end of a week the whole Scott family elected to adopt Eileen.

Immediately they ran into legal difficulties. It wouldn't be possible for the Scotts to adopt Eileen. All adoptions have to go through regular channels, during which other and possibly more prosperous people would be given a chance to grab her.

While we were in the Baby Ward that night it was seething with indignation over the case. Could Dolores and Jim Scott outsmart the law and get that baby? Or would she wind up with snobs who could afford to raise her to a life of hollow sham on Park Avenue? By the time we left the ward, Helen was quite frantic about the case. Even I, who would ordinarily have believed that such a soap opera couldn't possibly occur in real life, felt the suspense. As a matter of fact, it was to linger with both Helen and me for several months.

But we hadn't yet exhausted the melodrama going on that night at Bellevue. Guided by Nurse Kauffman, we entered the Children's Intensive Care Ward. And there Helen really came into her own. Some of those little creatures were pretty grotesque—one had a blown-up head and there were several with cleft palates. But there was a pretty little three-year-old named Maggie, who was a real "looker" with blonde hair and a truly vivacious personality. She might have been the picture of health except for a strange translucent pallor of her skin. She was doomed with nephrosis. At first sight of Helen, Maggie came up and solemnly presented her with a big pink rubber elephant, repeating the homage that children (and animals) always pay Helen.

We came upon a sad, wailing black baby with a terribly big forehead. His cry was so pitiful that Helen stopped beside the bed and spoke in her quietest voice—the one she uses in the theatre to dominate a scene without making too much sound. Pretty soon his wailing stopped.

"We may have to keep Miss Hayes here!" said Nurse Kauffman.

Helen beamed her thanks. "That remark is better than a rave review from Walter Kerr!"

We went through wards for grownups where, although it was now 10:30, patients were still allowed to watch television. We naturally were not invited into the violent wards, but as an indication of what goes on there, Nurse Kauffman told us that they have at least one case a month in which someone manages to break off a bit of bed spring and swallow it. This is generally done by patients who are about to be released and don't want to go home.

On our way out we came to the emergency department. Nurse Kauffman indicated a small platform at the end of the ward on which sat three men, a priest, a rabbi, and a Protestant minister. "That team keeps vigil twenty-four hours a day for anyone who needs their ministrations."

Whenever a doomed patient is brought in unconscious, all three spiritual guides join forces and say a common prayer for the poor soul. Helen fought back her ever-ready tears. "It must make those poor souls feel they're bound to get into Heaven through one door or another, doesn't it?"

Then she remembered a tragedy that had taken place in one of our city hospitals years ago. "It was when I was acting in Anita's play," she told Mrs. McCloy and Nurse Kauffman. "One night Dick Rodgers, who produced our show with Oscar Hammerstein, came into my dressing room. He was pale-faced and shaken. 'Oscar got a call from an unknown man during this afternoon,' Dick told me. 'The stranger had witnessed a catastrophe outside the I.B.M. Building at 59th and Park.

"A gray-haired man had suddenly collapsed on the sidewalk. Several people gathered and finally a policeman showed up; after examining the victim and finding no identification, the officer phoned for a city ambulance and kept guard over the prostrate man till it arrived. The stranger remained, however, until the ambulance took the victim away. It was then he noticed a card lying on the street near where the man had been lifted onto the stretcher. The stranger picked up the card, which proved to be from the American Society of Composers, Authors, and Publishers. And, along with an address, it bore a signature: Jerome Kern.

" 'I called you,' the stranger told Oscar, 'because possibly the card doesn't belong to that victim and I didn't want to alarm Mr. Kern's people at home.'

"Oscar phoned the City Hospital and learned that an unidentified man of Jerry Kern's description had just been brought in, suffering from a stroke. Heartsick, Oscar corralled Dick and they rushed to the hospital. They got hold of a young M.D. who escorted them into a ward where there were twenty or more beds, occupied by jibbering drunks and junkies who had been picked up off the street. At the end of the room was the inert figure of Jerome Kern.

"When Dick and Oscar told the young doctor who his patient was, he was shaken. 'Could he be moved at once?' they wanted to know. 'Not for several days, at least. It might be fatal.' 'But we can't leave him in this hellhole—we can't have his wife see him here. And isn't all this noise very bad for him?' Yes, bad it was and the whole situation was almost too much for the young M.D.

"But he finally rallied; he turned and faced the length of the ward and addressed the patients. He had to talk loudly to overcome their awful maniacal sounds. 'Fellows, listen to me! This new patient is very sick and he needs quiet. Do you know who he is? He's Jerome Kern, who wrote "Ole Man River" and "Look For the Silver Lining" and a lot of songs you know. Can you help him by keeping quiet? You can save his life. Please try!' The sounds began to dwindle away and presently there was silence. Absolute silence.

" 'My God, what it must have cost those tortured men to keep still like that,' Dick said. 'I think that those few hours of stony silence were a greater tribute to Jerome Kern than all the applause he ever got.'

"At length Jerry was able to be moved to a private hospital. You know the rest. He died there peacefully."

Approaching the signing-in department near the emergency entrance, we passed a sort of anteroom where an addict was being given intensive treatment by a black orderly, an intern, and two nurses—one black and one white. We peered through the half-open door. None of them noticed us. They were too intent on bringing that junkie back to life.

Then down into the signing-in room, where there was a haphazard group (all males, mostly young and pasty-faced) waiting to be admitted. These men were all wearing handcuffs. A couple of them glanced at us with total indifference, as if they'd gotten past shame. "I'm embarrassed to look at them," said Helen, "even if they don't seem to care whether I do or not." Several had plasters on their faces or some other kinds of patchwork. "God knows what violence it all stands for," said Helen, "but I take comfort in the fact that it's all being processed quite expertly."

While we were waiting for our car in the courtyard, an ambulance drove up to deposit an alcoholic who descended rather jauntily and then staggered toward the doorway as if headed for home. At sight of him Nurse Kauffman spoke up rather casually to mention that several weeks ago one of our foremost drama critics had arrived in an ambulance and been dumped into the alcoholic ward. Helen and I were not too surprised. "And I'll bet," said Helen, "that he had just murdered a new play before he passed out."

Several days later another blast against Bellevue came out in the New York *Post*, which declared that it could only have been inspired by Dante's Inferno.

"Now that's unfair," Helen said. "Yes, there's a lot wrong with the old building which will be righted in the new one. But we saw plenty of patients being healed. That's what counts. In all fairness, the *Times* should run an article headlined, 'Go to Bellevue and Live.'"

"Let's make a date with Nurse Kauffman," I suggested, "and get her own story of Bellevue."

We thought of taking her to lunch, but where? I suggested Brownie's on East 16th Street, a unique restaurant which was possibly the first ever to serve organically grown food in our town. And the cuisine is strictly gourmet; a vegetable Wiener schnitzel is so much like an animal one, you can't tell the difference.

"Nurse Kauffman might like Brownie's. It's the only place I know that's as wholesome as she is."

"But I think she deserves champagne," said Helen. "And Brownie's doesn't serve it."

"We can give her champagne another time."

"Fine. Then later we'll take her to Twenty-One."

Well, we picked Nurse Kauffman up at the side entrance of Bellevue. She was in a trim Alice-blue suit, and if she were strolling along Fifth Avenue she could be taken for a youngish matron from a small town in the unpolluted part of our land—a visitor agog in the big city.

Sitting over a banquet of goodies that allowed one to look all live animals right in the eye, Betty Kauffman told us her idea of Bellevue. She's been there twenty-seven years; first as a student, then as a registered nurse, and for the past five years as Director of Nurses. All that time she's lived on intimate terms with violence, pain, and despair. "Bellevue's the best training ground in the country for both interns and nurses. I've spent my entire career there. I intend to stay as long as I'm useful." She smiled. "As a matter of fact, we're all pumping ourselves full of vitamin pills so we'll last till we get into our grand new building."

Certainly, none of the despair that's attributed to Bellevue has rubbed off on Betty Kauffman. Helen spoke sadly of the three-year-old girl we saw in the intensive care section, suffering from nephrosis, and mentioned her as being doomed. "Oh, Miss Hayes," Nurse Kauffman corrected her, "no one is ever doomed! We're finding new ways to save life all the time. We never stop learning new wonders of the human body. Who knows but someday a man might have a baby—right in Bellevue."

"If that ever comes to pass," Helen said, "I'm sure you'll be at the helm quiet and unruffled, bringing the miracle off in fine style!"

I wanted to know the effect of the new abortion laws in our state. "Have you been stampeded with abortions?"

"We're doing just fine!" She sounded almost jubilant.

As a Catholic, Helen cringed. She hates that new law. "I keep thinking of all those souls who haven't been allowed to live. Some of them might have enjoyed their lives."

Betty Kauffman, along with other positive qualities, is a realist. On the subject of Bellevue harboring drug pushers along with its addicts, she admitted that it *is* half true. Many emergency patients

—appendectomies, stabbings, childbirth—are also addicted to hard drugs. They've got to be supplied, so Bellevue must keep them on hand.

Between staff, workers, and patients the hospital harbors about six thousand people. Among them there are bound to be some derelicts—even in the staff. So that's how thefts happen in the drug supply. And that's why they're sometimes sold to addicted patients.

But later, while we were indulging in coffee (strong, *real* coffee; Brownie is no sadistic faddist), Betty supplied the most surprising bit of information about nursing we had heard so far.

Hunter College has recently instituted a nursing course, for our city's retired *police* and *firemen*. They may study there three evenings a week and get their practical experience at Bellevue. "It's a whole new active life for men who thought their usefulness was over. In the first year there were a hundred and five starters and only ten dropouts. Ninety-five forged through to earn their caps!"

I felt obliged to warn Betty that one of those cop-nurses may, in time, take that job of a male accouchement away from her.

"Over my living body, he will!" said Betty.

After lunch we stepped next door into Brownie's health-food store where, as always, we went overboard on Mrs. Brownie's home-baked bread, cakes, and cookies. Nurse Betty ordered a pound of peanuts ground into butter right before our very eyes. As we staggered out with our loaded shopping bags, Helen said, "Betty, our next invitation will be for champagne and caviar at Twenty-One."

"If you don't mind," said Betty, "let's bring some champagne down here to Brownie's!"

GETTING LOST IN

NEW YORK IS A PLEASURE

*H*elen called up. "What a lovely day for the Central Park Zoo!" But I had already thought of a more unusual idea. "How about the zoo on Staten Island?"

"Is there a *zoo* on Staten Island?"

"*Is* there ever!"

By ten o'clock on that Sunday morning we were on our way, Gladys driving her station wagon with Miss Moore (age eleven), Helen, and me as passengers.

It requires some explanation as to why a little girl of eleven happens to be called "Miss Moore." She is a namesake of *my* Gladys, and when she came to live with us it added a second Gladys to the household. To have called them "Little" and "Big" Gladys seemed too complicated, so at the tender age of two the younger became "Miss Moore."

Fate didn't intend us to get to Staten Island in a hurry. As we were lined up waiting to board the ferry, something conked out in the car. While Gladys went to phone the Automobile Club, Helen suggested that she, Miss Moore, and I should prowl about the neighborhood. Miss Moore preferred to count herself out and, curling up on the back seat, dozed off to dreams of Superman and Popeye from whose images on TV she had been ruthlessly torn.

To be stranded anywhere in our town can only turn into an adventure, for either better or worse. That day it led us into the city's most satisfying spot for people-watching: Battery Park!

Up to then it had been so far outside our ken that we hadn't thought of including it in our plans. To the extent that we knew it at all, Battery Park was a place to cross en route to the Staten

Island Ferry. We were now to learn that, aside from its qualities as a wonderful human zoo, it harbors one of New York's few archaeological sites, a dramatic relic of New York's earliest days as a Colony.

We started to follow a man who was studying a small map and within a few minutes found ourselves at old Fort Clinton. It is completely documented with posters. The Fort had been constructed as our colonial defense against attack by sea. And built so well that it's still here. We wandered farther; learned that the Fort had suffered the fate of the Maginot Line—had become obsolete in its own day and was abandoned.

We next came to a piece of information that made Helen glow. "When its use as a Fort was over, it had been turned into that fabled playhouse known as Castle Garden."

"Just think, Anita, that the great P. T. Barnum held forth here as impresario. And it was here that he first presented Jenny Lind, the Swedish Nightingale. Can you imagine Castle Garden on such a glowing night, with its potted palms and arched glass roof and great crystal chandeliers?"

"Well," said I, "it doesn't really take much imagination when there are posters all over the place with illustrations of it."

Helen waved this aside; again we wandered on and then sat down to rest on a bench that faced the dazzling Harbor.

"Look at Miss Liberty," Helen exclaimed, "raising her torch high above the Harbor as if to light up the great meadow in front of Fort Clinton!"

She was interrupted when a transistor radio started pouring out a Strauss waltz. Then another radio tuned in the baseball game, and a whine of rock reached us from a distance. According to Helen, it all came together just fine.

Presently, a mild, elderly black man took a seat on the bench next to us and turned his transistor on to the latest kidnaping, followed by a couple of murders. But they only served to deepen our sense of present peace.

"This is the best example we've had, so far, of the amazing

81

heterogeneous mass that makes up the city," Helen said, waxing ecstatic over several Chinese groups with the living dolls that they call children. And there were Latin Americans, the fathers bouncing the little ones on their shoulders. Helen was also much taken by the Jewish family feeling—Grandma and Grandpa taken right along on the outing, free to show off their young with pride.

It was easy, of course, for Helen to spot the Irish. "I like to think the papas are off-duty cops. And, Anita, have you noticed, there isn't a sullen, angry look in the whole crowd?"

Helen then indicated a woman sitting to the left of us. She was typical of those lone souls one encounters all over the city. "But this one," whispered Helen, "had the good sense to choose Battery Park."

Noticing Helen's attention, the woman edged over and spoke so fervently to her that it made her jump. "May I ask you a question?" Having agreed to hear the question, Helen allowed as how she was really she. At which the woman thanked her, got up, and wandered away. Helen sighed in relief. "Just imagine! She didn't want to strike up a conversation! Just wanted to satisfy her curiosity. But unfortunately she opened with one of my unfavorite gambits, 'May I ask you a question?' The other infuriating one is 'Did anyone ever tell you you look like Helen Hayes?' They know damn well who I am, so why not come right out and say so? Why the coy bit?"

Perhaps I have given an impression that Helen is a humanized sugarplum. Not so. Frequently, with her face aglow, she will trill the most poetic accolades on things she finds sweet, beautiful, and yummy. And, then, boom, right out of left field, she can detest something just as violently as good old detestable me.

I think what really annoyed Helen about that poor woman was the intrusion into the delicious anonymity of that Sunday crowd.

We wandered toward the expansive meadow running the full length of the Park and found it far removed, in spirit, from what we are used to seeing in Central Park. Any number of perfectly normal families had set up small households on the grass, with folding chairs, ice buckets, lunch bags, beach towels, and transistors, not to mention a few portable record players. A fat lady in very short shorts had even brought along blankets and a pillow. She was a natural for Helen's emotions. "She's all alone, but she's going to have a delicious day, God bless her! All these things are happening for free at Battery Park. We're seeing New York relaxed and smiling like the outsized village it is."

Looking around, I added, "And not a single hippie in the lot."

But here Helen had to correct me. "Look, darling! Here come three of them, Daddy, Mother, and Baby Bear, and they've all grown long hair but Daddy has won with the bushiest." Her tone now tenderized, Helen continued, "See how he's carrying baby like a knapsack? And there's a look of old-fashioned bliss on their faces that only comes with love and from having a small being that you have made!"

I couldn't let that observation go unchallenged.

"That hippie father is 'wearing' his child as if it were an extra string of beads, and his blissful look could easily come from being stoned on pot."

"Have it your own way, love," was Helen's tolerant reply. "But do you know, as I look around here I remember another Sunday, at Alameda Park in Mexico City, and, may Father Knickerbocker forgive me, I thought how much more family warmth there was among those Mexicans. Fathers don't play unashamedly with their children back home in New York. Well, after this Sunday we know they do! And we know, too, that a lot of the picturesque experiences we go to look for abroad exist right on our own doorstep. All one needs is a pair of eyes for looking."

While making our way back to Gladys and Miss Moore, we strolled past the old Custom House facing the park which has been made obsolete by the World Trade Center, the towers of which loomed up in the distance. We stopped to admire the old building and the classical limestone statues representing the continents of America, Europe, Asia, and Africa in the guise of gloriously beautiful women of the type that's gone out of style.

"Wouldn't it be wonderful if the city moved those handsome sculptures up to Lincoln Center, to replace the fat circus ladies in the lobby of the State Theater?" Then, with her invariable fairness, she added, "Possibly those females were easier on the eyes as the artist created them, eighteen inches high, but twenty feet of them is just too much fat lady. And how utterly they fail to harmonize with the airy foyer."

" 'Airy's' right," I agreed. "It looks like a jail in Haiti."

Back at the station wagon, we found Gladys and Miss Moore still waiting for the Auto Club to come to the rescue, so we decided to board the ferry on foot, leaving the car to catch up with us at the Zoo after it had been repaired.

Approaching the ferry slip, Helen waxed philosophical. "Now that my future is shorter and time is of the essence, I simply can't use any of that precious commodity for travel by ship. I suppose that's why I look forward with such a happy sensation to this ferry ride. It's rather like starting on a European jaunt—that is, in the old days."

There's a paragraph about that ferry trip in the American Institute of Architects guide which we felt we ought to pass along: "This is the low-income substitute for a glamorous departure from New York by transatlantic liner, receiving Liberty's salute and viewing the remarkable wedding-cake silhouette of the Manhattan skyline. On a lucky day, you will plow through the wakes of freighters, ferries, liners, pleasure craft, and even an occasional warship. And you will experience one of the great voyages of the world . . . for only five cents."

As we got off the ferry, I became a guide to Helen. I had discovered the Zoo by chance one day when I went for an aimless drive with a friend and happened to wind up on the ferry. I'd never been to Staten Island, so we stopped at a filling station to ask if there was anything there to see. The attendant suggested the Zoo. I hadn't even heard about it so, on the way there, I remarked that it probably consisted of a coyote and a few captive pigeons.

How wrong I was. Small though it is, that Zoo, like Noah's Ark, has at least two of everything. And because there are not masses of animals, one sees them more distinctly, feels that because they've had so much personal attention, they've taken on a special friendliness.

Helen had visited zoos all over the country, had taken refuge in them when touring and tired of art galleries and what she called "their cold silence."

"I find delicious companionship in zoos, and have made some good friends among zookeepers. Invariably they assure me that animals are much better off in captivity. But they never make me believe that those powerful creatures pacing their small cages are happy in their lot. Keepers always stress that their coats are heavy and sleek, that they're never in danger of attack, that they enjoy a scientifically balanced diet and don't have to go on the prowl for food. They never convince me."

It was actually a matter of diet that caused our afternoon to end with an anticlimax. Every zoo features a star act, and on Staten Island it's the reptile collection. In we went, but Helen couldn't stomach the sight of those gluttonous snakes with little white mice struggling in their mouths. "They made me suffer as if I were a mouse myself," was her verdict.

Anyway, it was nearing five o'clock: closing time for the Zoo and not a sign of Gladys and Miss Moore. Perhaps they'd given up and gone home. I phoned my apartment. No answer. They must be on their way to Staten Island.

The Zoo closed. We waited out front for another half hour. Then, relinquishing all hope for our rendezvous, we left. Had something awful happened to them in that frightening Sunday traffic?

However chancy life may be in our city, at least it provides a workout for the emotions. Anything can happen after any parting: an accident, mugging, rape, or one of a dozen different kinds of violent death. While marking time for any reunion, the shadow of calamity never ceases to add suspense to the moment.

"Stop worrying, Anita, love! Let's enjoy our boat trip back to Manhattan."

We walked several blocks to a bus which took us down to the water past the charming early-American houses that dot the scenery. At the ferry I phoned the apartment again. Again no answer. "Don't look so gloomy, Anita, darling. Your Gladys and Miss Moore are all right—take your mind off them and watch this glorious crowd!"

Boarding the ferry, we watched a lot of young folk carrying bags with wet bathing suits and numerous families a little subdued perhaps but all ready to enjoy the ferry ride home. And still no hippies. My respect for the young began to rise.

There were more really beautiful people on the ferry than one could discover in any roundup of the Beautiful People of the World. We saw several girls who were prettier than the Vicomtesse de Ribes. Any one of them could have made a career of her looks, but it was obvious they preferred living to scheming on how to exhibit themselves.

Everybody was eating things that Helen loves—hot dogs, ice-cream cones, Good Humors. "Wasn't I good to buy only a bag of potato chips and a restrained Italian ice?" she boasted.

We then had the sort of experience which is, to me, what hot dogs and pickles are to Helen. Looking across the aisle, we saw a young man of such peerless beauty that he could have posed for any statue of the young King David.

"What a replacement for Marlon Brando!" exclaimed Helen.

That he hadn't already reached the movies must have been due to his extreme youth. He hadn't yet had time to circulate. Presently he became aware of our scrutiny and moved to a bench where we could see him better.

I could have approached him, explained who Helen was and that she felt he might have a career in show business. But then embarrassment overcame me. "What if he thought my interest was not cultural, that I was simply an old bag looking for a gigolo?"

86

"What if he's *right*?" suggested Helen. Be that as it may, I didn't have the nerve to approach him. "So much the better," Helen remarked. "He looked happy in his Schiaparelli pink shirt and his white canvas trousers, bent on nothing more portentous than getting home from a good time. Let someone else introduce him to glamour and vanity and Cardin neckties and frustration."

We got off the ferry. Looked for the spot where we'd last seen the car. It was gone. Should I take time to phone again, or hurry home?

The answer to that problem was supplied by the unbelievable sight of a Sixth Avenue bus, ready to bear us to the very block of my apartment building.

Home! We dashed into the elevator—unlocked my door—and there were Gladys and Miss Moore as safe and sound as when we parted.

It had taken the Automobile Club only ten minutes to fix the car, but they'd spent hours trying to locate it. Gladys had fretted as much about us as we had about them. And that's what I mean by a complete workout for the emotions in any single day of life in our fair city.

TRASH CAN BE BEAUTIFUL

*W*ith all due respect to LSD, nothing could be more mind-expanding than a trip Helen and I took with a load of New York City garbage. We were on a tugboat that was towing a fleet of sanitation barges down the Harbor. They were piled high with plastic bags full of trash, their brilliant colors glittering in the autumn sunshine: turquoise, aquamarine, and icy white, as if they were cargoes from a world of fantasy. Any single item that we were able to make out conjured up a mystery: to whom had it belonged; whence had it come; what would its destination be? And from time to time, Helen would exclaim, "Oh, why would anyone ever throw *that* away?"

Trash appeals to one of Helen's strongest instincts—thrift. A self-confessed hoarder, she has tucked away in her attic, closets, and bureau drawers a wild assortment of refuse being saved against the day when she can discover some use for it. And, while on this subject, I might as well tell all: she saves leftovers in the icebox, meaning to serve them up in some casserole of her very own concoction. So when I suggested that we investigate how the city deals with the problem of leftovers in a wholesale manner, she fell for the suggestion.

Of course, we had already learned a little about garbage disposal during our cruise around Manhattan on the Circle Line. Our guide had pointed out a small red vessel plying the Harbor. "That tugboat belongs to the Moran Towing Company. It has just towed a string of barges full of garbage over to Staten Island."

"How nice for Staten Island!" I had quipped.

At which, as if to reprove me, our guide continued, "The garbage will help fill in a swamp and give Staten Island several hundred acres of solid ground for a new park and gardens."

"What a constructive idea!" Helen exclaimed. "Coffee grounds as ground for new real estate!"

Well, we telephoned the Moran Towing and Transportation Company and invited ourselves aboard a tugboat assigned to towing garbage. And thus started one of our most revealing experiences. The offices of the Moran Towing Company are at the very tip of the Battery, and from their seventeenth-floor windows one can see the full sweep of the Harbor below. Actually, the view looks as if it were a scale model specially built for the Moran Company so that officials can sit at their desks and watch the numberless tugs at work among the ships entering and departing from the great Port.

However, on meeting the Vice-President of the Company, Mr. Lloyd Graham, we learned that he took a dim view of our ill-smelling project, and he now gave us a last chance to back out. "Why don't I send you ladies aboard one of our deluxe tugs that steer ocean liners into port and dock them at the piers?" he suggested. "Today you could sail down the Bay and help bring in the *Queen Elizabeth II*. You'd have just as superb a view of the approach to New York as if you were passengers on a luxury liner."

I was not to be dissuaded. We had recently had that selfsame view from the deck of a Staten Island ferry. "And it only cost a nickel," I argued.

At this point, Mr. Frank Weierich, a gentleman from the Sanitation Department, entered into the argument and warned that we might suffer some rugged moments. "Sometimes our load is a little ripe, and if the wind is toward us . . ." I argued that we'd endured some pretty ripe plays in New York lately.

"And because of my prominence in the profession," Helen added, "I'm denied the consolation of holding my nose." Just the same, however, Helen was sufficiently swerved to put the decision up to me. "Which shall we watch?" she asked. "The *Queen Elizabeth* or a garbage scow?"

I opted for the latter, "because," I explained, "it's so much more chic."

Which statement, later on, led to a little curtain lecture from my friend, who can't forgive me for resenting her frequent use of the word "yummy." "What about that speech idiosyncrasy of *yours*?" she asked. "Do you realize your chief standard of judgment is 'chic'? I have a feeling that if you get to heaven and find St. Peter short on chic, you'll back away and head in the other direction." I admitted defeat, but I won a victory in our argument with Mr. Graham and Mr. Weierich, who then confessed that they had been delegated to go along with us, no matter where.

Before starting out we were presented with copies of a booklet titled, "The Moran Story," which Mr. Graham said would explain the dramatic part played by Moran craft, not only in New York Harbor, but in the waterways of the entire world.

We were escorted to a small pier only a short block away and, once aboard the barge, our spirits really soared. The weather couldn't have been more entrancing: a bright October sun and the Bay just choppy enough to make us realize we were on an excursion. Our Captain and his crew of eight were in the best tradition —right out of a sea chanty. And our little tug, the *Martha Moran*, was "capital." Our only reminder of garbage was that our tug was trailing four enormous, zinc-lined scows. They were empty of trash except for one, from the crest of which a lone nylon stocking flipped impudently in the breeze and, by the way, stuck there until we bid it godspeed at the end of the day. That stocking looked as provoking and sexy as if it had been tossed aside by a latter-day Fanny Hill.

As we cruised along, the wind came from the direction of our scows but, even so, there was not a whiff strong enough to cancel out the eau de Cologne with which Helen and I had fortified ourselves. (Hers was Devon Violets, naturally; mine, a lush scent called Patchouli that is potent enough to cancel out the worst fumes that have ever risen from the Jersey lowlands.)

Standing on the upper deck of the *Martha Moran* with our two companions, Helen was moved to a confession. "For years I've traveled up and down the West Side Highway and watched these

90

chunky little tugs. (They reminded me of my grandmother on my father's side from whom I get my tendency to fat.) Then, one day when I arrived on an ocean liner from France, I watched them nudging our beautiful seagoing goddess into place and resented their impudence. 'I wonder if those dumpy little boats couldn't be done away with,' I thought. Later I had my answer during a tugboat strike when the Captain of the *Queen Mary* berthed her neatly all by himself."

Lloyd Graham objected to that statement. "Matter of fact," he said, "it was a great relief to the shipping companies when we could get back into action. Any docking without tugs is hazardous. It's a strain on the Captain and it's expensive. At night he loses precious time waiting out in the Narrows so he can dock in daylight."

Chastened, Helen said, "So there! I've learned *that*! I apologize to the little tugs. Now all of a sudden they don't look dumpy in the least. They're very gallant flaunting that proud white M on their smokestacks."

But when she later had an opportunity to read "The Moran Story" Helen completely lost the condescension with which she had figuratively patted the little tugs on the prows.

Few observers who see those boats scooting about the Harbor think of them as ever venturing into other waterways. And yet throughout World War II the Moran tugs regularly crossed and recrossed both the Pacific and the Atlantic Ocean. There was a certain gallant tug that bashed in the conning tower of a German submarine. Two Moran tugs were lost at sea with all their crewmen. And one that left New York Harbor on a ten-day job didn't get back for fifteen months.

World War II was, as a matter of fact, a fourth war for the Moran Company. It had been organized just in time for involvement in the Civil War. In the Spanish-American War, Moran tugs ran between Florida and the U. S. Fleet in Cuba. In World War II, Franklin Roosevelt got the Moran Company to assemble a fleet of craft to be sent to the aid of Britain. But Moran tugs really came into their own at that critical time in World War II when they aided in landing the Allied Forces on the Normandy beachhead.

To get those boats across the ocean was an unprecedented feat of engineering. A single tug wouldn't have sufficient weight to withstand heavy seas. The Moran experts worked out a plan by which tugs hauled railroad carfloats, one welded to the top of the other to constitute a vessel of sufficient depth and seaworthiness to face the Atlantic crossing.

Naturally, the Germans didn't let them accomplish those things under ideal conditions. And once the tugs reached the Normandy coast, they had to help in the prodigious job of constructing an artificial port. A huge mass of disabled ships and hundreds of great concrete pierheads had to be sunk offshore to create a huge breakwater and an artificial harbor for the landing of the Allied troops.

The head of the Moran family at that time was Edmond, and for his services he was made a Rear Admiral in the U. S. Navy. Recently, Admiral Moran has been quoted as saying, "Sometimes when I look out of my office window and watch our tugs crisscrossing the Harbor, I think of how we deposited that absurd collection of decrepit ships and cement blocks, one by one, on the Normandy beach. It's likely that such an operation will never take place again. So I say to myself, 'As far as I'm concerned, they can take that term "lowly tugboat" right out of the language.' "

Now we were nearing one of the so-called Marine Transfer Stations, thus named as a polite cover-up, for actually they are huge garbage dumps where that commodity is loaded onto scows. This one at the Brooklyn Bridge is adjacent to the grandiose Alfred E. Smith Housing Project. Our sanitation man eyed the apartment building balefully because its tenants had kicked up such a row about the odor that they succeeded in shutting it down. "People demand sanitation," said Mr. Weierich glumly, "but nobody wants to live next to an M.T.S." (M.T.S. being an abbreviation of Marine Transfer Station).

Sitting on the upper deck of the *Martha Moran,* we had a superb view of the Brooklyn Navy Yard, now defunct, but still harboring those two magnificent veterans, the first of the aircraft carriers, *Essex* and *Randolph.* "What heroics those two names bring to mind!" said Helen. Now the two rested, aged and deserted, on the water.

On the Brooklyn shore just above the Navy Yard there was a weird sight. It looked like a set for *Doctor Zhivago,* being a wide expanse of what appeared to be snow. It really is a store of rock salt that will be rushed to make the Brooklyn boulevards safe for travel in the coming winter.

Sailing past Brooklyn Bridge brought out all of Helen's eloquence. "It has such a look of magic," said she, "so spider-webby that it's hard to imagine it was ever constructed by toil, sweat, and muscles. Easier to believe that some fairy waved a wand."

We steamed up the East River and passed the Lloyd L. Seaman "Baby Barge"—a bright, white, pretty little barge that runs a child-care program from June to Labor Day under the auspices of St. John's Guild of Trinity Church. Children are taken by a parent for a day's outing, during which they get medical treatments and dental checkups. "That's a mean trick to play on the poor kids," I remarked, but Helen disagreed.

"Don't be too sure! I can almost see little Junior having a tantrum because Mom failed to get him an appointment with the dentist just so he gets on a ship!"

We next passed a bizarre sailing craft covered with Hebraic symbols painted on the prow and stern. It is tied up at 27th Street and is a Peace Ship from Israel. Heaven only knows how it got across the cruel sea to here, but our authorities refused it permission to go one mile farther into the U.S.A. So there it sits with a skipper dedicated to broadcasting footless peace messages in Hebrew from his ham radio set. "He's a little too close to the daffy ward at Bellevue to be safe," I commented.

Approaching Welfare Island, we were greeted by a splash from that enormous jet of water, put there as a thing of beauty and intended to beguile, but it really looks like a broken water main. And besides, it gave us a wetting.

At 91st Street, close by Gracie Mansion, we came to our first *active* M.T.S. Clearly our Mayor is in no position to register a complaint against the Sanitation Department.

But, bound for another M.T.S., we passed it by. Cruising along with our three empties in tow but out of our line of vision, we began to feel as pampered as guests of Mr. Onassis on the *Christina*. "The sights may not be as pretty as the Isles of Greece," declared Helen, "but they're nonetheless interesting."

"Not as interesting as Mr. Onassis," I cut in. "I once dined on the *Christina* and found him as devastating as Humphrey Bogart or any other Warner Brothers gangster."

At this point we were invited below for lunch. We had fancied that any refreshment served would be a matter of coffee and ham-on-rye and I had prepared myself for such a contretemps. "I couldn't possibly eat anything," I declared. "I had an enormous breakfast." But I had only done myself in: my breakfast left no room for the most magnificent spread of the year.

When we entered the saloon, the long table held an exhibition of Helen's favorite picnic fancies—or in more chic circles, hors d'oeuvres: olives, raw carrots, celery, deviled eggs, and pickles. Over it all there hovered the rare fragrance of homemade bread which, as it turned out, actually was homemade bread. It had just been taken from the oven by the tug's cook. Our respect for his cuisine rose high indeed; where, in any home we frequent, do we ever find homemade bread?

The cook had also prepared, from scratch, a wonderful pea soup with bacon, not from a can. There followed corned beef, cabbage, mashed potatoes, squash, carrots, peas, and salad. After which, Helen, feeling as overstuffed as a Castro convertible, had the choice of rice pudding, jello, or bread pudding—all home-made. We glanced at the small, seemingly inadequate stove, stuck back against the wall of the compact little galley and at the meager array of kitchen utensils.

Later on Helen told me she had thought of the parade of cooks who in the past ten years had wandered, discontent, in and out of her beautiful, big, perfectly equipped kitchen, with windows overlooking lilacs, dogwood, and the Hudson River. And then Helen admitted that it had crossed her mind to try to steal the *Martha Moran*'s chef. "But I had a strong feeling it would be hopeless. He was a sea cook, probably the son of a sea cook. He would never be content except on the water—like our Captain and the rest of the crew. Seafarers all. It didn't matter what sort of job they were doing, so long as they had the feel of water under them."

The only advantage Helen took of that sublime cook was to finagle the recipe for his deviled eggs. She edged into the subject by saying, "I made a batch at my house only last week, but they tasted sort of flat, so I thought I'd ask you for the secret of that unusually piquant flavor."

"I just mix mayonnaise and powdered mustard in the yolks," he said, and went no further.

"But that's exactly what I did, and they certainly didn't taste like yours."

He shrugged, turned away, and then slowly, torturedly, turned back and came clean. "I put in a squirt of sweet pickle juice."

It was inspiring to witness a man win a battle over his baser, meaner self. His galley would never again have exclusive knowledge of the best deviled eggs in the new world. And now Helen is printing his secret in a book. Oh, perfidy, thy name is Helen Hayes!

While Helen was working her wiles on the cook, I put in my time with our luncheon companions, the crew. Eight doughty men of a type I seldom get to meet on my restricted social rounds. The situation reminded me of a time in Hollywood when our kitchen oven started to smoke and, in a panic, I called the Fire Department. The fire laddies came, cooled the oven off, and left. But afterwards, my Gladys said to me, "That was the finest body of men you ever got into *this* house, Miss Loos!" On either Broadway or in Hollywood, one must look further afield for sex appeal.

95

Making conversation, I asked our Captain about a large brass cross that hung on the wall and asked if he were Catholic. "No," he said, "but one day the boys found that in one of our loads so we cleaned it up and hung it there." He added that there are more interesting things in garbage than it is ever given credit for.

"People often come to us for permission to search the refuse of their district for something they've thrown away by mistake," Frank Weierich said, "and the city's very co-operative. It gives orders for us to spread out a big tarpaulin on the dock and dump the whole day's load on it. You ought to see those folks—they'll wade through the whole mess for hours.

"Then, too, the police frequently have to go through our loads with a fine-tooth comb, looking for odd things . . . jewelry, art objects, bodies." I shuddered and changed the subject. For we were now getting close to our destination, the Southeast Bronx M.T.S., where we would pick up our first musty cargo. What if we saw a finger sticking out of it, or maybe a whole arm? If I'd been able, I'd have asked to go ashore.

As we were docking, Lloyd Graham gestured off to a big, low, spread-out building near the M.T.S., but only half completed. "That will be the new Fulton Fish Market when it moves from downtown. You ladies wouldn't want to come here again then! Fish garbage can make any other kind smell like a bridal bouquet!" (As yet we hadn't had a single nasty whiff.)

The maneuvering of the scows began. The *Martha M.* was to swap two empty scows for two loaded ones, after which she would proceed to the North Shore station in Queens, leave her two remaining empties, and pick up two more loaded ones.

We sat on the top deck and viewed the maneuver, entranced. It was as tricky as bringing the *Michelangelo* into dock. The first two scows, laden with garbage, were edged out of their slips at the enormous warehouse. The crew, following the Captain's shouted orders, leapt about from deck to deck like ballet dancers. They flung ropes back and forth with expert precision, always making their connection.

One member of that crew had attracted my eye from the very first. I've never gotten over my old Hollywood interest in talent scouting. This lad would be a boon to any Western. Browned by the sun, lithe and with the required rippling muscles, his hair not too long and just the right shade of gold. I nudged Helen and pointed him out. "What's he doing *here*?" I asked her.

"If I know you, love, you'll make it your business to find out."

During a lull in the proceedings I struck up conversation. His name, Michael Furlong, was quite "stagy" and just the right length for a marquee.

He told Helen and me that he had been at the job for several years and enjoyed the work. The hours suit him fine—six days on the water, living high on the *Martha M.*, fed by the cookery of Louis the master chef. Then eight days off. What does he do with the eight free days? He drives a hack in Central Park! "Have you ever thought of a career in movies?" I ventured. His answer withered me.

"I've seen those characters making movies in the Park. All they do is sit around and wait. Me, I like action!"

The young man's lack of interest delighted Helen. "I saw just such a character on a TV talk show recently," she said. "He was plugging a book he'd written. Asked how he supported himself while he wrote it, he said, 'I sell hot roast chestnuts in Central Park—still do. I like that work, too. It's just as groovy as writing.'"

When it was time to shove off, an alarming fact became evident. We had taken it for granted that we'd be pulling the garbage scows *behind* us with a good long hawser and, we hoped, the wind blowing in the opposite direction. We now began to realize that this was not the case. For the *Martha M.* began to nose her way *between* the two loaded scows. And it became clear that she was not going to pull that cargo behind us; she was going to push it ahead. We would be right smack in the middle of two mountains of garbage, at a distance of only a few feet, cruising up the river with a brisk wind blowing in our direction.

But once we were full steam ahead, we began to marvel that not a single unsavory whiff was reaching us from our cargo. It took an expert, Mr. Weierich, to explain the mystery. "Smells never cross water," said he.

"To think," Helen exclaimed, "that from the start, we'd been worrying about something that, thanks to a basic scientific fact, would never take place!" It reminded me of an old motto that Elsie de Wolfe used to embroider on satin sofa cushions: "Cheer up. It never happens."

It didn't take Helen long to wax even more philosophical. "I've always said that just about anything looks good in the sunshine. Did you notice how the most squalid sections of the East River shoreline took on gaiety and charm as we passed them? And now the sun is working its magic on . . . swill!"

And then, gesturing toward the elegant plastic trash bags, she observed, "Those must come from very fashionable neighborhoods." Mr. Weierich corrected her.

"Fashionable?" he exclaimed. "The Southeast Bronx? It isn't the rich who throw things away. Our men find that garbage from rich neighborhoods is scanty and uninteresting. The rich hold on to things—that's what made 'em rich. It's the poor who are extravagant."

One startling example on this poor people's trash heap was a monstrous pink teddy bear—the kind I've won at Coney Island when I hit an unlucky number and got stuck with a prize. But instantly Helen coveted it. She would have loved to salvage it and wait for a time when a soiled pink teddy bear came in handy.

I was particularly fascinated by typewritten pages blowing about our deck from the scows. Some of them looked like manuscript. "The tons of *that* I've contributed to trash!" I said to Helen.

"Of course, yours is more *chic*," she answered, "because of those different colors you use to keep track of the rewrites—pink, green, yellow." Mr. Graham thanked me gravely for my work of livening up the litter.

Presently we were greeted by an extra dividend of entertainment; at least a hundred or more sea gulls swooped in and settled on the cargo. Neither Helen nor I had ever before been able to watch the private life of gulls at close range. Now we had front-row seats. How elegant and spotless they were, in their French blue-gray and white. The females, a little subdued as usual in birds and beasts, stood respectfully by while their males had a first go at the litter. Most of them—bachelors and married gulls alike—seemed to have good manners and to obey the rules: no poaching on the other fellow's territory and no gulping. They picked among the trash quite daintily, and once in a while one would mount to a high point and stand there posing. We watched the struggles of a godlike male for ten minutes as he tried to get a bread crust out of a plastic bag. When he finally made the breakthrough, we all cheered.

The gulls are not the only pretty things among God's creatures who love garbage. A gorgeous orange butterfly fluttered over one of the loads all the way from the Southeast Bronx to the end of our trip. Helen knew that a butterfly only lives twenty-four hours, so it seemed foolish that this lovely thing was going to spend its entire life on a garbage heap. "Couldn't it find some lovely garden to hang out in?" Helen asked.

At which I replied, "Would you exchange this adventure for a routine day in any garden?"

"Of course not!" answered Helen brightly. "I'd never even think of it!"

Our journey was brought to a close by our return to the Bronx M.T.S. And now that we were landed, we began for the first time to experience the stench of garbage. It appeared that scientific fact had no mercy on the Bronx.

We left the *Martha M.* at the South Bronx station, and Mr. Weierich drove us back to Manhattan in his car, Lloyd Graham remaining aboard. The *Martha M.* was now ready for its last long haul to Staten Island, which it wouldn't reach until 9:30 that night. Had we been aware of our trip's many fascinations before starting out, we'd have arranged to stay aboard and witness the dumping of that load onto a Staten Island swamp. In addition, we would have had another delectable banquet with the crew of the *Martha M.*, one which would even have climaxed our lunch party, because now we were all pals. However, both Helen and I had commitments for that evening.

Now we reached that moody moment which comes at the end of a perfect day. And, looking ahead to the silly, superfluous world which would soon engulf us, I remarked, "Don't you think, Helen, that you and I have been spending an awful lot of time in the wrong places? And with the wrong people?"

Helen sighed, but, ever the optimist, she said, "Maybe, dear. But we'll never lose our memories of this lovely tugboat and the Sanitation Department!"

"Where men are men," I added, "and we are sufficiently unliberated to love them for it!"

BLOWING OUR MINDS

$\mathscr{T}$here is a variety of special institution of learning in our town that fires the imagination. Going through the Yellow Pages of the phone directory, I made out a list that staggered me. I read it to Helen over the phone. It staggered her. But more than that, it began to conjure up ambitions of which we had never before dreamed.

We found that we could take courses in astrology, poodle clipping, diamond setting, hypnosis, dry cleaning, Judo, stock brokerage, Yoga, skin diving, and chess. There is an Imperial School of Chinese Cookery and the Humanities, which is apparently out to gratify both the stomach and the soul. There is an old-world type of finishing school for young ladies run by some optimist out of the past who hasn't learned that most of today's young ladies are finishing themselves. There's the Ikebana Art Center for the study of floral arrangements. And, most broadening of all, the International Bartenders School.

"Just think," said Helen, "of the people who go to Paris for courses at the Sorbonne, and to the Royal Academy in London for acting or Kyoto for Zen Buddhism and Rome for art, when there's so much to learn right here!"

Our ambitions to study a new subject almost got out of hand. But realizing that at our time of life we couldn't hope to complete too large a number of courses, we decided to investigate at least some of them to the furthest stretches of our minds. We hardly knew where to begin. "Let's start alphabetically," Helen suggested, "with Astrology." So off we went.

The Lynne Palmer School of Astrology is on West 72nd Street in one of those offbeat neighborhoods that look like steel engravings of New York in 1880. Our destination was a ten-story office building which, in its heyday, had been a skyscraper. It frankly shows its age and the elevator wobbles.

We entered a room so immense that there was space to spare for twenty-five large round tables, each one of which accommodated four armchairs and a sizable ashtray. There was enough wall space for any number of astrological charts representing signs of the zodiac. At the end of the classroom stood an easel on which were placed horoscopes of the famous for study by the class. (Napoleon's was there that day, with an astrological alibi for Waterloo, no doubt.)

In no way did Miss Palmer conform to our visions of an astrology teacher. She looked not more than thirty, was feminine, cute, and pretty as a postcard. She wore not a smidgen of batik nor even an amber bead. On the contrary, her pink suit possibly came from Chanel and she sported a few tasteful jewels that looked hot off the workbench of Van Cleef and Arpels. The only manner in which she fitted our idea of an astrologist was that she hails from that capital of the world of whim-wham, Los Angeles. Where else?

Lynne apologized for her premises, saying that only in an old building could she find a room large enough for her classes. Hers is the only school in our nation, she told us, where astrology is taught en masse. Classes are held all year round with sessions for beginning, intermediate, and advanced students. "I have a special seven-weeks marathon course," said Lynne, "during which the entire subject is covered in depth and detail. All ages and types attend that class. I have a seventeen-year-old hippie whose special interest is Tarot cards and a professor of psychology from the College of the City of New York."

"When could one enroll?" I asked and learned that no enrollment is necessary. "One merely shows up at will and pays six dollars a day."

The beginner's course deals mostly with "chart erection." The intermediary course features advanced math but also includes a study of special horoscopes of, for instance, twins, psychics, astrologers, dogs, traitors, murderers, homosexuals, transvestites,

102

people who changed their sex, prostitutes, madams, sadists, nymphomaniacs, con artists, liars, drug addicts, movie stars, and writers. Among the last, Lynne's students learn all about Mark Twain, Rudyard Kipling, Billy Rose, Grace Metalious, Hedda Hopper, and Stephen Foster.

The advanced class studies births, marriages, assassinations, murders, cancer victims, unusual deaths, and presidential elections. The course ends with prognostications of what will happen during the next two years. And, at that moment, a future was being charted for Mia Farrow, Elizabeth Taylor, and Liza Minnelli.

Just to contemplate that list of facts was head crushing, but it was the subject of math that posed a main problem for Helen and me. I hopefully asked, "It's quite easy to do the required figuring by computer, isn't it?"

Lynne shook her head. "No," she said. "Computers aren't yet accurate enough."

"Hurray!" exclaimed Helen. "Any time I hear of a computer failing, I feel better about the twentieth century."

"But what about slot machines that give instant readings at airports and railroad stations? Don't they use computers?"

"They do indeed," said Lynne scornfully, "and there's the rub. There's no such thing as Instant Destiny. My students have to work everything out by the sweat of their own brains."

That was what turned Helen and me off following astrology any further. But at the same time it seemed possible that it might supply proof to an idea I'd had for years and never dared mention: that the Wise Men from the East who traveled to the Christ child were actually astrologers. I asked Lynne about this and she answered, "Of course they were! Naturally." Feeling that she might be prejudiced, I didn't yet quite believe I'd stumbled onto a truth. But a day or two later Helen called up from Nyack in a state of excitement. She had just come from Mass and wanted to read me from the Sunday message. "Listen to this! 'During the reign of King Herod, astrologers from the East arrived . . . Herod called the astrologers aside and found out from them the exact time of

the star's appearance.' " Astrology is backed up by the Catholic
Church itself, through the Gospel according to St. Matthew.

Lynne read us some brief descriptions of our own personalities
from her pamphlet on Sun Signs. Helen's hit her right on the button. And, in case I may do her an injustice during this reportage,
here is the astrological low-down on Helen Hayes.

Born *October 10th*

Libra:

You try to balance life . . . see both sides of every story . . .
strive for the beautiful . . . peace, justice, harmony, love.
Understanding and companionship are cravings that must be satisfied. You need love . . . beautiful love . . . not lust. [This rather
threw me off, considering the many times I've caught Helen lusting
for chocolate éclairs or an ice-cream cone.]
You give in to people . . . situations. You can't say "no." [This
is correct. Helen will gleefully attend a social event that could only
be pulled off by a sadist.]

On the subject of my birth, Lynne commented that its sign covers both Shakespeare and Hitler and she read as follows:

Born *April 26th*

Taurus:

You like to own . . . possess . . . hold on . . . determined in
every way not to give up.
Persistence is yours.

"That's really more like Hitler," I observed.
Lynne continued:

Often you are so quiet that you shut yourself in and no one knows
what happened to you.

"That explains why so little is known about *Shakespeare*," I
protested. "But I'd like to find out something that's more *me*."
Smiling, Lynne read on:

Taurus has its obstinate side. Don't be so stubborn!

104

I accepted this diagnosis, and we then went on to examine Lynne's framed collection of original Tarot cards that date back to medieval times. We failed to understand much of the information Lynne gave us on that subject, but Helen did copy the prayer which hung at the front of the classroom.

PROTECTION

I am resting in the center of the pure white light of truth, forming a wall of protection through which no undesirable or evil thought, force or condition, or any plane astral or physical can penetrate. My aura is sealed by the divine aura of the Godhead, shutting out all that does not vibrate harmoniously with divine Light.

But the key phrases of that prayer, such as "astral plane," "aura of the Godhead," "harmoniously with divine Light," puzzled us and plunged us back into those odd vibrations that emanate from Los Angeles and have baffled both of us from the time we had to live there. "I could never remember such a complicated prayer in an emergency," said Helen. "I'm afraid my favorite supplication will always have to be 'God help me!' "

On our search for culture, Helen and I, sticking to alphabetical order (and Taurus obstinacy), next accepted an invitation to visit a certain minor college. It is on Eighth Avenue near 43rd Street and, in looking for the entrance, we had something of an adventure.

The ground floor was occupied by one of the many expositions of pornography that are bent on destroying romance in the Broadway area. The two of us mistook it for our destination and were heading for the entrance when we were stopped by two policemen. "What are you 'ladies' looking for?" one of them asked with a bare modicum of respect.

"We're looking for the Atlas Barber School." This stunned the cop for a moment, and he then indicated a nearby door. It was only then that we did a double-take and saw the sign that read: "Peep Show."

105

"To be mistaken for a pair of hustlers at our age," I remarked, "is rather a compliment."

"It's all yours, love! When he said that he wasn't looking at me."

As a matter of fact I actually had investigated a couple of those peep shows one Saturday en route to a clean matinee with a respectable escort. The first was lined with book shelves filled with paperbacks. On their covers were the most lovely-looking girls and the handsomest boys in postures that turn sex into a boring monotony. In the center of that room was a group of those little boxlike machines invented in the first days of the penny arcade. But the price had been upped to twenty-five cents. Each box was labeled to describe the action: "Boy and Girl," "Girl and Girl," "Boy and Boy"; something for every type of bad taste.

There is another emporium for hard-core pornography called "The Mini Cinema" and there the entrance price is five dollars. The ultimate in physical relationship is shown on a movie screen with no attempt at artistic overtones. But there again the girls and boys were of peerless beauty.

What about the audience, however? What derelict, even in these days of government relief, can afford five dollars to enjoy those expositions? Looking about, I was more startled by the patrons than by the films themselves. Most of them looked to be in comfortable circumstances; staid, of middle age, and in the process of becoming dirty old men. Fear of growing old is so much more prevalent in men than in us, that the phrase "dirty old woman" has never entered our language.

"Just watch out, Anita, and see that you don't introduce it!"

We were now mounting the long, narrow flight of steps that led to the Atlas Barber School. It is rather large, in a small way. We entered a long room equipped as a beauty parlor and were greeted by an extravagantly coiffed blonde. She introduced herself as an instructress and explained that we were in the classroom where a course in beauty culture for ladies is taught: "Our students prac-

106

tice on customers who get their treatments at a bargain rate." But now that the day was near its end, the classroom was empty except for one lone client bent on being eternally a blonde.

We were led into the men's classroom and found it buzzing with excitement, for, with our usual good luck, we had walked smack into preparations for a party. It seemed that one of the operators was having a birthday. There were Happy Birthday emblems all over the place. "Just as there were in that vault at the Federal Reserve Bank," said Helen. "Celebrations in this city of ours never know when to stop."

We were invited to return as soon as the party got under way and then led into the office of the school's director, Mr. Matthew Raguso.

I wondered whom he reminded me of, until it popped into my mind that he looked like that character called the "Laird" as drawn by George du Maurier for his novel *Trilby*. Mr. Raguso's Vandyke beard was classic, under control, and just exactly right. Later Helen and I agreed that he must be one of the handsomest gentlemen in New York City. "Just as Mr. Perry Como was in Philadelphia," I added.

On the wall above Mr. Raguso's desk is his photograph as a young graduate in mortarboard and gown. "Was that taken at the time you graduated from Barber School?" asked Helen. It was not. It was his graduation picture from the University of Ohio.

There are, we were told, three branches of the Atlas Barber School. The one we were in is a sort of parent to a larger institution farther downtown, and there is a branch on Wards Island where barbering is taught to drug addicts after they are cured. We made sure of *that*.

The birthday party followed, with Helen promoted to be guest of honor. Only recently she had made her way through four separate sticky birthday cakes of her own, during a series of celebrations that went on and on like a Hungarian wedding. But Helen is such an ardent cake lover she can even take pleasure in a bad one. Since the afternoon was given over to celebrating and snap-shots of the Birthday Girl with Helen, we made an appointment for the following week to attend a class in hair styling for men.

We arrived at ten and met Mr. Michael Vee, the professor in charge. He had been acclaimed "Barber of the Year" by his peers at one of the International Barber Contests. His beard, like Mr. Raguso's, was elegant but a trifle more casual.

The pupils were a group of young barbers taking an advanced course. Among them were two pretty girls learning to be bar-berettes. I fancy that to have a barberette work on one's hair can bring a great deal of satisfaction to any man's ego.

Professor Vee chose one of his students for a demonstration. He was young and pleasant-looking, and, in our amateur opinions, his hair and sideburns seemed perfect. But the Professor went to work on him and within the hour we saw an Apollo Belvedere emerge. The transformation was accompanied by Professor Vee's lecture, delivered with the expertise and vocabulary of an artist. "My principal instrument is this pair of gold-plated sculpturing shears. And another important tool will be a mirror. Glance at it frequently.

"Every man presents a different problem. Study your problem and attack it as if you were a sculptor."

While he worked on his young model, the students bombarded him with questions. "Should we try to persuade a client to change his hair style?"

" 'Encourage' is always a better word than 'persuade,' " said Professor Vee.

"What is the proper hair length?"

"Two or three inches. With this length you can swing it, sway it, and bend it to your will."

Watching the Professor, I was inspired to compose an enco-mium on hair. When human beings are created they are endowed with features which, except for one, are permanent. It's impossible to change the color of eyes or the pigmentation of skin. And while

108

it's true that noses can be altered, it's always a risk. However, the good Lord, in his mercy, granted mankind one feature that's easy to monkey with. It can be bleached, dyed, arranged in any form, twisted, turned, added to, or thinned out at the fancy of the grower. Any brunette can turn blonde and be preferred by gentlemen. And the musical named *Hair* can break every international box-office record. All hail to hair.

We watched Professor Vee in awe as he demonstrated two of today's favorite stylings: the "Jon-Jon," named for the stepson of Mr. Onassis, and the "Prince Valiant," copied from the comic strip.

Toward the end of Michael's lesson, he described the process for transplanting hair. "And," said Helen, "that should settle any controversy as to whether men are more capable of suffering for beauty than girls."

The transplanting is sheer agony. Hairs are taken from the back of the client's own head, where it usually grows abundantly. A tuft of six or seven hairs is scooped out with a tiny, sharp, spoon-shaped instrument of torture, so that each hair retains its follicle or root; the identical instrument is then used to scoop a hole in the bald portion of the head, where the tuft is inserted and covered by flesh, exactly as in the transplanting of a bush.

The cost of a transplant is high. Five dollars for a single tuft, of which there must sometimes be several hundred. Only about one per cent fail to take root; the others sprout and spread until they eventually cover an entire bald area.

The Professor then brought in a young man on whom the job had recently been done. Obligingly, he pushed back his hair to show us the tufts, neatly spaced at identical distances, as in an orchard.

The operation is done scientifically by specialized surgeons, and results are a hundred per cent successful. But at what a cost! During the operation the pain is dulled by an anaesthetic, but once it wears off, a headache of atom-bomb proportion erupts over the victim and lasts for days on end. There is little difference between the pain of a transplant and the agony of a face lift. Truly we have become a unisexual race in more ways than one.

Next on our list was the Bartenders School. Here, both Helen and I would be on solid ground, although she had the advantage of several bartenders in her family, particularly on the Old Sod before the Hayeses migrated here. My connection with bars was fairly remote; as a child in San Francisco my Pop, in company with the novelist Jack London, had been a periodic but nonetheless thorough drunk.

We were now to enter a realm in which I find my greatest exhilaration: the world of manly males, the International Bartenders School. All atwitter, we entered the ancient office building which houses the school way down on West 24th Street and were greeted by its proprietor, Charlie Dempsey. He is a fine broth of a man to whom the Irish in Helen responded like an electrical connection. I needed no common ancestry with him to follow suit. We were off to a flying start. And it never slowed down.

Charlie introduced us to his equally virile assistant, Robert Lamb by name. Charlie's measure as a man can be gauged by the devotion of Bob Lamb, who told us in a burst of pride, "I want you ladies to know that Charlie here is a very great benefactor of the human race. He has lifted more mortgages in his time than any loan and trust company."

"My, my!" exclaimed Helen. "How?"

"He's run this school for over thirty years, and in that time he's given a proud profession to thousands of floundering men and even some ladies who were floundering too."

Beaming, Charlie interrupted to let it be known that, like every true Irishman, he has always had a weak spot for the ladies.

"That's neither here nor there," said Bob, "the guy's got a list of over thirty thousand graduates who've bought and paid for their own suburban homes, established families, and sent the kids off to college."

We learned that Charlie began his career in the prize-fight game, from which he had drifted into bartending and thence to teaching. Today he runs the only international bartenders school in the U. S. A. Many of its graduates go on to Europe, South America, and all over the world, carrying the great American dry Martini to the very farthest corners of the earth.

The course requires fifty-four hours to complete but, if necessary, a student can spread them out while he is working at another job to earn the hundred-and-fifty-dollar fee. Bob Lamb told us that Charlie can easily be talked into keeping a young man afloat when he can't afford the tuition.

"The story I like best about Charlie," said Helen when we later mulled that particular adventure over, "is the one about Mack the taxi driver." To drive a taxi in New York is a nerve-shattering business, and one day Mack blew his stack at a mean customer. The man wasted no time in reporting him. Mack lost his license, his profession, his savings, and had a nervous breakdown. But finally Charlie heard about his plight, helped Mack pull himself together, and enrolled him for a course, on the cuff.

"Just last week, after five years of bartending," said Bob, "Mack moved into his own home in Astoria and had a baby!"

"That's what I call a love story!" said I.

Along with supplying tuition, Charlie runs a department for job opportunities. On getting his diploma, a man is set for life in a gainful occupation with which neither season, economic situation, nor even panic ever interferes. "Sometimes," said Charlie, "panic even enlarges the field!" But in bad times or good, a bartender knows he can work as long as he can stand on his feet. "Furthermore," Charlie added, "tending bar is good for the psychology. A man learns when to talk and when to button up."

"Particularly when it comes to politics," interrupted Bob. "Charlie advises the boys never to mention Washington, to keep their noses clean and concentrate on sports."

"And what about discussing 'the fair sex'?" I asked.

"That used to be okay," said Charlie, "but the way things work out today, it brings up painful ideas, so I advise 'em to leave the ladies lay."

Bob started us on a tour of the premises. We first visited a very conventional classroom, with a blackboard and rows of desks. The course entails a lot of paper work, and there is a serious memory challenge in learning the names of exotic cordials and liqueurs such as Mexican Kahlúa and Israeli Vishniak.

There are wall mottoes which admonish, "Never drink while on the job," "Never serve a drunk," and "Don't argufy."

The principal classroom is fitted up to resemble a fair-sized saloon, and when Bob led us in we found nineteen students lined up behind a long bar. The bottles bore well-known labels, but they were filled with water which, in every case except for gin and vodka, had been tinted to look like the real thing by an artistic blending of vegetable dyes. Charlie is meticulous that the colors be identical with those of the booze they imitate, but an array of olives, cherries and lemons appeared to be for real.

The class, taught by an expert behind the bar, was learning to mix a Martini. Among the students were two young men Helen vaguely recognized as having seen before. She was right, for when we met them later they proved to be actors out of work. There was only one lady, a capable-looking blonde who owns a tavern and was taking a course in order to pinch-hit during emergencies.

After our session at class, we said a regretful good-by to Charlie the flirt. But when we parted from Bob, he supplied his boss with a much higher rating. "Always remember, ladies, that you've met a gentleman who in his day was the best club fighter that ever put on a glove!"

Next came the letter C, which, to me, meant the Charm School of Ophelia de Vore. I had seen its ad in the Yellow Pages of the telephone book and called up to make an appointment. The day we went there, we found more pretty girls than either of us could remember seeing under one roof. It was evident that to matriculate at Ophelia de Vore's you had to be black and you darn well better be beautiful.

That day it appeared that Miss de Vore herself was going to be late but we were taken in charge by Jim Carter, an extremely attractive and articulate young man with an Afro hairdo. He informed us that the school had been in existence since 1946, now has an enrollment of three hundred students, and includes extra courses for teen-agers and even children. "It's never too early to eradicate the inferiority complex with which little black babies are born."

The school consists of a series of extravagantly appointed rooms, among them one dedicated to make-up and another to cinema where the girls are able to watch themselves on screen.

In the lecture hall we met a number of students, quizzed them, and found in their answers a great deal of the purpose Miss de Vore has in mind. Any one of those girls could easily have a career in modeling on her looks alone, but that is not exclusively the point. They were there to give themselves confidence in a culture where they have been submerged for so many generations. One of the prettiest, Rovenia Styles, said she was a "home girl" without any ambition for a career. "I just want to learn to feel comfortable when I come into a roomful of people."

The arrival of Miss de Vore herself that day was like the *grande entrée* of a prima donna. A sepia version of Jolie Gabor, she was dressed all in flaming red, topped by a Borsalino hat with a soaring feather to match. She has a healthy, natural beauty with a skin so pale she could easily pass for white. "And that's just what I did," said Ophelia, "when I first got here from my home in Georgia."

Ophelia's idea had been to go on the stage but her family objected. "Only bad girls go on the stage," said they. So at the age of fifteen Ophelia began a career as a model. "I had no problem because nobody thought I was black, and I didn't bother to correct them." But then the idea struck her of opening up the field of modeling for her really black sisters. She started her school in the

113

very location it still occupies, and a great number of black beauties who have since been admired on TV and in advertisements are products of her establishment.

In addition to running her school, Ophelia is also the editor-publisher of the Columbus, Georgia, *News*, which was left her as a legacy by her husband and is one of the five Negro dailies in America. The U.S. Government frequently calls on Ophelia's talents in various widespread merchandising campaigns. And she helps Con Ed train their black employees in self-confidence, plus, she chuckles, in developing a sense of humor. And as if to prove that Elizabeth Arden and Helena Rubinstein are not the only women to have built empires, she manufactures a line of cosmetics for blacks which she demonstrates in tours throughout the country.

"However do you cover all that territory?" Helen, no mean traveler herself, asked her.

"Well," explained Ophelia, "my husband died three months ago, so I've taken his place and commute every week between my Park Avenue apartment and our country place in Georgia. I did have a lovely summer home in Connecticut but to keep up three places was a little too much. So I sold the Connecticut house to Mike Nichols."

We left Ophelia's premises in a state of daze and with some strongly developed white inferiority complexes.

D for Drama was now on the agenda, and that meant the American Academy for Dramatic Arts. It is on lower Madison Avenue in a district which, once charming, has been taken over by small industry and warehouses. The building was designed by Stanford White for the exclusive old Colony Club and, with its red brick exterior and chaste white colonnade, it now looks as out of place as Dolly Madison at a hardware convention.

When the Colony Club moved to its present uptown quarters, the lovely building began a downhill career and finally hit the bottom as a Turkish bath. Eventually even that failed and the

114

American Academy was able to buy it as a bargain. Then there followed the usual fund raising, spurred by a major gift from Helen Hayes herself in memory of her daughter Mary, who had graduated from the Academy in the days when it occupied a dingy set of studios in the basement of Carnegie Hall.

In this permanent location the Academy's appointments are complete and kept in immaculate order. But looking it over with Helen that day, I thought of the two young actors we'd seen learning to shake up a Martini at Charlie Dempsey's. I wished the Academy taught a more reliable way to make a living, because a young actor bent on marketing his wares is practically clamoring for rejection.

That fact, however, doesn't seem to limit attendance at the Academy in the least. Just as kids all over the country are drawn to Greenwich Village to loaf, those who love to work are drawn toward acting. No people in the world work as hard as actors. They keep on even when they don't have to. Groups of them whose jobs are exhausting will get together and organize a workshop which takes up every free moment.

There came a momentous period in Helen's life when she decided to auction off the contents of her twenty-room Victorian mansion and donate the money to her beloved American Academy. Yes . . . Helen decided to leave Pretty Penny forever. She had never ceased collecting furnishings for it during the forty years she'd lived there. From the time she played Queen Victoria, Victoriana had poured into Pretty Penny as tributes from all over the world. But steeling herself for the sacrifice, Helen put the whole lot up at auction.

On the first day of the sale, the premises were jammed, not only with buyers, but with the snoopy. One by one precious mementoes of Helen's past went under the hammer. Anguished, I stayed away from the historic occasion; but I kept in touch because the event was reported in all the news media and honored by a center spread in *Life* Magazine.

115

At the end of several days of chaos, Helen, alone in her empty mansion, called me up.

"Well," I asked, "is it all over?"

"Yes," she replied . . . but I thought a little gingerly. I asked how soon she was going to leave the house.

There was a very long silence which Helen finally broke. "You never really thought I could leave here, did you?"

Actually, I had believed up to that very moment that she was ready to go down the steps of Pretty Penny, lugging all that was left of her worldly goods in a couple of suitcases, a lone widow departing from her home forever. And Helen is such a competent actress that she had not only put one across on me, but even on herself.

The upshot of this is that Helen is still at Pretty Penny but the American Academy gained its most appealing acquisition from the proceeds of that auction.

On entering the lobby, a noble façade greets one, rising from the far end of a long white marble floor. Over its entrance is the legend:

MARY MACARTHUR
THEATRE

When Helen took me into that exquisite miniature playhouse, she had to apologize for her emotion.

"I'm sorry, but every time I come into this little place I get teary. It means to me that Mary will always be here in spirit to welcome new young hopefuls into this gracious showcase. It's all so different from the disheartening old studio in the cellar of Carnegie Hall where my Mary had to study."

Other improvements have been carried out inside the old building. The gymnasium has been transformed into a great rehearsal hall and its various assembly rooms fitted out for classes. And there is another and larger theatre in addition to Mary's small playhouse.

The entire premises are slick with prosperity; they gleam with that well-being which is produced only by a force of earnest scrub ladies.

A list of graduates prominently placed on one wall provides a warm feeling of security in even the most lackluster talents: Cecil B. De Mille, Jane Cowl, Spencer Tracy, Grace Kelly, Edward G. Robinson, Lauren Bacall, Rosalind Russell, and Anne Bancroft.

Contemplating that list, Helen launched into speculation. "Sometime I'd like to take a refresher course here: try out my theory that actors should periodically start afresh with a whole new approach and training. It's awful to feel yourself imitating performances you've given before because you can't think up any new way to express an emotion."

I myself look on the theatrical profession less as an art than as an anodyne, a sort of cure-all such as Lydia Pinkham's vegetable compound used to be. I've had friends who lost loved ones on whom their lives were centered, who've been threatened with nervous breakdowns and even death itself, but were completely cured by a plunge into show biz. If rich, they can become backers. If indigent, they can join a summer-stock company and help to sanitize the rest rooms. I have seen many a weeping widow suddenly turn joyous and start to whoop it up at a Newport Jazz Festival. So, to that extent, I give the theatre full marks.

But I felt it only fair to look through the Academy's brochure and give it a chance to fight my levity. The catalogue almost convinced me I was wrong. The Academy's list of sponsors is august. I know full well that its mentors are experts at their trade: Frances Fuller, Worthington Miner, Lillian Gish, Helen's close friend and godmother to her son Jim, and all the teachers are experienced theatre experts.

But then, at the end of the brochure, I found excerpts from graduation addresses by two rare, intelligent souls, Josh Logan and the late Moss Hart.

Said Josh: "The only people who can exist in the theatre are those that nothing can stop. If anything can stop you, it should."

And Moss: "You will quite easily learn the tricks of the trade—

they will come as naturally as breathing the musty air of dressing rooms. . . . But there is one art that no school of drama ever teaches. It is the art of survival."

When we reached the letter F, which stood for the Fine Arts Institute of New York University, we were, in a roundabout way, going among friends. The Institute occupies the old James B. Duke mansion at 1 East 78th Street, which had been presented to the city by his granddaughter, Doris.

Doris Duke is an eccentric whose eccentricities are all based on the greatest common sense. As a mere girl she passed up all the frills the Duke family accumulated in the Eighties and, according to recent information, is now enjoying life as a member of the choir of a black church over in New Jersey.

The Institute is devoted to the history of art and archaeology, with special courses in the restoration of art works of all kinds— paintings, ceramics, statuary, books; everything. It had sent a team to Florence after the Arno flooded, to aid in salvaging and restoring works of art.

"Those young students were successful in saving a lot of rare books with irreplaceable bindings," Helen informed me.

But she hadn't yet told me about her personal association with the Institute.

"You've heard me mention an 'almost' daughter of Charlie's and mine?" Helen asked as we made our way there in a taxi.

"Perhaps. But you've got such a lot of 'almost' daughters."

"This one's special. She's been studying for two years in the Ancient Near East Department of the Institute. And now she's qualified for field work, in places like Erech and Lagash." In response to my vacant look, Helen added, "That means Mesopotamia and the Euphrates Valley, stupid!

"Well, at the end of the summer of '46 Charlie, Mary, and little Jamie were returning home by ship after a summer in London. It was during my engagement in *The Glass Menagerie* at the Hay-

118

market Theatre. The children had to get back for school, and it would be a couple of months before I'd be free to join them.

"Aboard ship they met the Geary sisters—Joyce and Phyllis, two gay, pretty girls from San Francisco who had been vacationing abroad. They were just Charlie's style and he had a glorious time with them. At the New York dock Charlie met their parents, who had come all the way from San Francisco to meet their daughters. Joyce, it seemed, was to remain in the East to enter Sarah Lawrence College, and Charlie promised the Gearys to look after their ewe lamb. Mrs. Geary was grateful but warned, 'Don't get ideas about a ewe lamb—you're more apt to find yourself with a tiger by the tail.'

"The Gearys returned to San Francisco and, as so often happens with shipboard friendships, the girls just became pleasant memories. I vaguely remember Charlie mentioning those nice Geary kids when I got back from London, but that was the end of it.

"Three years later our Mary died. One evening soon after, when Charlie and I sat numbly in our East River apartment staring at the walls, the doorbell rang. I dragged myself to the door and was confronted by a total stranger—pretty, young, with a timorous smile. 'I'm Joyce Geary, and I met Charlie and Mary and Jamie on the ship, and I'd like to extend my sympathy and . . . is there anything I can do?'

"Joyce came into our lives at that moment and was a part of our family for the next eight years. After her graduation she moved out to Nyack with us. And it was by frequent sessions of gin rummy (my Charlie's only card game) that Joyce and the young people she attracted helped two lost souls find their way back to life. I used to talk a lot for publication about Faith and Work and the lofty things, but our own secret recipe for survival, Charlie's and mine, was the support of that gallant girl. She remained our house guest until we saw her married at Trinity Church to a bright young lawyer, Kenneth Volk.

119

"A little while after Charlie was gone, I invited the newlyweds on a tour of the Greek Islands and the Peloponnesus. We traveled over ancient territory by plane, boat, car, and, in a pinch, donkey. Joyce had brought along a small library of books on Crete, Mycenae, the Greek Islands, Homer, and the plays of Euripides in order to enhance our understanding of the past. But as we went our way, Joyce began to realize that what we were doing meant more to her than a mere holiday trip. She wanted to devote a lifetime of study to archaeology.

"Ken Volk, being a man of culture, was thrilled to learn this new dimension of his bride's character. But Joyce waited until they had had two babies, then she waited until they reached school age, during which time she mastered German, which would be a requirement of her future course.

"At long last Joyce was free to matriculate at the Institute, where she has now become a qualified professional archaeologist.

"How proud I am of Joyce," exclaimed Helen, "and how grateful that our carefree holiday trip put her in touch with her destiny and partly returned the great blessing she'd bestowed on Charlie and me."

We reached the Institute a little too early for our appointment with its Director, Craig Smith. The premises were buzzing with students, all very young and attractively "mod," but they were too busy to pay us any attention, so we felt free to snoop all over the place.

On our progress through the old mansion, Helen began to form an insight into the character of the American tycoon who built it. "The house is altogether too big," said Helen. "I'm sure this entrance hall was designed to strike terror into the heart of every guest who came through that big front entrance. Right away it put old man Duke on top of the situation—a rival tycoon or even a belted Earl, who'd just been admitted by an icy-faced butler, would be inclined to tiptoe for the duration of a miserable evening. Personally, I'd have cut and run."

We gaped at the wide marble stair curving up from the hall

which required no one less than Gloria Swanson to be descending it—in feathers. As to the ballroom, how humiliating to be caught in it without one's tiara. And just try to imagine the Duke family huddled in one of these caverns for a quiet evening at home!

When it came time for our appointment with Director Craig Smith, we found his office to be a lofty Louis XIV anteroom where trembling guests used to wait before they were admitted to the presence of old man Duke.

Director Smith took us on a tour of some of the workaday areas of the old mansion. Its library occupies the gorgeous stairwell on the second floor. School hours were over but there were a number of students earnestly going about their business. One girl was balancing on a ladder which, although it made her miniskirt seem a little precarious, was getting no attention from her peers. Most of the boys wore their hair long but it looked very well combed.

The Director next took us to a classroom where the restoration of ancient Chinese documents and works of art is taught. The room was empty except for two doll-like Chinese girls in miniskirts, seated at desks writing. They were far too pretty to belong there, we thought. We thought it all the more when the Professor in charge informed us, "Before beginning this course, a student has first to have a working knowledge of an ancient Chinese dialect."

I gestured toward the two Chinese dolls. "And do they qualify?" I asked.

"They wouldn't be here unless they did," said the Professor.

"And to think," said Helen, "they might easily get jobs in show business."

"Well, Helen," I remarked, "sometimes all the world is *not* a stage and all its men and women merely players."

It was when the Professor led us into the basement that I think we both felt more at ease. It is a labyrinth of pantries, kitchens, laundries—the intestines of a great house. And there we came upon Joyce, looking like a schoolgirl in her work smock. The studio was full of others all earnestly engaged in mending things:

Meissen porcelain, an oil painting, an antique Chinese scroll, and old jewelry. Such precision, such patience! Watching them, Helen whispered, "But they look so cute and frivolous, don't they?"

Presently, the Director indicated one of the girls who had just been awarded a fellowship for further study in Greece. When we were introduced and congratulated her, she nearly dropped a Tanagra figure she was mending. "Oops!" she said. "Last night the class gave a party to help me celebrate! And look how my hands shake." But she was incredibly expert for one so hung over.

As we started to leave the Institute, its pompous front entrance put Helen back on the subject of the Dukes. "What a giveaway that second floor was with the balcony overlooking the stairwell and, off it, all the family bedrooms. There's only one word to describe them. They're downright *dinky*. What about that, Anita? This whole setup of Fifth Avenue Dukes was designed for psychological warfare."

Then suddenly Helen stopped dead, right on the front steps. "Something's just hit me that makes me fighting mad!"

"Like what?"

"Like people who say this age is so mechanized; that handwork has completely disappeared from our culture. And yet right here are hundreds of young artisans who are earnestly planning to make it their life's work!"

Then she added rousingly, "Three cheers for our darling Doris for handing her home over to the right people. If only I were forty years younger, I'd sign up to join them."

We had now reached the letter H on our list. That meant Hypnotism, and we set out to learn how to do it. But the school of hypnotism was as different from what we had imagined as was the school of astrology.

Miss Palmer's classroom holds a hundred students, while our professor of hypnotism takes them one at a time in a small studio in a modern apartment building on West 57th Street. Mr. Albert Hall is everything in appearance that a hypnotist should be. He is tall, dark, rather dreamily handsome, and was dressed in a casual outfit with a Byronic blouse of snow-white silk. At first glance he looked capable of leading us right into another world. But we were wrong again. For Mr. Hall couldn't have been more down-to-earth.

We listened entranced as he told us the story of his life. "I started out as a singer and had a profitable career in concert until I developed arthritis. I was so badly crippled I couldn't appear in public. I tried one specialist after another without any results, and then, all by myself, I started to practice a sort of mental affirmation of health. And then, as it succeeded, I began to realize I was using self-hypnotism."

By the end of his cure, Mr. Hall was obsessed with the need to pass his experience on to others. His pupils are from all walks of life; people who lack the self-confidence required to succeed. "It might be more simple for *me* to hypnotize *them*. But the method I prefer is to teach my pupils how to hypnotize themselves—autosuggestion."

"Could you teach Anita and me?" asked Helen, all agog.

"Well, first of all, you'd each have to bring me an order from a physician." Then he laughed. "Secondly, I couldn't teach you anything because you two were already experts at it when you were in the cradle!" We gasped. "All normal babies hypnotize themselves," he went on. "Then, when they begin to talk, their behavior patterns are called 'fantasies.' But life does its best to deprive them of imagination, so by the time they grow up they're case-hardened adults intent on doing their own dull thing without benefit of vision."

He centered his interest on Helen. "If you hadn't clung to the knowledge of self-hypnotism you were born with, how could you ever have become Queen Victoria on stage? Or the teen-age Cleopatra?" He then turned to me. "How do you concoct those plots of yours?" he asked. "Where did that dopey blond Lorelei come from, except out of some hypnotic nightmare?"

"Does the fact that I'm a self-hypnotist mean that *you* couldn't hypnotize me?" asked Helen.

Grinning, Mr. Hall took up the challenge. "Put out your arm," he ordered. Helen did as she was told. "Do you think you could lower your arm?" Helen nodded. "Well, I'm telling you that you can't." Helen tried to lower her arm; it might as well have been the branch of a tree. "But now your arm has suddenly turned into lead." And down it went!

"I'll be jiggered!" was Helen's response.

As we descended in the elevator, Helen waxed philosophical. "Well, Anita, we've met some people who'd be nuts anywhere else, but here they're just typical New Yorkers!"

A VERY SMALL PORTION OF HAM

"The Arts Institute is my favorite New York school," said Helen the day we were leaving there. I knew full well that it would be replaced sooner or later, so I wasn't surprised when I heard her declare, "The Professional Children's School is my favorite place of learning in all New York!"

"I'll let that statement stand," said I, "until the day we get around to the academy for clipping poodles."

"Just keep still," said Helen, "and let me tell this in my own way."

Helen's choice really is unique, for the reason that no other U. S. city, with the possible exception of Los Angeles, has so many youngsters who are professionals or children of professionals.

On the day when Barbara Bemelmans, the daughter of our dear friend Ludwig, graduated, Helen made the commencement address there. "I told the class that day, 'You belong to the only true aristocracy left in the world: the aristocracy of professionals.' I meant it then and I still do, more and more fervently.

"Sitting through those commencement exercises was an occasion to remember. Young Master Dimitri Toufexis approached the piano to play a bit of Mendelssohn and we all rested easy, knowing we'd hear something of concert standard.

"The same thing happened when Master Lavery of the School of American Ballet astonished us with his technique. And then when a group of pint-sized Shakespeareans began a scene from *A Midsummer Night's Dream*, we relaxed, feeling sure the Master was in safe hands. For these kids are pros living in the world of pros. They have discipline and style!"

The School was created fifty-six years ago, and it began in one small room where classes were held at hours to suit the unorthodox life pattern of its pupils. Those who were on tour were supplied with lessons by mail.

Oddly enough, the School was organized by two women who were not of the theatre but came from a religious background. They were Deaconess Hall of St. John's Cathedral and a Mrs. Robinson, the daughter of Bishop Greer.

Today, that one-room school has grown to be a seven-story building in the Lincoln Center complex of New York. It has hundreds of students, mostly working in TV, modeling, pupils from the Juilliard School of Music, or those studying dance at the School of American Ballet or Balanchine's New York School of ballet. Their regular three R's are fitted into times when they're free from jobs or rehearsals, and the courses are so well planned that the students not only pass the Albany Board of Regents exams with flying colors, but they gobble up college scholarships like popcorn.

That these little hams are very special children can be proved by listing only a few of the school's graduates: Joan Blondell, Milton Berle, Elliott Gould, Ruby Keeler, Patsy Kelly, Gene Raymond, Beverly Sills, Suzanne Farrell, Allegra Kent, and Allan Arkin.

While talking about the Professional Children's School one day, Helen remarked, "I'd love to take lunch at the school cafeteria and listen to their chatter. I wonder what they talk about?"

"What do they say to you," I asked, "when you're backstage with them or at rehearsals?"

Helen thought a moment. "Well—I believe they tell me about their games or toys or maybe their lessons."

"Then, Helen, they're putting you on! The last time I heard a small actor talking to another, he was saying, 'Take my advice and steer clear of a major agency. It'll wrap you up in a package deal with some no-good author and a lousy director they're trying to push and then sell you down the river.'

" 'And what if they try to gyp you on program credits?' his little friend inquired.

" 'Just get a competent theatrical attorney, like Arnold Weissberger, and bring suit.' "

Ah, the naïveté of childhood on Broadway!

A SPREE IN BROOKLYN

*T*he day we had set apart to inspect a school for poodle clipping it looked as if we were in for some glorious weather, so I called Helen up. "I think these schools we've been visiting are making us seem highbrow. What do you say if we take a look at Brooklyn?"

The very thought of Brooklyn turned Helen on. "Yum yum!" she exclaimed.

There's a trace of the erotic about the way we Manhattanites regard Brooklyn. The Bronx may supply guffaws, Queens make us yawn, and Harlem start us jiving but Brooklyn touches our very libidos. Among the innumerable graffiti that have been scrawled on Brooklyn Bridge by strolling couples, there ought to be one, spelled out in lights, that reads: "Manhattan loves Brooklyn."

The two lovers are so ill-assorted that their affair has real fillip. Typically Miss Manhattan is a tall, liberated young woman with the stride of a man, a pony face, and long stringy hair. She is too self-sufficient, snobbish, and opinionated to be messing about with a Humphrey Bogart character like Brooklyn. But the two seem to magnetize each other; to be truly yin and yang. And in one particular way they are excessively unlike: Manhattan forever runs itself down while Brooklyn is supercharged with pride in Brooklyn. During the time when the Brooklyn Dodgers held forth at Ebbetts Field, this pride used to come to the surface in a sort of paroxysm, so barefaced as to be disarming. But Brooklyn never fails to amuse its fellow borough and, in a sneaky way, Manhattan shares in its vainglory.

It was manifest that our Spirit Guide arranged that trip to Brooklyn. We were to be under the auspices of the Downtown Brooklyn Development Committee, from which we'd had a letter.

Dear Misses Hayes and Loos:

We saw a note in Leonard Lyons' column that you are interested in offbeat cultural spots. Hope you won't forget those in Brooklyn. May we help?

Sincerely,
Donald Moore
Executive Director

We had made a date with Mr. Moore for lunch, but we left Manhattan in plenty of time for a visit to Brooklyn's chief pride and greatest joy, the Brooklyn Museum.

At its entrance, we were welcomed by Henri Ghent, a friend of mine who is Director of the Museum's Community Gallery. This is a unique feature of the Museum, a place where talented Brooklynites who fall a little short of genius can still gain a measure of acclaim.

I had tried to prepare Helen for Henri but, even so, she blinked at sight of him. "He could walk right into the role of Othello without any make-up," she exclaimed later. "Hurray for Brooklyn that it can turn out such culture, urbanity, and *diction*!"

"Well, it *did* have some help from Paris and a course at the Sorbonne."

As he led us to the Community Gallery at the rear of the ground floor, Henri said, "You're in luck today, there's a very special show on." "Special" was correct. It was dedicated to "The Art of the Elders of Brooklyn" and a wide variety of works from several Jewish geriatric centers was on exhibit.

We particularly admired Gussie Wadler's hooked Menorah, Rose Kreshefsky's pottery, Julius Gluck's mosaics, Neddie Danishefsky's weaving, Tillie Feinstein's embroidery, Rose Schmaefsky's dolls, Max Slutsky's sculpture, and the oils of Laura-Short-Everneaser (whose signature went to prove that an artistic Hebrew lady can assume three names, just like an artistic Gentile).

All the paintings were refreshingly nonchalant; folks who have reached a certain age are relieved of pretensions. But our favorite painting, as well as that of the *New York Times,* which had reproduced it, was an oil by Gustave Klumpp entitled "Burlly" (the artist's abbreviation for Burlesque). The picture shows eleven extremely busty babes wearing minimal garments and standing in pyramid formation on a staircase. The subject was obviously inspired by the dear, dead days when men were men and traveled to Brooklyn to see a lusty production entitled *The Beef Trust*. At that time sex appeal was measured by heft, and the weight of an ideal chorus lady approached three hundred pounds. Looking at that Klumpp, I could only philosophize, "How impotent men seem today when they can only handle women who've been skeletonized by diets."

We learned from our catalogue that Klumpp is sixty-nine, which means that he couldn't have been more than twelve when he was inspired by *The Beef Trust*. But obviously it had an enduring effect, because the artist's reaction to those Brooklyn babes of long ago is still that of an incredibly precocious twelve-year-old.

I coveted that painting and what's more had just the right spot to hang it, next to a Constantin Guys of several ladies in a parlor being inspected by some lewd gentlemen. "How much is this Klumpp?" I asked Henri. "I'd like to buy it."

He only laughed. "If that painting were for sale," Henri said, "there'd be a line from here way over to the Botanical Garden. But the artist is keeping it for himself."

"He's no fool," exclaimed Helen. "It's more stimulating than any other art around today."

At length we tore ourselves away from those geriatric marvels and made for the Egyptian collection. Threading our way through it, Helen stopped at a Pharaoh in alabaster and grew lyrical. "Look how its planes and contours are picked up by these baby spotlights," she exclaimed. "How lucky we are to live in this age of electronics. One can almost feel he's breathing!" I agreed that Pharaoh seemed alive and well in Brooklyn.

Helen assured me that the Museum's Egyptian collection is one of the three finest in the world—"Not the largest, mind you, the *finest*. Every piece here is a great treasure and that's because the

Department's head, Bernard von Bothmer, is one of the world's top Egyptologists."

(A few years ago Helen joined the Museum's trip to Egypt under the guidance of her friend Bernard. The purpose was to visit Abu Simbel, the site of the two temples that had been carved out of a stone cliff in the reign of Ramses the Second. Then three thousand years later Nasser the First had given an order for it to be flooded by the waters of the Nile after the Aswan High Dam was finished.

"Our whole trip was marvelous, thanks to Bernard's knowledge of Egypt and of how to pass it on to us. Best of all, he was able to pass on his enthusiasm.

"Another exceptional thing was the warm hospitality of the Egyptians. They couldn't do enough for us—parties, special trips, official receptions; there had even been a band at the airport to greet us. Seeing that we were a very private party, we'd been mystified by all the attention until the Cairo correspondent of the International News Service showed us a copy of the local paper. It had come out the day of our arrival and flaunted a headline in Arabic across the whole front page. Our I.N.S. correspondent translated it:

" '125 Millionaires from Brooklyn Flying in Today.'

"None of us disclaimed the lie that had given us such a wonderful time. And it was my considered opinion that the Museum's Public Relations Department sent out that story. Now, isn't that just like Brooklyn?")

The Museum's important collection of American paintings, including the Hudson River School, is Helen's special delight. Living on the Hudson as she does, everything relating to her river evokes ecstasy in Helen. But after my recent exposure to the school of Klumpp, those paintings looked pretty mingy.

Helen stood before a dark brown landscape that had a tan sky, a grove of chocolate-colored trees, and a waterfall that flowed with gravy. "My," she exclaimed, "when it came to art, our early American painters certainly didn't drag their feet, did they?" I agreed but felt it was because their feet were stuck in mud. For which I got a dirty look.

Finally even Helen got a little tired of prowling the dark forests of early Americana, and we went out into the sunshine.

The Botanic Garden is a mere few steps away. We wandered about its vast area on that bright November day and never met a soul. The great masses of chrysanthemums were of special interest to Helen as a pillar of the Nyack Garden Club. We had learned from our gourmet friend Mort Gottlieb that the Garden has an extra-special feature that few people know about. Adjacent to the grounds is an institution called the Brooklyn Botanic Beekeeping and Benevolent Brotherhood, a club that was brought into existence some years ago by a group of Wall Street brokers who, incredible as it appears, happened to be mutually hung up on bees. They got permission from the Botanic Garden to establish an apiary there.

Helen and I tracked down a guard and asked if we might see the apiary. He apologized but said the Club was very exclusive and it would take more pull than we could trump up at the moment. However, the guard must have reported on our snooping, because the following week we were each the recipient of a case of Brooklyn honey.

The labels on the jars read "This honey was produced at the Brooklyn Botanic Garden under the supervision of amateur beekeepers."

We were further informed that bees must gather nectar from an average of nine million blossoms to make a pound of honey, which means that a Brooklyn bee in her six weeks of life provides the Benevolent Brotherhood with less than half a teaspoonful of honey. We also found that, unlike most of the specialties of the borough, its honey is mild to an extreme. That's what I mean about Brooklyn: for all its manly vigor, it occasionally comes through with a delicate surprise.

When time came to keep our lunch date, we made for Gage and Tollner's on busy downtown Fulton Street. We were met by a delegation from the Downtown Committee, Mr. and Mrs. Moore and Mrs. Worthington, Director of Public Relations, there to brief us on a great deal we didn't know about Brooklyn.

Looking about the restaurant, Helen remarked, "Why, we've stepped right back into the comfortable Nineties!" Because, for all its ninety-two years, the mahogany at Gage and Tollner's still shines and its crystal chandeliers shimmer. No present-day black-out can harm a feeling of security, for the original gas fixtures are still in place, ready to be turned on whenever Con Ed fails us. There still remain clusters of large wooden hooks in "S" shape, put there for the plug hats of early-day Brooklyn swells.

Donald Moore recalled that he had first been taken to Gage and Tollner's as a toddler, but on the momentous day that he could reach up and hang his plaid cap on one of those great big hooks, he suddenly felt he'd become a man.

The place was crowded with businessmen who were not eating the quick lunch of Manhattan—they really meant business. When I, overawed by the lengthy menu, said diffidently, "I'd like cottage cheese and Melba toast," it earned me no prestige. Helen met the spirit of the place head-on and ordered a Brooklyn lunch, starting with oyster stew, followed by steak and french fries, and topped off by apple pie garnished with old-fashioned American cracker-barrel cheese.

After lunch we were guided by our new Brooklyn friends across town to the Academy of Music. On going through the front entrance there we were greeted by the gigantic gilded Heracles, with a poised bow, who hovers over its vast marble lobby. He is on loan from big brother Metropolitan Museum in Manhattan.

Inside the Academy, there are three large theatres. Its main one is as grand as an opera house but painted white, picked out with silver, and with velvet drapes and upholstery the color of American Beauty roses, it is both airy and gay.

I had first come to know the big auditorium on an occasion in the summer of '65. At that time I happened to be in Montecatini, where the municipal casino was advertising a Festival of International Ballet. I went to see the Czechoslovakian and Israeli groups and found both of them dreary to a degree; audiences were small and many customers left before the ballets ended. So I canceled my tickets for the remainder of the season.

One morning I went down into the lobby of the hotel and found practically a mob scene round the concierge's desk. When I asked what it was all about, I was informed that people were trying to order tickets for a ballet company that had opened the night before. Now rather curious, I queued up at the concierge's desk to make inquiries. "It's that famous Alvin Ailey Dance Group." Never having heard of them, I asked where they came from. It surprised the concierge that I didn't know. "Why, the United States, of course," he said.

That night I went to see the troupe. There were not more than twelve dancers, all black, but at times they filled the stage as if there'd been a hundred. At the end, the audience, wild with enthusiasm, gave them a twenty-minute ovation.

I couldn't wait to get home and let my New York friends in on my discovery. We waited in vain for the Ailey troupe to show up until we learned it had been corralled by the Director of the Brooklyn Academy, Harvey Lichtenstein. Manhattan had overlooked a troupe that had been acclaimed in Europe, Asia, and Africa. But Brooklyn had offered it a permanent home.

There is a second theatre in the Academy complex which is almost as large and festive as the main one. It harbors musical groups and movie classics borrowed from the Museum of Modern Art in Manhattan.

The third theatre, high up in the attic, is occupied by the Chelsea Theatre Center of Brooklyn, which had already sent one success across the river.

That day we stumbled into a rehearsal where some young, earnest, and hairy actors were rehearsing their play, *Tarot*. After watching the rehearsal for a while Helen said quietly to me, "I've got a hunch this play is not for us." As it turned out, *Tarot* was not for anybody.

133

After its quick exit, Helen's invincible optimism overcame her. "I'll bet everyone connected with that production grew in stature!"

Eventually we made our way back to the big main theatre to watch Elliot Feld's Company rehearsing for that evening's ballet. The company was beguiling as the very young can be when they are beautiful, earnest, proficient, and thin.

During a lull in the proceedings, Helen looked about the vast auditorium and waxed nostalgic. "I played here myself when I was a lot younger than those kids," she said. "It was fifty years ago, and the Academy was just as grand as it is now." She gestured off toward the right-hand stage box. "That's the spot where my heart was broken for the very first time!" She sighed. "The Lew Fields production of *The Summer Widowers* was about to take to the road for our winter tour after the summer layoff. We had been called here early in the day for a brush-up rehearsal before the opening. Mother and I were waiting in that box while the cast strolled on stage. But I was looking for only one of them: my fiancé, Vernon Castle. I sat there with a lump in my throat and finding it pretty hard to breathe.

"At first Vernon had been my best friend in the company. He was handsome and tall, with a sophisticated British accent, and when he treated me as an equal it made me forget I was only a child. At every performance I'd station myself in the wings to watch his comedy turn. And when he came off, Vernon would ask very seriously how it had gone. After hearing my compliments Vernon would scoop me into his arms and carry me up the three flights to my dressing room. In no time at all I was madly in love.

"One evening I asked diffidently if he was ever going to be married and he answered, 'Not until I can marry you!' Which naturally meant we were engaged.

"Is it any wonder that I was all atingle that day waiting for him? Suddenly he strode onto the stage with the easy grace that before very long was going to be familiar to all the world. As he greeted the company, he was all the while looking around for

134

somebody. Then I heard him ask, 'Where's my girl?' I rose from the shadows of the box and called out 'Yoo-hoo!' He called back, 'I'll be right there, small one!' And added excitedly, 'I have a surprise for you.'

"A surprise—it could only be one thing. My engagement ring. I could hardly endure the time it took for Vernon to make his way through a back passage to the box. I fairly leapt into his arms, felt the strength with which he was hugging me back. But then presently I became aware that someone else had materialized out of the darkness behind him. Vernon looked around. 'Here's my surprise,' he said, 'someone you're going to adore!' I turned and saw a vision of pure loveliness, of the kind of beauty I knew in an instant I could never hope to have. 'Meet Miss Irene Foote,' said *my* fiancé. 'She's promised to marry me and she's going to go on tour with us in the show.'

"The drums of doom started to beat in my heart as he continued. 'I've arranged with Mr. Fields for you and Irene to share a dressing room, so that you can look after her. You see, she isn't a pro like you. It's her first time on the stage, ever.'

"Maybe Shakespeare, who could write the death of Cleopatra or Juliet, could have put my feelings at that moment into words. I had, however, a built-in talent for survival. In the midst of all the agony, I could still thank my lucky star it was too dark in the theatre for anyone to see me being jilted."

Helen's anguish waned as she continued. "Before the tour ended, Irene and I got to be real friends. And then, after Vernon was shot down in the Royal Flying Corps, Irene sent me a photo of herself and Vernon dancing together. It was inscribed, 'To Helen, with love from us *both*.' After Vernon had been killed, Irene was sharing her love for him with me."

Helen's voice trembled and I could tell she was getting set for a state of gentle melancholy that might last for the remainder of the day.

So, consulting my watch, I suggested we might have time to visit the Children's Museum of Brooklyn (its pet name being

"Muse"). To get there meant driving through the Bedford Stuyvesant district, which, as the newspapers reveal, is the scene of
constant violence and is the grimmest area of Brooklyn. But our
route to Muse was on the wide main avenue, and we recall only
sunny streets with children playing.

Muse turned out to be a darling museum which, in spite of its
small size, provides a treasury of instruction to fascinate the
young. There's no limit to the subjects taught there: piloting a
plane, ceramics, acting, collage, native Afro dancing, photogra-
phy, and the writing of TV commercials, to name only a few.

What's more, the children are allowed to handle all the exhibits.
Helen, like the sensuous woman she is, spotted a fourth-century
Roman doll made out of basalt and said, "Maybe I've never ma-
tured, but I yearn to touch that thing!" We both tried on Civil
War bonnets and just generally messed about into everything. A
visit to Muse is a great rejuvenator.

At dusk, on our way home, we stopped to take a walk along the
embankment and watch the lights come on in Manhattan, across
the water—maybe the best twilight sight in the world. Behind us
were the elegant old houses of Brooklyn Heights.

They reminded Helen that, not too long ago, she and Lillian
Gish were on the Heights making some exterior shots for a television production of *Arsenic and Old Lace*. Whenever Helen is on
location, she spends her lunch hour inspecting the neighborhood.
That day her costume bordered on the outrageous. She was made
up to look ancient and daffy, in lavender and old lace, with mitts
and a poke bonnet. Oblivious of her appearance, Helen was studying the superb architecture of Victorian Brooklyn when a foreign
sports car pulled up at the curb and its puzzled driver called over
to her, "Do you always go around looking like that?" For a moment Helen was too surprised to answer. But then, assuming the
character she was playing, she said, "You'd better buzz off, young
man! I'm a killer!" At which the startled young man quickly
drove away.

One of the most gracious mansions on the Heights belongs to

our pal Oliver Smith, New York's foremost scenic designer. Oliver's house, a vision of Edwardian splendor, has made history in a sort of special, personal way. It was there that his friend, Jackie Kennedy, trying to assuage the grief of her terrible bereavement, went to take lessons in painting from Oliver. During the time when Truman Capote was writing *In Cold Blood,* he occupied the basement floor of Oliver's house. In summer Oliver gives garden parties. But the fly in that particular ointment is a rather plebeian roominghouse that has been erected right smack against Oliver's garden wall by the religious cult, Jehovah's Witnesses, which has its headquarters in Brooklyn. Now, it appears that they expect the world to end almost any day, and when Oliver gives a party they take their places at windows where, peering down their beards, they witness the sinful festivities in Oliver's greenery and sense the beginning of the end.

Not long after our visit to Brooklyn, the *New York Times* carried the story of a near-riot in the lobby of the Brooklyn Museum. Its director, on hearing that the City of New York was about to short-change the Museum in the new budget appropriation, called a meeting in its marble halls and roared out a noble threat to close the Goddam place at once. For a few days the New York papers had a lot of fun reporting the situation.

Four months later, when I phoned the Museum for final news of the outcome, I learned that the appropriation had been restored by dipping into some frozen funds, and all was running more or less smoothly across the river.

But that ruckus in the Museum's lobby might sum up the spirit of Brooklyn: a love for art that can only be adequately expressed by a poke in the nose.

THE THREE METS OF NEW YORK

I had never been to a ball game in my life but Helen, that Renaissance woman who numbers baseball among her countless enthusiasms, had been trying to put me *au courant*. It was a late afternoon in September and, as we were driving out to Shea Stadium, Helen said, "You've sure got beginner's luck in your first game. It's the high point of the season." Then Helen added some statistics about the night's event: a clean sweep at the box office; fifty-one thousand tickets; a million-dollar take.

The fans were already streaming in. Perfect weather had been predicted so, naturally, about 5:00 P.M. it had started to drizzle —a fact that hadn't deterred thousands of early-comers from the risk of getting wet and a threat that there might not be a game at all.

Our own reason for arriving early was pretty overpowering. Helen had accepted an invitation from the owner of the Mets, Mrs. Charles Shipman Payson, for dinner before the game. It was to be in the Board of Directors Club, high above the grandstands. We entered a spacious suite of rooms that smacked of masculine hospitality: furnishings designed for comfort as well as luxury; chairs that girls could sink into and feel pampered. We were met and greeted by Joan Payson herself. In addition to being owner of the mighty Mets, she is a leader of society, a patron of the arts, a breeder of race horses, and, as is boasted on a plaque over her desk, the Nation's Number One Baseball Fan. "What an improbable woman," remarked Helen. "The only one I ever knew who can turn a problem of overweight into charisma."

On this important occasion Mrs. Payson was simply dressed in a plain dark suit but, as jewelry, she wore one single, outstanding piece. Unable to examine it closely, I felt pretty sure it was an authentic Mickey Mouse watch. And this I report with something like awe, for they had ceased to be manufactured and have become museum pieces. Today, a genuine Mickey Mouse wrist watch is definitely a status symbol.

Joan's guests that night were Manhattan's true elite; none of the jet set that wings about the airways chasing its own witless fantasies. These were people of purpose who have found a very rational purpose in baseball. For in these days when it's stupid to try and figure out what's going on in politics, art, science, and even fashion, how sane, pure, and uncluttered baseball can be. I'm sure that without sports to relieve its confusion the great public would flounder in a mess of total insecurity.

The atmosphere in the clubrooms was tense. It was now 6:30 P.M. and the game which would be so vital to the Mets was due to start at eight. Near the bar there was a large closed-circuit TV set focused on the playing field. And it was showing a steady sprinkle of rain. The field itself was protected by an acre of tarpaulin but, even so, it revealed puddles that made it look like a map of the Great Lakes.

Guests continued to pour in. Joan greeted them all with a superbly casual manner and glanced only infrequently toward the dismal picture on the TV. Nobody mentioned the dubious situation; there was only small talk concerning such matters as the hanging of a new show at Joan's art gallery in Locust Valley and of the dress problem in those early days of pants suits. "Imagine me in pants," grinned Joan, "or wouldn't you care to try?"

Waiters were quietly passing caviar and hot hors d'oeuvres, and, as the drinks kept coming on, I recklessly ordered a spritzer, causing Helen, who nursed a heartier drink, to chide me. "You wouldn't go any further than white-wine-and-soda if we two were to win the Nobel Prize for Literature," said she.

The conversation ran on at an easy pace. I, as a novice, asked Mrs. Payson how she ever came to own a baseball team. She

139

shrugged. "I really don't know," she said and added with a chuckle, "Just lucky, I guess." She was quoting the tag line of what must be a favorite joke: the prostitute's reply to a client who was startled by the *magna cum laude* diploma on her bedroom wall and asked, "How did a cultured girl like you ever get into *this* business?"

For dinner we were served with all the proper sportsman's fare: roast beef, steak, lobster, cheesecake, pie à la mode, and such substantial American fare. But the TV monitor was so placed as to be in our line of vision and we were always conscious of its relentless picture of the weather. About fifteen minutes before game time, Joan, looking as bland as a pink bonbon, confessed, "I'm a little nervous inside. I don't know why."

And then at 8:30, just half an hour after the official starting time, a miracle hit Shea Stadium. The rain stopped as if Jupiter Pluvius himself had suddenly turned off the tap. Our hearts rejoiced for Joan and for the damp fans who had been waiting in the stands all afternoon. As we finished dinner, we could now watch a work crew on the TV screen expertly folding the acre of tarpaulin that had kept the field itself moderately dry, then carrying it off and putting everything in order.

We threaded our way through the maze of iron and concrete galleries, past boxes on which the nameplates are a combined Social Register and Who's Who (it was a thrill to read our publisher's name on one of the most prominent), and reached Joan's box at center front just as the game started. I couldn't understand what was going on, but I used restraint and not once did I venture to ask anybody, "What's he doing that for?" The drama of the game, however, got through to me, and I had the advantage of watching the antics of the crowd without being distracted by the plays.

I had already been briefed by Helen with descriptions of how the fans carry on. During baseball's more classic years when the Dodgers held forth at Ebbets Field, Helen used to go to the games with a crony of ours named Mark Hanna. Mark, raised in Hell's

Kitchen, had gone to his first ball games when he was a small boy under the aegis of a Ninth Avenue bartender, who was his dearest friend. That was before he became a very tony fellow and a society wit, at which time he attended games with Marie Harriman, Marie being a more avid baseball fan than any bartender. "Mark told me," Helen reminisced, "about the early days when the Yankees were still known as the Boys of Coogan's Bluff. In those days the denizens of the bleachers all looked the same: brilliantly striped shirts, celluloid collars, sleeve garters of pink or baby-blue satin, straw hats (Chevalier type), and their expressions ranged from innocent to dumb.

"Mark was there with his bartender friend the day they first introduced the custom of singing our National Anthem before the game. It was Madame Margarete Matzenauer, a Wagnerian diva of monumental heft, who was escorted to home base before the start-off and there launched into the 'Star-Spangled Banner.' A moment of hesitation occurred as the crowd didn't know the right thing to do, but eventually they all straggled to their feet, doffed their straw boaters, and looked solemn. Madame finished verse one and the crowd, sighing in relief, sat down. But then Madame began verse two and confusedly the crowd rose again. She finished verse two and the crowd slumped back into their seats. But now Madame started verse three, and as the fans again straggled to their feet Mark's bartender called out for all to hear, 'For Chrissake, somebody give that dame a base on balls!' "

But Helen's memories of baseball were sometimes colored by sentiment. "In the Thirties Charlie and I attended a World Series game at the Yankee Stadium, otherwise known as the House That Ruth Built. A minute before starting time there was a great stir and gradually every soul in the packed stadium was on his feet, all looking off in the same direction. There was a mighty roar as we saw a massive figure attired in a white polo coat and white cap to match standing in the box above the Yankee dugout. It was the Babe.

"That was the Babe's first public appearance since a severe

heart attack. I have subsequently seen royalty enter theatre boxes in London, Presidents appear in them in Washington and New York—even movie stars—but never have I heard anything like that ovation for the ailing idol of Coogan's Bluff. I can close my eyes anytime and still hear Charlie whistling through his fingers."

Helen remembered the Dodgers' old Simp-phoney Orchestra which, in the days of Ebbets Field, assaulted the ears at moments of climax. But that night at Shea Stadium, I learned that Mets fans have provided a substitute. During a moment of high play, someone in our vicinity sounded a klaxon to draw attention, at which another loyalist took charge and went into action. He was a fine figure of a gentleman from Queens by name Karl Ehrhardt. Karl may be a sign painter by profession, for he had arrived at the game tugging a stack of six-by-ten signs with words of cheer for the Mets and the vilest sort of insults for the opposition. At every sound of the klaxon, Karl rose and held aloft a sign that was specially written to fit some moment of play. One such read, "Bless you, Padre!" (in reference to Al Ferrara). And when Al scored again, the message read, "Twice Blessed." At one climactic moment an eye-popping superlative flashed out "Super-calis-tragilistic-epi-ali-docious."

It is sad to report that at the end of the game all those prayers for the triumph of the Mets, all the confident cheers of the beginning, turned out to be of no avail. "While we were praying for that drizzle to stop," said Helen, "we should have asked Providence to turn it into a hurricane and prevent all this agony."

The Mets played the game and lost the game. "It's much too sad," remarked Joan as we left the stadium, but she added with true sportsmanship, "We couldn't even temper our grief by being mad at anybody." There was no booing of old enemies that night. The Mets had given their all and lost out to a better team. It was as simple as that.

We joined the fifty-one thousand other stony-silent New Yorkers who trooped out of Shea Stadium and went home that night to weep into their pillows.

THE SECOND MET

When it came to the subject of the old Metropolitan Opera House, it was I who wept while Helen actually chortled. For I grieve over my memories of the old Opera House whenever I pass its site on Broadway. The building that replaced it has less character than a vacant lot. I had joined the committee that hoped to save the Met but we had failed, so it was clobbered into dust.

One day when Helen and I were strolling past an old brownstone in the throes of being shattered, I observed, "That big black iron ball ought to be the official emblem of this day and age." I was referring to the old Metropolitan Opera.

"It was about time for the old place to go," said Helen vindictively, "that ugly warehouse of a building." Then she corrected herself. "To call it a warehouse is a compliment. It had so little storage space that scenery had to be moved to the sidewalk after every performance and then trucked all the way across town to a really honest warehouse."

According to Helen, only an architect who hated opera could have designed a balcony where the posts cut off all view of the stage. Helen remembered that when she was a child her mother used to scrimp even on food to get her into the opera to see great acting performances like Jeritza lying on her stomach as she sang *"Vissi d'arte."* But they never saw Jeritza. Instead, they were looking at a post. And they had heard tantalizing reports of Caruso being so confident of his vocal powers that he sang Rodolfo's narrative in *La Bohème* gazing out over Montmartre with his back to the audience. But they never saw Caruso, they could only hear him. "We were probably the only two people in the world," Helen commented, "who ever complained about *listening* to Caruso."

In my own memory, the old Met had no resemblance to a warehouse. It was a sensuous and ornate spot where audiences were dressed to match. Never shall I forget a night when Duse played a farewell performance there—more years ago than a phony sou-

143

brette like me cares to remember! The lush auditorium held an unmatched collection of celebrities, stage and screen stars outdoing each other in jewels and extravagant gowns. But the demure little Gish sisters, Lillian and Dorothy, stole the show, in prim street dresses, horn-rimmed sun glasses, and shod in patent leather ankle straps. When I tried to solve the mystery why they, as foremost stars of the silent screen, didn't wear their Mainbocher evening gowns that night, Lillian told me in her usual precise manner, "*We* did not go there to attract attention."

Helen and I have our most lively differences of opinion on the subject of modern architecture. I sometimes challenge her by saying, "Why is it that in this age when building materials are more tough and pliable than they have ever been before, architects have to copy the outlines of a packing case?"

"The outlines of a packing case are basic and pure," Helen will counter, "so if the proportions of a building are good and it's made of sleek, shimmering glass, what's wrong with *that*?"

"The first thing that's wrong," I contend, "is that it's a gyp! Construction companies use glass because it's cheaper than masonry. But as soon as a tenant moves into one of those 'sleek glass buildings,' he's got to block out the glare with wall-to-wall window drapes at his own expense."

"Get you," exclaimed Helen, "trying to put down God's good daylight!"

At which I cockily remind her that light can be a blight and is actually one of the most fiendish means of Chinese torture. "Furthermore," I go on, "employees who work in a glare tire very quickly. They require extra coffee breaks, at the cost of their health. And," I add, "by doing away with walls, art is removed from modern living. You can't hang paintings on a window curtain."

A prominent modern designer backs me up in my contentions. My friend, Robsjohn-Gibbings, finally reached a point where he could no longer tolerate glass walls and semipartitions that let the noise in. "I want to live in a culture where one can enter a room,

close a door, and block out the public," said Gibby. So he relin-
quished his eminent career in modern design to settle in Athens,
where the walls are stone and within them one can listen to one's
thoughts.

Be that as it may, Helen managed to get to the Met's grand
opening, "by accident" as she phrased it; she has a theory about
accidents. "As I look back on my life, Anita, it seems that nearly
every good and wonderful thing that ever happened to me has
been an accident—like going on the stage and falling in love with
Charlie. And I'm forever reading about some scientist who hit on
a great discovery when he was actually looking for something else.
Maybe that's the true secret of success—being accident-prone, in
a nice way."

Helen's theory was put to a triumphant test at the opening of
the Met when a doctor friend of hers was forced (or was he or-
dained by Fate?) to send a patient to a hospital. Now it so happened that the unlucky man was the owner of two tickets to the
opera, which he passed on to the very doctor who had done him
in. ("I'd have given him a sharp kick!" said Helen, using the
vocabulary she's learned by playing all those racy old ladies on
stage and screen.)

And that was the happy accident by which Cinderella Hayes
got invited to the grand event. Incredible as it seems, a Met opening had never been within Helen's reach. By November, she was
either working in New York or off on the road.

So like most other mortals, Helen had always got her news
about the opening from the front pages of the evening *Journal* and
the morning *American*—never bothering, she says, about the
music critics. The Twenties, in her recollection, were the best
years of all. At that time it wasn't enough to be glittering in black
velvet and jet from the House of Worth—one had to *do* something
as well. Mrs. Henderson, that active septuagenarian, made news
by sitting with her feet propped up on a table in Sherry's Lounge,
while she puffed on a fat cigar. Richard Knight, the odd-ball socialite, in white tie and tails, took to standing on his oversized

head on the sidewalk. Hope Hampton, more circumspect, merely
added an inch or two of diamond bracelets each year, which were
duly recorded in prose and picture. A favorite of Helen and her
Mom Brownie was Mrs. Vanderbilt, mistress of the great Fifth
Avenue mansion, wearing her famous trademark, the "Headache
Band." It was a swatch of expensive textile pulled across her forehead and tied Indian-style at the back of her pure white coiffure.
"This year," Helen's Mom would solemnly read, "Mrs. Vanderbilt
selected silver lamé for her headache band."

And it was in this year of our Lindsay, 1970, in the month of
September, that Helen finally made it. And here, verbatim, is her
report:

"I had a gorgeous gold lamé by Count Sarmi and a chinchilla
shrug cape; I was free of commitments, I was escorted and on my
way with a silent prayer: 'Oh, Brownie, I hope you can see me
now!'

"My friend is not a society doctor and his 1953 Plymouth has
seen a lot of hard wear, but it got us there. At least it got us to a
curb between Tenth and Eleventh Avenues, on 60th Street; that's
Hell's Kitchen territory—dark, dirty, and scary. We started to
pick our way through the litter toward the Opera House and in no
time we had acquired our first followers; two little Puerto Rican
boys, hypnotized by the glitter of me, fell in behind. By the time
we reached the back of Lincoln Center, word had spread through
the neighborhood that something wondrous, never before seen
afoot in the vicinity, was on her way through and we were heading
a fairly noisy parade. It was happy noise—full of wonder and
admiration.

"I often have to make the decision of how to meet such a moment. Shall I give in to the normal embarrassment of being a lone
goldfish in a big bowl, or shall I try to enjoy the situation? Well,
that night I made the decision to steel myself and enjoy it. Anyway, we marched into Lincoln Center in pretty noticeable fashion,
and I was only sorry I couldn't drag my sidewalk following into

146

the lobby with me. I might forever have erased the memory of Mrs. Henderson and her big, black cigar.

"We entered that lovely lobby of the Met—airy in its proportions, elegant with red, gold, and crystal, gay with the Chagall murals. It's a grand place for an entrance, I must say! The press cameras are given a perfect shot as one descends the red-carpeted stairs to the orchestra lobby. Above us were those three balconies circling the enormous chandelier that shed a glow on us heroines of the society columns as we trooped in. When I stopped on the staircase to be photographed, fans from the tiers broke into applause and called out, 'It's Helen Hayes! Look!' I had never known such a feeling of triumph and fulfillment at one of my own openings. Maybe I had always wanted to be Hope Hampton. Or one of Brownie's *grandes dames* of the social whirl.

"I happen to adore the interior of the new Met because it has everything: comfortable seats, space for your knees, good sight lines, and perfect acoustics. The only thing we miss here is the entr'acte in Sherry's Lounge at the old Met, that heaven of red brocade and portraits of opera stars in dusty gold frames. Even though I'd never made an opening night there, I recall other occasions when I'd sip coffee or toy with an ice while showing off my décolletage in public, unhampered by a coat.

"The doctor and I tried twice between acts to find our way to a restaurant, any one of the countless eating places by any staircase we came upon. We discovered several little champagne bars tucked away in odd places but no proper tables or chairs. And then, during the last entr'acte, we got into an elevator, desperately punched all the buttons, and ended up in total confusion in the Board of Directors Club, in company with Mayor and Mary Lindsay and members of the Board whose names jingle like gold pieces to the ear, drinking champagne for free with Rudolf Bing. But, much as I regret having to join my carping pal Anita, there were no chairs, the only furniture being a makeshift bar. When I asked a director friend, Mrs. Lewis Douglas, about the bareness of the

147

room, she said, 'Oh, we removed the furniture to leave more space for the guests tonight.' And she added with pride, 'Normally, we have a big table for the Board Members with a dozen armchairs around it.'

"I recalled Joan Payson's board room at Shea Stadium, so well-equipped for a party, and the gracious board room at the Los Angeles Music Center, with its exquisite paneling, antique furniture, and thick carpets, all donated by friends of the Music Center. It occurred to me that most of the people in that naked room could have searched their attics and prettied it up a bit. I hope they do. I don't like Los Angeles getting ahead of us in anything.

"More important, however, the back-stage faults of our Opera House have been ironed out since its first season. We had just listened to Martina Arroyo sing Verdi's *Ernani,* totally unaware of the stage hands' efforts to switch from a castle in Spain to a barren cave and then a convent. And I recalled the calamity of that first performance four years ago, when after the desert scene the Sphinx in *Antony and Cleopatra* refused to budge and had to remain onstage for the next scene, which happened to be the Forum in Rome. And Leontyne Price, trapped in the Sphinx without air or light, was forced to wilt in her Egyptian hotbox until intermission, when help could get onstage to release her. But then, at the finale, Leontyne, with a gallant twitch of her robes, and a pat to her crown, had coolly sauntered onstage to accept her standing ovation. I thought of the cumbersome, temperamental divas of the past and of the advantage they would have taken of a chance to faint or have hysterics or sue the Met. But not our Leontyne!

"And I thought, too, that it wasn't so long ago that great voices like those of Leontyne, Grace Bumbry, Martina Arroyo, Marion Anderson, Paul Robeson, and Roland Hayes could only be heard in concert or on records. Yes, our Met, which was once the most reactionary of all institutions, has taken giant steps in the right direction. Bravo, Bing.

"As we were blocked by the crowd leaving Lincoln Center that night, I looked about and realized that there were still plenty of show-offs. All the eye-catching tricks were being flagrantly practiced. See-through pajamas were in evidence and some minis so short as to make you flinch. But, after all, there were no antics, which was just as well; we see plenty of those on TV from college campuses. Once inside and seated, that opening-night crowd behaved like angels. What's more, they actually listened to the opera."

THE THIRD MET

Possibly Helen and I know the Metropolitan Museum as well as the average New Yorker. We've seen every special exhibit of the past years where, under the direction of Thomas Hoving, works of art take on an ethnic and historical meaning over and above their value as art. For instance, the Italian frescoes of '68 and "Before Cortez" in '70.

Then there was the exhibit of "Masterpieces of Primitive Art" gathered by, among others, the Rockefeller family—a show in the grandest sense, in selection, arrangement, and drama. "Isn't it just like Ted Rousseau," Helen remarked, "to exhibit those fearsome war masks and voodoo talismans against a delicate background of baby blue! And to give program credit to the savage artists who designed them."

"I could love any sculptor with a name like Ooga-ma-goola," I observed.

It was also good to know that after that special exhibit was over it will become permanent, in a new wing constructed especially for primitive art. The exhibit has special meaning for the Rockefeller family because it was while helping assemble the collection that young Michael was lost in the New Guinea jungle. It is in his name that the exhibit will be given to the city.

Another special show everyone will remember was "Masterpieces of Fifty Centuries," in which every modern technique of electronics was put to use. Small objects, such as T'ang figurines and ancient jewelry, were shown on revolving platforms, at eye level. It was next best to holding every precious object in one's hand. "Had they been shown as they usually are," said Helen, "badly lit and in obscure surroundings, they'd have looked no more glamorous than a lovely woman with uncombed hair and a dirty apron bending over the kitchen sink."

And Helen's hackles rose higher when we heard the Met criticized for making art too sensational. "Why shouldn't art be dramatized?" she demanded. "Great art is sensational, and here at the Met people are jogged right into a realization of what they're looking at!"

Helen's feeling for the Met has an extra and personal dimension which she loves to relate. "It began a good many years ago," she recollects, "when I was in the midst of my long run in *Victoria Regina*. One day I was on my way to a matinee when a couple of theatregoers approached me. The woman nudged her husband and whispered, 'That's Helen Hayes.' But no sooner had they passed than I heard the man exclaim, 'That's not Helen Hayes, for God's sake!' His tone was so scornful, it caused me to look down on myself. I was wearing a rather curled-up nutria coat that had been through several winters of rain and snow.

"During the next two blocks to the theatre I did a lot of thinking. I might be giving my all to my public onstage but offstage I was letting them down. They were paying tribute to a star; I was paying them back by looking like a dowdy housewife. When I reached my dressing room, I picked up the phone, called Revillon Frères, and announced that I wanted to order a full-length sable coat.

"By the time the matinee was over, a tall, very impressive man arrived at my dressing room wearing a fur-lined coat with an astrakhan collar. He introduced himself: he was one of the Frères. He carried a briefcase in which there were half a dozen sable pelts for my inspection. We carefully chose the most becoming color for my complexion and then he divulged the price. Twenty thousand dollars. Well, I ordered it. No one was ever going to say, 'That's not Helen Hayes, for God's sake' in that tone again.

"On my way home for dinner, my taxi was stalled on 57th Street and there in the window of the Durand-Ruel Galleries, all alone and shimmering in beauty, was Renoir's *Girl in the Lace Hat*. Her message flashed to me across the sidewalk and through the taxi window. I paid the driver, got out, and stood with my nose pressed to the window, gazing at her entranced, like Stella Dallas. You see, that painting looked just as I thought our Mary would look when she reached the age of *The Girl in the Lace Hat*. And I said to myself, 'By rights that picture *belongs* to Charlie and me because it's a portrait of our daughter.' The gallery was closed but the next morning I phoned and found out that the picture cost the same price as the sable coat. So I made a switch. I bought the painting; I called off the coat.

"Afterwards, I had my regrets and told Charlie I'd let my public down again. But he was ready with a quick solution. 'You can always march off to matinees wearing the Renoir as a sandwich sign.' So that's how we came by the Renoir.

"Many years passed, and when Mary grew up she looked just like her portrait by Renoir. But after a while, Mary was gone and then we didn't want to stay home so much. We were forever traipsing off on long trips and our *Girl in the Lace Hat* was left all alone in the house. Finally Charlie suggested lending her to the Metropolitan for a year. I called Theodore Rousseau, Curator of Classic Painting, and made the offer. Ted was delighted, so she went over to take up her residence at the Met.

"A little later I had a call from Ted. It seems that when the Met borrows a painting, it must go through a series of tests to determine if there are any damages of which the owner must be told. Ted had found that one corner of the canvas had buckled and the X-ray machine revealed a flaking of the paint so minute that it wasn't yet visible to the eye. Would I permit them to treat it? I would indeed. So our Mary's portrait was saved intact and the Met became one of the most precious friends we'd ever had."

On various occasions Helen and I visit the Met for purely acquisitive motives. Recently we went there on a shopping spree. "We ought to find Christmas presents in the gift shop for our house-proud friends," said Helen. "And, besides, the Christmas cards and calendars are so high-toned, they'll reflect credit on us." We went early in October to beat the Christmas crowds. It was pleasant in the card department because everybody, clerks and shoppers alike, had museum manners and were most polite; no shoving ahead or snapping at each other, and the cards were artistic reproductions of illuminated manuscripts and paintings.

"There's not a cute poodle or a jolly Santa in the lot!" Helen exclaimed. "These cards reflect the true meaning of Christmas!" To my mind, such high art is only appreciated if a person gets one single card at Christmas, for any two of them look exactly alike. And more than two are nothing but a medieval blur. However, Helen's choice came in the form of bookmarks, so that anyone stuck with a dull book might take a closer look at Helen's Christmas card.

Passing on to the department for reproductions, we found grand and expensive gifts that were calculated to boost any donor's prestige. There were copies of Metropolitan treasures— Paul Revere silver, Egyptian faïence, ancient Greek, Roman, Peruvian jewelry in look-like-gold; that sort of thing.

Helen remembered a small Greek horse she once bought there. It looked so much like a toy that it could delight even an art hater. Now, it happened that Helen was obliged to give a present to a certain monstrous brat who could smash anything softer than bronze, so she decided to outwit him by buying him that horse. But now she ran into a hurdle. The saleslady, lowering her voice, said, "You've brought up a rather embarrassing subject, Miss Hayes. One of our new officials has discovered that the original little Greek horse was a . . . fake."

"No!" said Helen, in a shocked tone that matched the saleslady's, except that Helen was kidding her.

The saleslady sighed. "It's been a great loss to the gift shop. The little horse was a best-seller for over forty years!"

The subject of fakes had fascinated me from the time I was involved with that magnificent Hungarian swindler, Elmyr de Hory, who sold millions of dollars' worth of his forgeries to galleries all over the world. I had been introduced to him by my pal Zsa Zsa Gabor, and he later begged us to pose for portraits, saying they would be presented to us, compliments of the artist.

Elmyr required Zsa Zsa to bring a number of evening gowns to his studio so he could select the one he wanted her to wear. But he could never decide on a choice, and no wonder; for he suddenly decamped, taking all Zsa Zsa's evening gowns with him. It was obvious to us that he intended to wear those spangled dresses himself. So Zsa Zsa and I discovered that Elmyr was a crook several years before Clifford Irving made him a hero of that book called *Fake*. And the circumstance caused Zsa Zsa to philosophize, "Men may be more intelligent than us women, but we're smarter!"

That day when I inquired of the embarrassed saleslady what the Metropolitan did with fakes, she replied, "Oh, one wouldn't like to inquire. They disappear, presumably into the basement."

"Dear, dear!" exclaimed Helen. "I once gave that little horse to a very distinguished friend and now I'll have to tell her to make it . . . disappear." Thoroughly convinced that we had discovered the Achilles' heel of the mighty Met, we wandered on.

But Helen couldn't get that little bronze horse off her mind. "How presumptuous to say that, after forty years of delighting art lovers, he's suddenly supposed to lose all beauty and be banished," she fumed. "There's nobody can be as blind as a dyed-in-the-wool expert."

To make her point, she launched into a story Charlie had once told her. When he was a young reporter he had been sent to interview Caruso. And the great tenor told Charlie that whenever he sang in concert, the public refused to leave until he sang "Santa

Lucia." Caruso was fed up with "Santa Lucia," but if he wanted to get rid of the audience, he had to come out with it.

One time when he was to sing at Carnegie Hall, Enrico conspired with an Italian friend whose voice could just about make it with Neapolitan street songs. The friend was to hide behind a screen on the stage and when the usual cry went up for "Santa Lucia" Enrico assumed a stance in front of the screen. And there he mouthed the ballad while his friend on the other side sang out with everything he had, which wasn't much. When Caruso finished the house went mad with delight.

Next day a leading New York music critic asserted that the Great One had reached the top of his vocal glory in "Santa Lucia." "That song is Caruso's own," he pontificated. "Nobody else should ever be allowed to sing it!"

"Nothing's either true or false," concluded Helen, "but thinking makes it so!"

That day we spent some time in the Museum's bookshop, where we chose our Christmas presents for each other. For Helen I picked out that fat volume titled *Museum*, the history of the Metropolitan written by our friend Leo Lerman. For me Helen bought *Merchants and Masterpieces* by Calvin Tomkins. While waiting for Christmas, Helen read it herself, and she couldn't resist telling me what was in it. "Why, that book has more suspense than a Hitchcock movie," she declared. "It tells how the Met was founded by a self-educated tycoon who got rich by manufacturing varnish. His first move was to acquire a former dancing academy on Fifth Avenue and then he hung his own collection of paintings in it.

"Nobody took him seriously and, as the book follows his struggles to keep the Museum going, you're all aquiver, wondering will he bring it off or will he not. You forget that this solid pile of masonry has been here ever since you can remember."

"And," I cut in, "that one of the most tremendous collections of loot the world may ever see is safe inside it!"

Helen was almost grateful for a remark that allowed her to get furious. "Loot!" she exclaimed. "What a false statement!" It seemed that without intention I had struck a crushing blow at my friend's chauvinism. "I refuse to join the mourners over our looting of the treasures of the Old World!" Helen was really carried away. "If we buy art works, somebody had to sell them to us, didn't they? And we take care of them as nobody in Europe ever does, don't we? Why, right here in the Met's Egyptian collection are six statues of Queen Hatshepsut that had been smashed to pieces and abandoned in a sand pit in the desert at Luxor until the Met found them and put them back together. They're as good today as when they were new in 1500 B.C. Now, who's the villain in that situation?"

To bring down Helen's blood pressure, I harked back to Leo. "What fascinating things he knows about this place that nobody else does!" I exclaimed. Which gave Helen an idea.

"Why don't we ask him to take us on a tour of the spots that are out of bounds to the general public?"

"Places like the basement where the fakes are?" I asked.

Helen grinned. "Well, why not?"

So before the week was out Leo was escorting us on a guided tour of the Met. En route there our taxi driver turned out to be a vocalist and started to sing the popular song that goes "People who need people are the luckiest people in the world." "Not true," Helen said. "It's the people who need *things* that are luckiest. Give your heart to beautiful things and they'll never let you down!"

"And if they're beautiful enough," said Leo, "they'll land in the Met and their upkeep won't cost you a dime!"

As we approached the Museum, its fountains, extending on either side of the façade, were splashing gaily. Out in front idlers were relaxing, under trees, in small iron chairs which made the scene look more like the Tuileries Gardens than Fifth Avenue. Also, people of all shapes, coverings, and uncoverings had draped themselves along the magnificent stairway.

In the cool lobby with its islands of exotic plants at either end (a gift from the incredible Mrs. DeWitt Wallace) we were met by Jack Frizzelle, the Met's Director of Public Relations. He supplied us with small plastic buttons that clipped on our lapels and dignified us as guests, free to enter any area. Our venture into the unknown began.

Helen wanted to see the Costume Institute first because she had only recently been made a member of the new Visiting Committee and "with my usual luck I was away making a movie when the first get-acquainted meeting took place. I always miss out on the exciting things." Leo allowed that making a movie might seem to some more exciting than a committee meeting. Mr. Frizzelle guided us toward the still-unfinished Costume Institute in the basement. The rooms were quite bare, in the throes of reconstruction. A number of mannequins were grouped under a big canvas, as naked as debutantes in the center fold of *Playboy*, but more sexy.

Leo Lerman had a brainstorm. "Helen Hayes must see those items from the wardrobe of Queen Alexandra—after all, Alexandra *was* her daughter-in-law." Mrs. Stella Blum, assistant curator, looked bewildered until Leo reminded her of how long Helen had played Queen Victoria.

A large dress box was unearthed and Mrs. Blum reverently unwrapped its contents from their tissue paper and allowed us to touch them . . . almost. What wonders of handwork! A dress of palest lilac net over silk was trimmed with infinitesimal handmade flowers of silk appliqué as a wide border around the hem of the skirt and on the train. They were repeated on the bodice and on the wide-puffed sleeves with silk lace flowing from the elbows. The lingerie of fine lawn was embroidered so extensively that there didn't seem room for one more stitch, which also went for the stockings. "Or should we call them hose?" There was not a remote possibility that they would be seen by anyone outside of the Queen's dressing room, yet they were embroidered from the insteps to the knees.

No wonder fashionable ladies were always going broke and being driven to sinful intrigues in those Victorian and Edwardian novels. It must have cost an indecent amount to clothe oneself decently.

I had actually seen Alexandra once in London. She was driving through Hyde Park in a calèche: a frail, tiny old lady of pastel coloring, much prettier than royalty need be. Moreover, I can now report a historical fact that has gone unrecorded up to this moment. Edward VII might have neglected his Queen to romance Mrs. Keppel but, through my connections in the movies, I happened to know the Dowager Queen had a mash on a Hollywood film star of Grade B Westerns named Eddy Polo. The London distributor of his films had an order from the Palace to rush every Eddy Polo feature straight to Buckingham Palace as soon as it reached the office. What was sauce for England's royal gander was just as tasty for Alexandra.

Helen asked Mrs. Blum what she would name as the main treasure of the Met costume collection. "Our great treasure," she replied after a pause for thought, "is an abstract. It is the historical and geographical scope of our collection, the variety, from queens to peasants, which is unmatched in any other museum of costumes. We have, for instance, a comprehensive collection of children's clothes of the nineteenth century. And it recently came to light only by accident while we were making a survey of our boys' underwear. We had no idea before."

A department at the Met in which Leo takes great pride is the repair shop for arms and armor. And there we met two gentlemen who are possibly the only practicing armorers in America: Theodore Cuseo and Robert Carrol. They were engaged in repairing a fourteenth-century suit of armor, doing the job with tools 250 years old which they told us had been unearthed in Dresden. Their shop talk contained words that had been used by their predecessors centuries ago. "Listening to them," said Helen, "made me feel like Mark Twain's Connecticut Yankee."

Over in a corner was a pretty blonde girl painstakingly polishing a corselet with Ajax cleanser. With long straight hair and

157

miniskirt, she had the total look of Now. Helen, immediately forsaking the experts at the sight of youth, learned that Miss Jean Tibbet was all of sixteen, a junior at a high school just outside the city, and was working with the Met armorers as her summer Humanities project. "I work five days a week—9 A.M. to 5 P.M. and I'll get credits for it," she said. "I chose working in this department because I've always been interested in medieval culture."

"Well, knock me over with a broadsword," Helen said when she rejoined us. "Maybe this is the most interesting young generation the world has ever known! The unseen and unsung underground that restores something with cleansing powder instead of blowing it up with dynamite. How she heartens me!"

I was intrigued by another aspect of the scene. "How can armor that's merely on exhibition ever get out of repair?" I inquired.

Mr. Cuseo shook his head. "The New York air," he said lugubriously.

"Do you mean our air is as destructive as an attack by Saracens?" I asked.

"Oh well," he replied, "every age has its own public enemy!"

In an adjoining room we were shown an exact reproduction of the furnaces in which armor was once forged, its fire blazing and ready for use. But there we also discovered one concession to modern technology: an apparatus for cleaning chain mail by electricity. It is a huge cylinder containing a quantity of gritty substance that looks like coarse sand. The armor is put into the cylinder, which slowly revolves, and rust is scraped away by the gravel, which is of a lot more use than moon rock.

Helen and I felt much more at home in the upholstery department. There we were introduced to two Senior Restorers, Charles Anello, head upholsterer, and John Canonico, the cabinetmaker, who preside over a storehouse of antique hardware and fabrics. Working with those ancient things and loving them so obviously seemed to have given the two an old-world look. "Their faces are like those one sees in tapestries," I whispered to Helen. "Surely they must have come from Europe." But when Helen inquired, we learned that one of the aficionados was born in Brooklyn and the other in Queens.

Talking shop with Mr. Anello, we realized it would be unthinkable for him to reupholster the Museum's treasures in anything but the real McCoy. He led us to a wall cabinet in which there is a store of precious brocades, velvets, cloth of gold, and embroidery, stacked as neatly as linen in an old Dutch wardrobe.

However, there was one item in the cabinet about which Mr. Anello had to apologize. He showed us a quantity of the narrow braid which conceals the raw edges of upholstery. "The braid we use is a reproduction," he admitted. "You see, the wear and tear of centuries has destroyed practically all the ancient braid. But even so," he added, not without pride, "these reproductions are done by hand in Paris, at a cost of seven hundred dollars a yard."

"Did you say *seven hundred dollars?*" Helen gasped.

Mr. Anello nodded. "Every inch of it is both woven and embroidered by hand!"

Then he let us in on a Museum secret. Hundreds of yards of this braid have come to the Museum as a gift from a certain fancier of furniture who is one of the great experts of the world and, necessarily, very, very rich. She shall be nameless here because, as Mr. Anello explained, "She doesn't want her generosity known." (This is a mystery, because her less worthy pursuits are constantly in the gossip columns.)

Leaving the world of Mr. Anello, Leo led us to the room where textiles are washed. Every precious thread has to be taken into consideration. The washtub there consists of a zinc receptacle covering almost half the floor but only four inches deep. A tapestry was submerged in it. Tending the laundry that day was the Met's Master Restorer himself, Mr. Edward Rowe. He explained that he was substituting for an assistant, Miss Nobuko Kajitani, who was away on holiday. Mr. Rowe glowed with pride when he spoke of his young Japanese aide. "She is so expert," said he, "that I never have to supervise her work. I just hand her a dirty tapestry and she takes over. It comes out as fresh as it was the day it left the loom, several centuries ago."

Ed·Rowe has a philosophy which seems to me the quintessence of human wisdom. Summed up in a few words, it says, "Select whatever interests you most in life and then take it as far as you can go."

For our next venture we proceeded to the top of the Met where the photographic department spreads over the entire attic. For it is under the Museum's own roof that the objects reproduced on postcards and in brochures and art books are photographed in color. The head photographer took us in charge and showed us about. Mr. William Pons and his staff work in the greatest discomfort, for this part of the Museum is not air-conditioned and, like all attics, it is stiflingly hot on a summer day. That afternoon, they were engaged in photographing a Persian rug so large that it hung from the ceiling and had to be photographed in sections. Every object that comes into the Metropolitan Museum is photographed by the Pons team and the color transparencies are kept in the hundreds of filing cabinets lined up and down the great gallery.

By now the hour was getting late and we were scheduled to visit two more places, the laboratory for the restoration of paintings and the basement. "There isn't time to cover them both," said Leo, "so which would you rather see?"

I cast a significant glance at Helen. She returned it. Then, in unison, we replied, "The basement."

And so the climax of our tour took us deep underneath the Museum into a world which was a mystery even to Leo. It consists of a seemingly endless tunnel low enough to produce instant claustrophobia. This tunnel is what remains of an underground passage leading to the Reservoir in Central Park. The aqueduct was filled in during the 1820s, except for the section used by the Museum for storage.

The portion we visited has for years been a storeroom of miscellaneous works in the Museum's collection which do not require temperature or humidity control. This includes some fakes and objects of pure kitsch which the Met had to accept because they were given by misguided millionaires whose cash was as welcome as their taste was not. Running almost the length of the tunnel are shelves for small objects, some worth no more than what one might buy at Woolworth's. But possibly they couldn't be gotten rid of without calling a Board meeting, so they are left to gather dust in the tunnel.

A pair of the Met's fakes have been too greatly publicized to be kept under wraps as was the little bronze horse. They are larger-than-life terra-cotta sculptures, known as the "Etruscan Warriors." Placed on display in 1933, they became a lively center of interest because of the warriors' size and belligerent attitudes. They also served as a lesson in anatomy to little tykes who, dragged to the Museum willy-nilly, picked up interest at once when they saw those Etruscans, who were nude in just the most interesting spots. The purchase had been made by the head of the Met's Classical Department, John Marshall, a man of taste and erudition who was responsible for the Museum's superb collection of ancient Greek and Roman statuary.

Almost immediately after their installation the international art world began to attack those Etruscans. A Roman taxi driver with the flowery name of Fioravanti boasted that he had helped two brothers named Riccardi to manufacture the warriors in a workshop near Orvieto. Then an Italian critic announced that the clay in the statues contained ground-up glass from Peroni beer bottles. A distinguished professor named Cagiani had visited the Met and, when asked if he cared to look at the Etruscan Warriors, he replied, "No, thanks, I know the man who made them."

Marshall staunchly held his ground against all that criticism. And his position was bolstered by an interesting fact: in Italy every new archaeological find is guarded by the authorities, and when Marshall first went to Orvieto to investigate the statues, he was stopped outside his destination by a cordon of police.

161

Marshall, of course, looked on the police as proof of authenticity. But what he didn't know was that the Riccardi brothers, who had more cousins than a Mafioso, had put them all in uniform and stationed them outside the studio for Mr. Marshall's benefit.

The Italian art forger has nothing to worry about, even when he's caught. Italy has stringent laws to prevent the exportation of authentic treasures and also a sneaking admiration for anyone who can fool experts in the U. S. A. But finally the Riccardis themselves started to boast that they had taken in the great Metropolitan Museum, and in 1961 the Met conceded that its Etruscan Warriors were fakes and they were banished to the basement.

We departed from the Met that day without finding out how paintings are restored, but in the cab on our way home Helen regaled Leo and me with the story of a fascinating job of restoration in which she herself was involved.

"Several years ago," she said, "I got notice of an auction up at Catskill of paintings by Thomas Cole, the Hudson River Master. It was a wonderfully exciting opportunity, so, all primed to acquire a Hudson River School, I drove upstate. But luck was against me: every big gallery owner in New York was there, bent on running up the bids, so that no private collector could buy a Cole for less than he'd have to pay on 57th Street. And as the auction proceeded, pictures were being bid in at prices from six thousand to around twenty thousand dollars.

"Just when I was about to give up in despair, the auctioneer introduced a painting called *Girl with Sheep*. It had a hole in the middle, one side was entirely black, and in the foreground one could make out a girl and two barely visible sheep. It was a mess. There was nary a bid. Finally I heard a timid, squeaky voice offer two hundred and fifty dollars. There was no further bidding and, as everyone turned to look at me, I realized that the timid, squeaky voice had been my own. I had just paid two hundred and fifty dollars for a piece of blackened canvas with a hole in the middle.

"There was someone in the throng, however, who took pity on

me, an authority on Thomas Cole from Harvard University. When the auction was over, he approached me, introduced himself, and said, 'Take my advice and don't hand that painting to a restorer. He'd charge a fortune. First have the hole mended by a reliable framer; then buy some Winton Cleaner and some Q-tips and go to work on the picture inch by inch.'

"Well, I took my painting home to Nyack and got a local weaver to mend the hole." Then, sitting outside because it was summer, Helen started to clean her painting in the bright daylight. She was thrilled when she saw a lush green valley emerge out of the grime. It didn't even distress Helen that the girl with the sheep turned out to be wearing an Italian peasant's costume and was playing a mandolin. "You see," explained Helen, "all the landscapes Cole painted when he was abroad look exactly like the Hudson Valley."

But when two male figures began to emerge in the lower right-hand corner, a problem arose: the paint had flaked off, leaving only a bit of shoulder, a wrist, a knee—just enough to indicate their positions and to show that one of the men was definitely playing a flute. At long last the picture was clear and well defined except for those two male musicians where the canvas was bare.

"Well," said Helen, "I went to an art shop and bought myself a box of oil paints and some brushes."

"Brava!" spoke up Leo.

Helen took a bow but went on modestly, "Oh, I admit it took a week to get up courage for the first brush stroke, but once I started I cheered myself along by thinking, 'It's my picture, after all. And I don't mean to sell it. Even if I did, I'd put a label on it stating Thomas Cole, as restored by Helen Hayes.'

"Everyone who came in the back entrance—the milkman, mailman, and dry cleaner—stopped to look and advise and admire. We—the picture and I, that is—became celebrated locally. Finally, at the end of six weeks' effort, I had myself a beautiful Thomas Cole! And if you ever hear, dearest Leo, that the Met has acquired a black canvas with a hole in the middle, will you let me know? It might open up another career for me, now that I've re-tired from the theatre."

"Darling," declared Leo, "you'd better forget about saving the Hudson River School. Because, if you ever *really* retire from the theatre, how can you keep on retiring?"

Helen grinned and said, "Oh, well."

SALVATION FOR US ALL

$\mathcal{T}$he Salvation Army lives and works in the dark corners of the city. We followed it into a pretty dark corner at Thanksgiving time. So far as I know the Army doesn't have a public-relations staff, which sets it apart from every other charity in Manhattan. How it feeds, clothes, and repairs so many tattered souls with so little fuss is one of the great miracles of our town. At Thanksgiving the Army serves a turkey dinner in more than one of its centers. We chose the Wilhelm Loewenstein Memorial Cafeteria, between 10th and 11th Avenues on 48th Street, because we meant to *eat* our dinner at whichever center we went to, and, much as we wanted to see life in the raw, it wouldn't have been fitting to have barged into the Bowery hostel.

The Loewenstein Cafeteria occupies the ground floor of a rehabilitation center for homeless and helpless men. When we arrived at the building there was a long line of people, two abreast, halfway down the block waiting in the cold to be admitted. I looked them over and found that not one of them was without an overcoat. And this I relayed to Helen. She was truly surprised. "Really?" she remarked. "I couldn't bring myself to more than glance quickly at them. I was too embarrassed." I hadn't thought of embarrassment in my surprise. Up to that point I'd harbored feelings of guilt over being warmly clad and, instead of hunger, merely having an appetite. Inside the gaunt auditorium we found no reason for guilt, either. The staff that met us made me feel that the greatest thing the Army does is not its work for the poor, but its ability to corral so many super-spirits who keep alive a cheerful acceptance of life, good or bad, that one finds in all Army personnel.

The rehab center is equipped to house and feed a hundred and thirty-five derelicts with only one proviso: that they really want to better themselves. When we entered the cafeteria there were a number of them behind the steam table: their rehabilitation had reached the point where they could expertly dish up the turkey, mashed potatoes, and gravy—no easy job, because fifteen hundred guests were expected and they were barging in at the rate of a hundred or so every half hour.

"How few dinner parties we get to where we're really fascinated by the guests," said Helen. "I doubt that there's a bore in this entire lot!"

It appeared that we were not encouraged to sit down to dinner and this suited us fine. By this time we were more interested in the company than in the food. And it then transpired that the Army expected us to help in the serving. So we joined a crew of volunteer hostesses and learned from their conversation that they show up every year. All of them glowed with contentment. First of all, they were a big cut above the diners; secondly, they were being confirmed in the knowledge that they were important to the world. Helen remarked that she envied every one of them. "I've found out that the hardest thing in life is to feel important to the world!"

A very correct type of elderly lady took charge of us. Judging by her competence, she might have owned the joint. "This is my thirty-fourth year of serving at Thanksgiving!" she announced as she led us to our station at the pumpkin pie table.

Our responsibility was to put a paper plate with a piece of pie on each tray as the guests passed by from the steam counter en route to the tables. It was a great vantage point for us, since it gave us a chance to study the guests at close view. But presently we became aware of a subtle antagonism on the part of one of the regular waitresses. Our first hint of it came when we began to be avoided by the tray bearers; they were skirting our pie table as if it were a swamp. Studying the situation, we then realized that their trays had already been supplied with pie. We speculated on the reason. Presently Helen got a clue. "Look at that fat little hostess with the red wig!" I looked. She was sneaking the paper plates containing pie from behind our backs, carrying them to the steam counter, and plunking one down on every tray. But why?

"It's purely a case of professional jealousy," I ventured. "We're newcomers, crashing in on her territory." My viewpoint was confirmed when we overheard the young lady remark to a fellow "regular," "Who do those two dames think they are?" I was all for meekly accepting the situation. Helen was not. She appealed to the Dean of Hostesses who was our friend. Mrs. Red Wig was promptly stationed at the entrance on the far side of the room and once again our pie post gained its supremacy.

We encountered every sort of outcast. There were the shabby but polite who thanked us with dignity when we gave them their pie. Two unexpected types were befringed hippies, and there was a sort of Black Panther who was outfitted in a slick mod getup and Afro hairdo. There was a reasonable number of families. There was a black lady with three children who really shouldn't have been so cute because it was too easy to spot them when they sneaked around a second time. And there was a young white couple with two rather fancily dressed offspring who looked so prosperous and domestic that Helen was curious. "How do you happen to be here today?" she asked the Mama. "We just ain't got no turkey at home," the bad housekeeper answered in a matter-of-fact manner.

There was the anticipated number of bleary-eyed gents who were redolent of booze. Their deportment was slightly formal, although they seemed to be more at home than any of the others. I suspect that the Loewenstein Cafeteria is more or less their regular stamping ground. We were told that anyone can get a good, filling breakfast there for twenty-five cents with hot or cold cereal, doughnuts, and all the coffee one can hold. And, if one happens to be short the twenty-five cents, that's all right too. Everybody who passed our table seemed at peace with the world on that cold day; nobody complained of the menu, except one rather *grande dame* type who wanted mince pie instead of pumpkin. And, feeling that her preference was of interest to us, explained, "Pumpkin gives

167

me gas." As she moved on, pieless, Helen said to me, "I like her the best!"

I was so interested that day in the goings on that I failed to note a sense of preoccupation on the part of Helen. But as we were walking back to my apartment, she unburdened herself. "All the time we were there," said she, "I was morbidly afraid of locking eyes across the pie with someone who had acted with me somewhere." I had to admit that there were plenty of old girls in the crowd who looked like aging actresses. The type is rather prevalent on the west side of town. "They live out their lives in the grubby apartment houses of the Forties and Fifties," Helen remarked, "and can be seen any sunny day strolling up Eighth Avenue garbed in their ancient fripperies on the way to their favorite benches in Central Park." Then, as usual, Helen resorted to optimism. "Maybe I'm wrong in pitying them," she said. "They look fairly content. Their way of life may not be all that melancholy. At least it has continuity and rhythm. And the struggle to put up a front, to be a principal or spend at least a brief moment downstage-center, has all been removed from their existence. No more that dread humiliation of being programmed among the 'Omnes.'" Helen sighed. "What a delicious relaxation! What a happy last act for any play."

Well, we'd seen how the Salvation Army comforts the "oldies," now to investigate the other end of the generation gap. We took to the phone book for help. The list of branches was what Helen calls "a startlement." "Heavens to Betsy!" she exclaimed. "The Army has more branches than Woolworth's or Chock Full O' Nuts!" I suggested going to the top and phoning the boss. "Why, of course," she said and she went right about calling her friend Brigadier Andrew Miller. (Helen knows all the best people, just as I know all the scamps.)

The Brigadier suggested we visit a center on Stuyvesant Square where the Army, through a new method of social therapy alone, is working to rehabilitate delinquent girls, to whom they have given a new classification. Here they are not called dope addicts. The

Army begins its first treatment with the face-saving technique of calling them "drug-dependent."

Reaching the center, we ran into a situation we'd been experiencing from the time we started casing the city. Helen and I are always finding ourselves integrated into the past. We were met by Lieutenant Elizabeth Baker, who heads the staff there, and shown into the parlor. "This house was built at the beginning of the century as a home for wayward girls," said the Lieutenant, "and it was completely financed by Helen Gould."

"Well," exclaimed Helen, "that sort of ties me right into the project. Helen Gould was my mother's idol. And that's how I came to be named Helen."

We found out that there were about forty girls in residence, all in their teens. The rule is that they must apply of their own volition and agree to sign for the entire cure, which takes eighteen months. The girls, for the most part, stay the full course.

The treatment is a new but idealistic form of the old "cold turkey" cure, which means that no drugs are used to deaden the agony of withdrawal. In fact, the only medication employed at all is for such infections as have been caused by dirty hypodermic needles. After they have been cleared up . . . nothing. The patients are on their own and God help them. Which is just what the Army counts on. Lieutenant Baker shrugs at the mention of methadone—"Just a bad habit replacing a worse one" is her opinion. "The only medicine we use here," said the Lieutenant, "is the help of God." She laughed. "And we therapists need it more than the girls do, because only our faith can supply the determination that carries a patient through to the end of the cure."

A large part of the treatment is supplied by group therapy; it somehow seems to stiffen the backbone, permits the gripers to let off steam, and they are allowed to prove in front of witnesses that they're all equally important.

The really important members of that rehab center, in my opinion, are the magnificent human beings who run it. One such character is Elizabeth Baker.

Helen and I were allowed to eavesdrop behind a door on a group therapy session. It sounded like the caterwauling of a thousand cats at midnight. A richer variety of oaths couldn't have been thought up by a crew of striking teamsters. Presently the door burst open and a raging-mad girl whipped out, passing us as if we weren't there. "It's Rosita again," the Lieutenant sighed. "I was afraid so." It appeared that Rosita wanted out. "We're trying to keep her as long as we possibly can," said the Lieutenant. "The other day *I* screamed at *her*," she added. "I had to restrain myself hard to keep from socking her." Lieutenant Baker doesn't exactly speak the language of Salvation. She knows that the ears of her girls are soundproof to anything that doesn't pack a wallop. She can only reach them by using terms of the street, of pushers and hookers and all such human trash.

"It's pretty indicative of these girls," said Lieutenant Baker, "that when they decide to get out they never say, 'I'm going home.' Any home a girl may have is a disaster area. So, she'll always say, 'I'm going back to the street!' That's the place they all long for. When a girl gets that 'street look,' it means trouble."

She told us of another girl like Rosita, a rebel and a troublemaker who wanted out bad. One day she got word that an aunt had died in Newark; a family funeral would be an excellent chance for a breakaway. She was naturally told that the only way she could go was with an attendant. "What are you trying to do to me?" she screeched, in a flood of tears. "Make me go to that ___ ____ funeral with a keeper? What kind of a front can I put up with that ____ ____ square family of mine? They'll take me for a ____ ____ tramp, that's what they'll take me for, you ___*__!__**!__."

Just thinking of that diatribe made Lieutenant Baker wince. "But hostile as she was," the Lieutenant continued, "I never gave ground. I shouted as loudly at her as she shouted at me. I wouldn't have given a nickel for my chance of winning that contest. But then all of a sudden, she went mute. She glared at me silently for a long time—it seemed a very long time. Then she said, 'All right, Baker, I'll go with you but nobody else.' "

"After all those names she called you?" I exclaimed.

The Lieutenant smiled. "Probably because of all those names *I'd* called *her*. You've no idea how grateful these kids are when somebody cares enough about them to howl them down. That's what's wrong with our family life, from Park Avenue to the ghettos. People just don't care enough about each other to raise a little hell.

"Well, the upshot of it was that I took my girl friend to New Jersey. I changed from my S.A. uniform into civvies; she left off her white lipstick and we looked more square than anyone in Newark. Auntie's funeral turned out to be a howling success. And that's just what it was—howling."

But that isn't the only type of problem with which the Lieutenant has to cope. Next door to the center is a rather quiet-looking hotel. A pusher, bent on opening up a likely market, moved in there and took up a post on the sidewalk opposite the shelter. For days he stood there, making signals to the girls in the upstairs windows.

When they left the house by twos and threes in charge of an attendant for their weekly shopping tours, he grew bolder and, in sign language, indicated that he could help them shop much closer to home.

"One day I whammed across the street," the Lieutenant told us, "and I grabbed that pusher by both his elbows and I shook him. I shook him until his brains clanked. And I said, 'If I catch you here tomorrow, you'll get much worse than a shake! Because I'll call a cop!' "

Lieutenant Baker grinned. "Of course, that threat was a calculated bluff. I hadn't a scrap of evidence that could call for his arrest. But the bluff worked. That night he was seen, suitcase in hand, quitting the neighborhood for good."

The Lieutenant took us to the dining room while lunch was in progress. It was for all the world like a refined boarding school for young ladies; one difference was in the quality of the menu—here it looked better.

The chief difference, however, was that the girls were all black or Cuban or Puerto Rican. Some of them were downright beauties. Seated at tables for six or eight, they were chattering and laughing, even Rosita, the rebel who had broken out of the group therapy session.

While the girls were still at lunch we went to see some of the rooms. They were just like the rooms of any "home girl" in a small town, decorated with pinups of movie idols and glamour girls from the fashion magazines. Propped against pillows on some of the beds were the awful sort of dolls that I thought went out with the Thirties. And on the dressing tables there were beauty aids galore. It all spoke of a fierce striving for impossible ideals and brought Helen near to tears. It didn't help her when we heard the story of two illegitimate kids who had recently been baptized by the center's chaplain. The mother was a drug-dependent girl of eighteen who no doubt had conceived them in her desperate attempt to get money for heroin. But she had given her unwanted babies the names of Mark Antony and Victoria Christine.

On our way back from Stuyvesant Square, Helen spoke her thoughts. "There must be something very wrong with a system that drives girls like those to drugs in order to escape the inequities of life."

"On the other hand," said I, "there's something very right about a system that can produce the Salvation Army!"

Helen laughed. "You love to be perverse," said she.

"Not at all!" I argued. "It's just that I'm an optimist. To my mind, everything is for the best in this worst of possible worlds."

HIS EMINENCE AND HIS HONOR

$\mathcal{T}$here we were, on a chill Sunday afternoon, sitting stiffly in the drawing room of a Prince of the Church and more than a little overawed. For some as yet undisclosed reason His Eminence Terence Cardinal Cooke had invited us to lunch at his residence on Madison Avenue behind St. Patrick's Cathedral. Now, Helen is a Catholic, which should have eased the tension for her, but didn't. I was trying to hark back to my girlhood when our Episcopal services were so High Church as to be almost Catholic. But in my case the ritual was secularized because of a mash I had on our young priest. Years of nonchurchgoing had followed and now, remembering my unchastened youth, I felt guilty and uncomfortable.

Helen and I met at my apartment whence we had to walk to our date. That Sunday Mayor Lindsay, bent on proving that air pollution could be reduced by cutting down on motor traffic, had declared cars off bounds on Fifth Avenue. So, booted and furred against a biting wind, we trudged down Fifth Avenue, seeing no cars on the way.

It was certainly one of the world's delights to walk down the middle of Fifth Avenue without fearing for your life. We had only to dodge groups of boys playing touch tag and jumping on and off mini-trains that bumbled along at the speed of a slow walk. The Mayor had borrowed some from the Bronx Zoo and dug others up out of storage where they'd been stashed away since our World's Fair. And the ride was free, compliments of the city. Any extremity brings out the small-town spirit that so easily surfaces in New York; people were talking to strangers and cracking jokes as if they were old friends. Fifth Avenue had the feeling of a carnival —a quiet one without any calliopes.

173

The vendors of hot chestnuts and bagels were out in full force and Helen, caught up in the holiday spirit, decided to buy the Cardinal a bag of chestnuts. "I'm sure it's years since he's taken a carefree walk and had a chance to buy a bag of chestnuts. It'll be a real surprise for His Eminence!"

"It would be a bigger surprise to take him a bag of bagels!" I suggested, not to be flip but to assuage a mounting sensation of awe as we neared the appointed hour.

We arrived at the stately home of His Eminence, which seems to share the dignity of the Cathedral behind it. The door was opened by a young maid who was certainly Irish, impeccably starched, and glowing with satisfaction in her job. (I also felt she glowed with interest in us two characters from a world far removed from the rectory.)

The maid was so correct that Helen began to feel a little abashed at carrying the grubby bag of chestnuts, and after we'd been deposited in the drawing room, Helen whispered, "I feel as guilty as if this bag concealed a bomb!"

"Sh," I admonished her, "maybe the place is bugged."

Staunch Catholic that she is, Helen giggled. And that's what's so great about being a Catholic: the Church always wants you to be cheerful.

His Eminence's double parlors are, in Helen's words, "extremely high-toned Catholic." The woodwork is Victorian Gothic, there are stiff Nottingham lace curtains, heavy brocade upholstery, and oil portraits of His Holiness the Pope and a number of other Church dignitaries. They looked so imposing that Helen lost even more nerve about that bag of chestnuts. "Oh dear," she said in muted tones, "it looks as if I'm trying to be cute!"

At which point a young man in priest's attire entered briskly and introduced himself as Monsignor Clark. He explained that he was an aide of His Eminence, who would soon be free to join us. The Monsignor was so handsome and vital that I put him down as a churchly version of a public-relations man, they being among my favorite people. It seems to me that when politesse and consideration dropped out of personal behavior, the P.R.'s of the world picked them up and are salvaging good manners which otherwise would disappear forever.

Monsignor Clark then explained why His Eminence had asked us for lunch. He had heard a rumor about our search for the good things that exist in our city and it happened to be one of his favorite topics. "Whenever His Eminence is interviewed by the press he asks why more space isn't given to the pleasant side of life here. Of course he knows that the press sometimes plays up sordid things because they sell papers. For a long time he's tried to spur somebody on to write a book on 'What's good about New York!' But such best-sellers as *Last Exit to Brooklyn* train a magnifying glass on a single, scabrous element of life as it exists in any large city." Monsignor Clark smiled wryly. "We like to think that readers of a book like that are no worse than curious or perhaps enjoy a 'holier-than-thou' sensation reading about degradation." He shrugged his shoulders in distaste. "And then, many writers, like most other people, want to make money."

Encouraged by the Monsignor's confidences, Helen handed him her bag of chestnuts. "I bought these for His Eminence on a misguided impulse," she said, "but if I've done wrong please get rid of them and say nothing about it."

Monsignor Clark laughed and said he thought His Eminence would enjoy them. "If you'll excuse me," he added, "I'll take them to the housekeeper."

Further encouraged, Helen began to snoop and to examine the drawing room in depth. Many objects were labeled with little brass plaques indicating they were gifts to the residence from some worthy donor. Although they sort of institutionalized the place, at the same time they made things seem more human. On a rather pompous boule desk, picked out with brass curlicues, I found a plaque announcing that it had once served in the office of Major Bowes, at the Roxy Theatre, when he conducted his Amateur Radio Hour. Broadway had invaded the Catholic formalism. "Now that is a real New Yorky thing!" Helen whispered.

Presently, flanked by Monsignor Clark and another Monsignor of about the same youth, Cardinal Cooke entered. His Eminence, of a hearty, substantial build, exudes well-being. His hair is graying and he wears old-fashioned gold-rimmed spectacles. He greeted us by our first names, which immediately put us at our ease. His Eminence might, in fact, be one's devoted uncle, provided the uncle is a great many degrees smarter than uncles usually are.

In these days when a mayor may look like a movie star, a bishop like a tennis pro, and a Wall Street tycoon like a long-distance runner, Cardinal Cooke looks as if he belongs exactly where he is . . . in the Church. And this, despite the fact that no air of sanctimony hovers about him. He speaks quite often of spiritual matters but in a sort of factual tone that makes them all the more impressive. Here's a true intellectual, I felt, to whom deeply religious feeling is a normal way of life.

Lunch was presently announced by the maid and served by her and another maid in identical crisp caps and aprons. We found that the usual type of American food is served in that churchly dining room: plain bouillon, broiled chicken with vegetables, and vanilla ice cream. But if the fare was undistinguished, the conversation was not. His Eminence is on intimate and I may even say loving terms with every phase of the city. He is informed on endless subjects outside his Church; he knows the problems of city government as well as our Mayor himself. But his deep concern over them is graced by humor and sophistication. I didn't dare express my opinion of the Cardinal until Helen and I were out on the sidewalk. "His Eminence is so . . . so hip!" I said. "How exhilarating it is to be in the presence of such a man!"

Helen, happily rattling away during our table talk, was inspired to tell of our outing in Battery Park and the discoveries we'd made there. "We were terribly interested in a charming little colonial brick chapel with a graceful curved staircase out front. It was tucked in between two enormously high skyscrapers and looked so pinched that we could believe it would yell 'Ouch!' any moment.

When we crossed the square to investigate, we saw that one side of the house was a chapel. Mass was just letting out and we met two Sisters who supplied us with information. The chapel is a shrine to Mother Seton and the house is the birthplace of that great nun."

During Helen's account, the Cardinal bristled with eagerness to put in a word. And after she'd had her say, he exclaimed, "Mother Seton's home is where my mother slept on her first night in America. She arrived here from Ireland in 1905 among a group of young women who got off the ship wearing tags on their blouses with their names on them. They were directed to Mother Seton's hostel near the dock, where they were welcome to stay until some relative or employer showed up to sponsor them. It was Mother Seton who protected and guided my mother in her first steps toward becoming an American!"

Presently, changing the subject, he asked, "What are you going to call your book?" We had considered any number of titles but had settled on none as yet. "Perhaps you should call it *The City of Hope*," he suggested.

His Eminence may have sensed that both Helen and I thought his title a little bit corny. For, as if in defense of it, he continued, "New York has symbolized hope to millions and millions of people, from the time the first pilgrims came here to escape persecution, down to the most recent searcher after fame in some worldly context like show business." Smiling, he continued, "Not that it doesn't require more ambition and harder work here than in most places! I sometimes think that New York is made up of superpeople. They even walk more quickly in the streets than others do, because they know where they want to go and can't wait to get there!"

Helen mentioned that she'd recently seen His Eminence himself in some pretty rapid action. "I was watching the broadcast of a ping-pong game," she explained. "It was in a celebration of the twenty-fifth anniversary of Your Eminence's ordination, given at the Orphanage of Saint Loretto on Staten Island."

177

The Cardinal beamed in memory of that game. "My opponents were eight to ten years old," he recalled, "but they were murdering me! And, to add insult to injury, the cheering section went wild in hailing my defeat. There wasn't a yes-man in the lot. That's the sort of disloyalty one can be proud of!"

We asked about the Orphanage and learned that it harbors nearly eight hundred girls and boys from broken homes in New York. "Some of them are not actually orphaned," he explained, "but they're all desperately in need of some place to belong."

His Eminence promised to arrange for us to visit Saint Loretto, and we asked if he'd suggest other Catholic institutions we might investigate. "There are so many," he answered, "that it would take months to cover them. There's our camp at Pawling which takes shut-ins for a holiday in the summer." He mentioned an old man who hadn't been out of the city hospital for thirty-five years until he was sent to the camp at Pawling.

"And there are institutions like the hospital run by the 'Servants of Relief for Incurable Cancer' up in Hawthorne; and 'St. Rose's Hospital in Manhattan' where, in this era of ever-spiraling hospital costs, our workers ask no money for their services. Our 'Visiting Sisters' provide the poor with nursing; then there's Grace Institute, on Second Avenue, an institution for girls of modest means which has earned the reputation of turning out the finest secretaries and typists in all New York City."

"But it's not only our institutions that are important," spoke up Monsignor Clark. "Every day we run into individuals who lead lives of extraordinary dedication. I've just met a young couple, Maryjo and Peter Hopkins, who have sacrificed a private life with their own two small children in order to make a home for twenty dependent teen-agers."

"Then," put in the other Monsignor, "a couple with three small children have taken in a little girl and her epileptic brother."

"It requires a special kind of sacrifice to accept a handicapped

178

child," His Eminence interrupted. "This family did it in order to keep the little girl and her ailing brother together."

We were then told of Tom Casabianca, a blind staff member of the Lavelle School for the Blind who has set up a ham radio station and is teaching twenty blind students to operate it. They recently relayed an urgent call for medicine for a ten-year-old girl in Yugoslavia. And their daily messages from servicemen in Vietnam to their families are giving these young blind people a better sense of "belonging" than any other activity they could ever do.

It was at this point that one of the maids brought in coffee, followed by the other with a silver covered dish which she placed before the Cardinal. And what did it contain? Well—to use Helen's own homespun language—"those dratted chestnuts!"

As His Eminence looked at them askance, it was obvious that he'd never met up with a chestnut in his entire life. Monsignor Clark came to the rescue and explained their source. The Cardinal thanked Helen and, rather perplexed, he added, "Well, they must be a New York specialty, aren't they?" Then, good sport that he was, he attacked a chestnut with his fruit knife and fork! It was agony for Helen to watch His Eminence struggling to subdue the hard, slippery chestnut.

But a bad moment eventually comes to an end, and this one was followed by something good. When it came time to leave, His Eminence presented us with elegant little red leather etuis. They contained bronze medals with the Cardinal's insignia and a bas-relief of St. Patrick's Cathedral and are inscribed: "Terence Cardinal Cooke—December 1, 1970—25th Anniversary of Ordination." Helen and I will always treasure those medals; mine occupies a place of honor on my coffee table.

Sometimes after Helen and I finish a day's adventure, we return to my apartment, where she waits for her car to take her back to Nyack. And, sitting on my couch, we discuss the experiences we've gone through that day. "You, Anita," said Helen, "were taken with the Cardinal's intelligence. To you he explained our city as a place for inspiration and achievement. I will be forever grateful to him because he made me aware of its soul." Then, inspired by His Eminence's words, Helen grew lyrical. "Have you ever flown into the city at nightfall, Anita," she asked, "when the lights are coming on in the tall buildings, and as the plane loses altitude you look down and the skyscrapers seem to be gesturing up toward the sky, a gesture of affirmation in steel and stone that will always endure? At that moment, I feel I'm glimpsing the Spirit of New York. A spirit of excitement and *hope*. Now, when I view that stunning, exclusively New York sight from the window of a plane, I will remember that little Irish immigrant who lodged at Mother Seton's and came to be the mother of a Prince of the Church. Perhaps the Cardinal was right when he said we should call our book *The City of Hope*."

I begged Helen to be less lyrical and face a fact. For as the Cardinal took us to the big front door, he suggested another title that was more in line with our meager talents. It was the three words which now decorate the title page of this volume.

Helen accepted my suggestion and exclaimed in reverence, "Bless His Eminence's heart!"

But I said, "Bless His Eminence's *mind*!" For in my own book of anatomy, the heart is in the head.

How does the first couple of New York City live during its rare moments of privacy? We hoped to find out on Friday, July 14th, for we were to lunch quietly with John and Mary Lindsay at their charming, old-world mansion on the East River. But on Thursday the morning papers published plans for the funeral of the greatly loved Louis Armstrong. Our Mayor was to be an honorary pall-bearer. The rites were to be held in Satchmo's parish chapel at Corona, and the hour would be twelve noon. On the phone with Helen, Mary Lindsay changed our date from lunch to a five o'clock drink. "John will be home from the office by then for certain," said Mary.

Helen visits Gracie Mansion more frequently than I; the pre-

180

vious time I'd been there was for a grand party the Mayor gave in honor of Helen's fiftieth year in the theatre. (How John Lindsay loves the theatre!) It had been a smashing occasion. His Honor had caused two fire-fighting boats to be anchored at the riverside and they turned into the most impressive fountains. Dotting all the lawns were circles of small flowers about three feet in diameter and set flush with the grass, giving the effect of an enormous polka-dotted carpet. There were hundreds of guests and, among others, I had made a speech about my girl friend.

But this was to be just a cozy afternoon. We arrived on the dot of five. Mary greeted us and conducted us to the rear of the wide veranda that surrounds the gracious old white clapboard house on three sides. We settled into the chintz-covered porch chairs; settled, too, on our drinks—iced tea for Mary and Helen, and, for me, the usual, soda water. An attractive little dark-eyed maid passed things meant to go with cocktails, as if we'd been a more sporting group.

Talk was desultory, as it should be among good friends on a shady porch of a hot July afternoon. At the foot of the sloping lawn, the East River was busy in a quiet way. One of our friendly Moran tugboats chugged by and we waved vigorously—hoping it was our intrepid garbage-towing craft, the *Martha Moran*. The river churning and curling under Hell Gate Bridge was the only other activity out there. Nearby the shade trees rustled because a welcome breeze had sprung up. A few squirrels scampered over the lawn on their everlasting search for last year's buried treasure. The sounds of the city were so distant as to be hardly distinguishable: "a sort of blurred hum like a far-off lawn mower," Helen remarked. Just enough sound to remind us that other people were busy while we were luxuriating in quiet, which, of course, made it all the nicer.

"You know something?" Helen said to her friend Mary. "I might even swap my house in Nyack for this!"

"Don't forget that the job goes with it," Mary cautioned her. Saying which, she was reminded that John wasn't home yet and it was well past five. "He swore he'd be on time, and I warned one of his aides who always takes *my* side against the city's, to push him out of his office at four thirty." She sighed, "Oh well—so much for influence!"

We asked Mary about Satchmo's funeral, which Helen and I had each viewed on TV at noon. We had watched Mary, clutching John's arm among the mass of V.I.P.s from many different walks of life. The Governor was there and numberless greats from show business, all looking bereft. Satchmo had taken a happy part in such a lot of people's lives! We would miss him.

Helen had her very own precious memory of Satchmo to share with us: "I was in Chicago once and had been tapped to appear on some sort of benefit. I hadn't paid any attention to the arrangements until I drove up to the old Shrine Auditorium in a limousine and, looking off, spotted a large banner that read '*Helen Hayes and Louis Armstrong*.' Was I ever thrilled! I'd adored and admired him for years, and there I was, costarring with the one and only Satchmo!

"That night I wondered how best to tell him of my adulation, he who was so used to it in every public form. But when we met backstage before the show, he gave me no time to search for words. Satchmo launched into a message for *me*. And it wasn't about my art. It was much more personal and private. 'Young lady,' he said—although young I was *not*—'listen to the words of this here cat and always pay attention to your bowels!' While I was struck dumb listening, he went on to give me his advice for keeping as well and active as he was. It all hinged on open bowels and it appeared that the happy state could only be achieved by a special diet he had followed religiously for years. Right then and there he outlined that diet. I listened earnestly, and such was the hypnotic influence of Louis Armstrong that I promised I'd follow it all life long, even though my innards have always been darling.

"I naturally forgot Satchmo's diet, as I do any health program that requires will power; I only remembered that I was to avoid ice-cold drinks as if they were the devil's brew. Well, here I sit, unregenerate, sipping iced tea and mourning the end of one of the world's great Forces of Nature who was my junior by three months. The moral of that tale escapes me, but my heart grieves at its sadness."

Mary spoke up with her report on those last sad rites in Corona. It had been unbearably hot in the small overcrowded chapel, which was evident even on TV. It now prompted me to make a suggestion. "If they want to establish a memorial to Satchmo, why not air-condition that chapel? It was the church he regularly attended and it would bring comfort to his widow and such a lot of his close friends." Helen mentioned an obstacle. "They'd never do it because it just makes too much sense. They'll probably settle for a statue of him in the Hall of Fame."

Just about now a small boy tootled by beneath the rail of the porch vigorously ringing his tricycle bell. And he provided us with a revealing glimpse of how Mary Lindsay copes with a problem shared by a good many other New York wives—household help.

"That's José," Mary explained. "He's three years old and the son of that pretty girl who served the tea.

"When the weather is good, José has the run of the garden, with one of us keeping an eye on him. When it's cold, there's fortunately an attic playroom we arranged when we first moved in and our children were young. Now Katharine is married and the two other girls are away at school, so only John Jr. and his friends and José and his friends use the playroom.

"The playroom and yard are also used by a group of young mothers who formed a play group for their children and José. The mothers take charge of the activities, the children love it, and it has provided some playmates for José."

Now that we knew the solution by our first couple of one typically New York problem, Helen broached another and more important one—how to keep a very busy father in touch with his children.

"How do you meet that situation?" asked Helen.

"At the beginning, I asked John to try to get home for at least one half hour of undivided, uninterrupted attention to his family. I must say he's really been very good, and the children and he are very close. But I *am* sorry about this afternoon!"

Mary suggested a tour around the house and we started out. "I'm always delighted to take a look at Gracie Mansion," Helen said. "It reminds me of visits Charlie and I so often made with little Mary in Charlie's arms. At that time it was the Museum of the City of New York."

"It hasn't altered much," Mary said. "When it was turned into the Mayor's residence during Fiorello La Guardia's term, the architects mercifully made very few changes in the look of the house inside or out."

The Mayor arrived just as Mary was showing us into the small sitting room. He must have been terribly tired but you'd never have known it from his brisk "Hi" and that vigorous handshake. "Mary's giving us the grand tour," said Helen, "but now we'll cut it short so you can relax."

"Not at all, Helen. I'm a first-rate guide. Let me take over."

As we proceeded in his wake, Helen remembered a previous occasion when His Honor had entertained her. It was at a theatre way up on Broadway at the beginning of the Puerto Rican district and he read the narration for a musical version of Dickens' "Christmas Carol." "The house was packed with school children, all from so-called underprivileged homes, but the production had a cast of top Broadway actors. And John's performance didn't suffer one bit by comparison! He was superb!"

(Later, on our way home, Helen brought that subject up again. "I get furious when I hear people say derisively, 'John Lindsay is an *actor*!' You're damned right he is—and isn't it fine? Abraham Lincoln spoke *his* part pretty well too. So did Churchill and Jack Kennedy. I can't see why some people think it's contemptible for a political leader to face up to facts with grace and a show of wit.")

Presently, His Honor stopped at a couch and indicated two small needlepoint cushions. "Look, Helen! Mary's mother gave me these for my birthday."

184

Helen Hayes in *Happy Birthday*

Vandamm

At the South Street Seaport Museum. From left: Anita Loos; Joe Canta-
lupo, Carting Corporation; Val Wenzel, historian of the South Street
Seaport Museum; Helen Hayes; Peter Stanford, President of the South
Street Seaport Museum

Harbrace/Jim Theologos

In the Children's Ward of Bellevue Hospital with Nurse Betty Kauffman

The tugboat *Martha Moran*
with garbage scows

Jeff Blinn

The Atlas Barber School

Courtesy Matthew Raguso

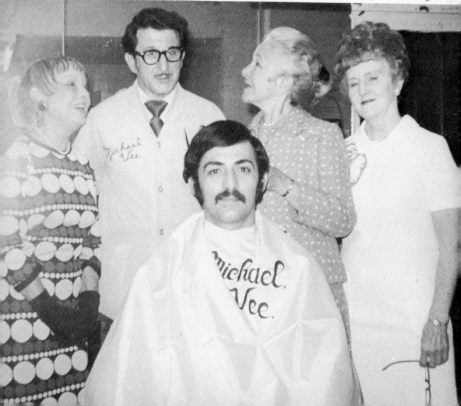

Ophelia de Vore's Charm School

Christmas at
Rockefeller Center

Courtesy Rockefeller Center, Inc.

Inspecting the armor at the Metropolitan Museum with Leo Lerman

Harbrace/Jim Theologos

The United Nations Gardens

Luncheon of the Friends of George Spelvin. Standing behind the authors, from left: Morton Gottlieb, Leo Lerman, Clive Barnes

Puerto Rican market in Spanish Harlem

There was a motto on one of them that Helen copied to embroider on a cushion for her daughter-in-law. It reads:

A Mother-in-Law's Prayer

Please God help me
not to be
Helpful

Mary led us over to a recent addition to the drawing room: a large petit point screen. "This was a present to the house made by a group of ladies who labored on it for ages as a work of love and appreciation for the city." Each of five panels represents one of our boroughs and illustrates its main feature, among them the Brooklyn Bridge with its web of suspension cables, Manhattan's United Nations, and the Bronx's Zoo. The shield of the city shines like a great golden sun at the top of the center panel. "How I love that shield!" exclaimed Helen. "Fifteen years ago Mayor Bob Wagner bestowed one on me. I forget why I got it but I was so taken with the Indian and the Dutch burgher holding up the emblem of Manhattan that I had it set in gold and diamonds by Verdura, to wear as a lapel pin. It's a little large for that but I wear it lovingly. I notice people staring at it, sometimes in alarm, wondering if I am a deputy sheriff, no doubt."

We explored the living quarters all the way to the kitchen, which has been so newly decorated and well equipped that it has no personality whatsoever. And we again encountered José (whose early dinner occupied a tiny pot on the stove) and all of us, the Lindsays included, got off a bit of tentative Spanish to him and his *madre*.

Then His Honor escorted us into his own special domain—the little City Hall which occupies a new wing of the house. There the furniture is the finest type of Federal, a gift of Historical Societies and other New York City enthusiasts. An air of elegance pervades the premises, but it isn't the chilling kind.

The conference room where top-level city meetings are held is gracious and very different from the awesome auditorium at City

Hall. In the midst of this old-world charm is a room that reminds one that the time is the electronic *now*. There are three TV sets, broadcasting equipment, and mysterious electrical units all over the place.

"Do you spend much time in here?" I asked His Honor.

"Oh yes! The news, you know!"

"John covers all the stations," Mary added, "most of the time simultaneously." Remembering how hard it is for me to stomach one of those disturbing newscasts, my heart melted in sympathy.

Finally we wandered back to our porch corner for what we anticipated as a cozy and, at the same time, illuminating chat. Something nosy, like would His Honor, perhaps, seek a Presidential nomination? The Mayor sank into his comfortable chair with a sigh of contentment. "What are you all drinking? Iced tea? Good! That's for me!" *Now* he *could* relax!

The tea arrived but John had managed only a couple of sips when the phone at his elbow rang. From his expression this seemed to be an emergency. "I'll be right down!" he said and hung up. "There's been another wreck at Penn Station," he explained. "The second in forty-eight hours."

As he swallowed a last gulp of tea I asked, "What ever led you to take on this job?"

He grinned and said, "Anything's better than having to work!" At which our Mayor set resolutely off to another scene of disaster.

Shortly after, we two were off to our own peaceful homes. On leaving, Helen allowed to Mary Lindsay, "I see your point about the job that goes with Gracie Mansion. I guess I'd better stick to dull old Nyack."

CHRISTMAS IS FOR ADULTS

*P*ossibly the gauge of any Christian culture is the way folks behave at Christmastime. In Hollywood, for instance, Christmas is an orgy: Santa drives down Hollywood Boulevard (renamed Santa Claus Lane) in a custom-built sports car with one arm around the foremost current sex pot, in a flurry of cornflakes that simulates snow and won't melt in the December heat.

Of course, veterans of old Hollywood movies like Helen and me regret the sex element that has crept in, remembering the Christmases of our youth when Santa was anything but a dirty old man and his girl friend was Baby Peggy instead of Raquel Welch. But once permissiveness starts rolling, who's going to stop it?

The Christmas spirit in New York is a matter of expert organization. The thousands of ad agencies and public-relations firms see to that. But this being the case, the typical New Yorker fights against giving in to it—up to a point. And then, along about the twenty-third of December his resistance cracks and there's more Christmas love, cheer, and uncontrolled giving than anywhere else I know. Once Christmas hits New York, it hits hard.

At Yuletide of the previous year I, together with my closest friends, had organized a non-Christmas Club; there would be no exchange of merchandise to boost department store sales. We escaped all the frenzy of buying and the bewilderment of choosing something that wouldn't finish up at the Actors' Fund's thriftshop. And we felt very superior about it all.

Even Helen, who is the epitome of everything that's Establishment, loves to grouse about the holiday just like the rest of us. And of late years she's even taken to running away at Yuletide whenever possible to her house in Cuernavaca. "In Mexico," she informed me, "Christmas is still regarded as the birthday of the Lord."

Which doesn't keep her from shopping for Christmas all year round, especially when she's traveling. Not that this really solves the problem. "When I fetch those 'treasures' down from the linen-room closet to be wrapped, a more squalid display couldn't be imagined! A clock that looked cute on the boardwalk at Atlantic City is suddenly revealed in all its crass vulgarity. I wouldn't even give it to someone I hate. And I finally stuff the whole collection back in the closet, where, by now, there's hardly room enough to put a toothpick!"

"Well," I suggested, "why not make an adventure of shopping; go places where we've never shopped before, and discover gifts that might be unusual?"

The first odd place we discovered was a brand-new boutique close to Saks Fifth Avenue. But peering in the windows, we found it was the branch of an old standby of ours, the Lighthouse for the Blind, set up temporarily for the sale of Christmas gifts.

Once inside, Helen glowed over finding all sorts of fancy kitchen aprons she could give young friends who are just learning to cook, not to mention a few old-timers who'd never gone near a stove before in their lives.

"Isn't it amazing, Anita, how hobbies change? A few years ago all our friends were painting pictures. At parties the women got into huddles and discussed new techniques they'd discovered or spoke very professionally about their palettes. But the palates they talk about today are in their mouths. Everybody's exchanging receipts.

"Oh, it's all right with me if they'd only stop there. But every amateur chef I know is writing a cookbook. I wouldn't mind eating their concoctions, but I'll be darned if I want to pay six ninety-five to find out what's in them."

Just the same, Helen loaded up on swanky kitchen aprons.

On our way out we met up with a long-haired merchant who had the sublime impudence to spread his mod jewelry on a blanket just fifty feet from Cartier's front door. A homemade sign in the blanket's center announced "Anything on display $1.00," which made me feel that here, at any rate, someone was making a serious effort to combat inflation.

Our second venture led us back to Brooklyn and the gift shop of the Museum. Helen, bedazzled by its tempting jumble of strange knickknacks, recklessly filled a tote bag with what she called "goodies" from India, Persia, Austria, Czechoslovakia, England, and Mexico; embroidered pillow covers with little mirrors worked into the design; cigarette boxes in lacquer; toys for her grandchildren's stockings—Austrian angel orchestras and antique silver miniatures from England. A number of them reminded me of the Atlantic City boardwalk but I kept my mouth shut.

I tried to find something for a friend of mine who is both a beauty and a Romanoff Princess. But somehow a Mexican doll made out of corn husks didn't seem right. (*Au contraire,* it seemed definitely Left.) So I remained in good standing with our non-Christmas Club and was the richer by twenty cents.

Our next tour brought us to the gift shop of the United Nations, which was full of tourists buying the same exotic commodities we'd found in Brooklyn, though the toys here were bigger and there wasn't a single corn-husk doll that I remember.

One purchase of Helen's was an embroidered camel that was too big for her tote bag and she had to carry it under her arm. "Whom did you buy *that* for?" I asked.

She hesitated a moment and then leveled. "If you've got to know, I've wanted an embroidered camel from the time I first saw them in Egypt but couldn't get one to fit into my airplane luggage. So this is my Christmas present to myself." As I visualized that camel among Helen's Victoriana I could hear her say, "What have I done *now*!"

But Christmas really made its *grande entrée* in New York on Monday, November 30th, when the greatest Christmas tree on earth was due to be raised on its platform at 8:00 A.M. I, being an early riser, found no problem in being at Rockefeller Plaza, but

Helen had to come all the way from Nyack. Even so, she made it. Christmas trees rank high among her major passions.

We were met by one of the public-relations staff, Caroline Hood, a delightful girl who turned out to be the daughter of a prominent New Yorker we had known. (He was Raymond Hood, the architect famous for the *Chicago Tribune* Tower.) Caroline proceeded to guide us and dispel a lot of misinformation we had collected.

I had read a children's book about the Plaza Christmas tree which had led me to believe that every year the search for a tree was conducted by helicopter over New England in order to spot the biggest pine in all its forests.

"That," Caroline said firmiy, "is indeed a fairy tale. A perfect tree rarely grows in a forest, where crowding and neglect interfere with its symmetry. The most perfect trees come from large estates whose owners may happen to have a splendid specimen sixty-five or more years old and in its last span of life. Since such a tree may topple in the next big wind, it can be given a more glorious fate if it's dedicated to bringing joy and beauty to the whole of New York."

Helen was ready to grieve over the premature death of those mighty giants, but Caroline added, "Just as soon as a tree is cut down, a small one is planted nearby to take its place.

"The biggest tree we ever had was ninety feet tall," Caroline further informed us. "It came from an estate near Mount Kisco. And then, for four consecutive years, we got our trees from the Tranquility Farm estate of Peter Stuyvesant in Allamuchy, New Jersey. Once a tree is located, it takes a 'corseting' crew three days to bind the branches close to the trunk. During the cutting it is braced against crashing by an enormous crane and then eased onto a fifty-foot log trailer for the trip to Manhattan. Several days before its journey begins, the route has to be checked with highway authorities to avoid traffic jams and to measure the bridges and viaducts along the route."

We turned to look with awe at the tree that now stood on its platform high above the skating rink at the end of the gardens. A glittering white star, four feet tall, had already been secured in its place at the top. There was a scaffolding around the tree for a crew of workmen who were wiring it for lights. "There are twenty-four electricians on the job right now," said Caroline.

"We have to take great care about the decorations," she explained. "The tree has to stand for over a month in wind, rain, sleet, snow, and smog. All the materials have to be thoroughly tested during the summer." These experiments arouse great curiosity in office workers who can look down on the terraces. "Imagine the surprise of a staff member of the passport office coming to work on a sizzling August day and seeing icicles eighteen inches long dangling in the heat from a linden tree."

The décor of the Channel Gardens is changed annually, to provide New Yorkers with a dazzling new show. And the Center starts planning its next Christmas display on the 26th of December. Each decorating scheme has to be dramatically different from its predecessor. One year, Caroline told us, there were twin rows of fountains juggling plastic balls. Another, there were gigantic candles, flickering with actual flames (the sort used to mark highway construction at night). Another memorable year the Plaza organ was piped into the tree, giving the effect that the Christmas carols were pouring forth from the tree itself.

"For the Christmas of '41 a unique and stunning effect had been planned. The lights in all the windows of the Center were to be in graded colors, from bright red at the top through varying shades down to blue at street level. But before that scheme could be put into effect came Pearl Harbor and the great brownout."

"Please God," said Helen, "that future brownouts will be caused only by Con Ed!"

As we wandered on, Caroline assured us that the whole project was made worth while by the thousands of thank-you letters that come from all over the world. She cited the case of a homesick American serviceman stationed abroad who had actually addressed a cable to the tree itself. It read: "You are more than ever in my thoughts at this time. God be with you until we meet again. Signed: A Soldier Overseas."

"Just think," said Helen, "he may have been an orphan and these Christmas trees were the only ones he ever knew!"

This is a statement that can be rightfully doubted, for the city literally bristles with Christmas trees. One evening Helen and I joined the mass of sightseers strolling along Fifth Avenue to inspect the Christmas storefronts. A fierce competition always develops between the big shops—which is another side of the Christmas spirit more reminiscent of Herod than the Christ Child, Helen remarked—and this year Saks Fifth Avenue was boasting "the biggest tree in the world."

But the public-relations department had gone a little bit overboard on that. True, the tree reached the entire width and height of the building and was tastefully decorated in green and white. But it was, alas, only the bas-relief of a tree. "A flat one leaves me cold," said Helen. "A Christmas tree should be as round as Santa himself." As we were examining the glittering displays in Saks' big windows, Helen grew pensive. "The most sensational Christmas display I ever saw," she said, "was about an inch and a half in height and there wasn't one little flick of glitter to it. I was strolling with Charlie and the children down Fifth Avenue when we stopped to look in the window of Schrafft's. There were several cakes on display, the center one a towering *Baumkuchen,* the traditional Christmas cake of Germany. As the MacArthur foursome stood looking it all over, Jamie suddenly let out a whoop of joy— jumped up and down and pointed wildly at the *Baumkuchen.* For, climbing up the side, like an intrepid mountaineer scaling Mount Everest, and using the elaborate icing for its footholds, was a tiny mouse. As he climbed higher and higher, my Jamie's ecstasy got louder. People began sauntering up to find out the reason. Once they discovered it, they joined the cheering section. Bets were made on the time it would take our mountaineer to reach the top.

"Now there was no backing on the shop window, we could see

right through to the restaurant beyond, and there we met the eyes of a puzzled manager, joined by a couple of curious waitresses. At that point Jamie spotted them. 'Jiggers, everybody,' he exclaimed, 'pretend you're looking at the other cakes.' Everybody quieted at once. I smiled at the manager through the window, nodding at the cakes and miming our approval. His face cleared, his eyes shone. I'm a pretty good reader of expressions and I unhesitatingly interpreted his as saying, 'Well! Our cakes are the most exciting Christmas display on Fifth Avenue!' He was so right. Some people drifted away, but the MacArthurs remained to see the drama through to the end. But then it kind of petered out. That mouse wasn't trying for the top at all. He was only looking for an insecure bit of cake that he could break off, which he found about halfway up. Then he scampered down and off with Christmas dinner to the folks at home, no doubt."

But let nobody think that the two of us were mesmerized only by Christmas on Fifth Avenue. We had wangled an invitation to Macy's Christmas party for orphans, the subject of orphans being anyway much on our minds, sensitized as we were by that very particular orphan Eileen, whom we had met so dramatically at Bellevue Hospital. We had followed Eileen's career in the *Daily News*, that organ which publishes all the comforting things that happen in New York, just as the *Times* delights in heralding our disgraces. Of course coverage by the *News* naturally favors events that smack a bit of the sensational, and for three months we had read of Patrolman Scott's struggles to get legal possession of the baby he found in that bathroom wash basin, in which the entire Scott family, James's wife Dolores and their three children, had now joined. Little Suzy Scott had written a note, addressed to nobody in particular but meant for the whole wide world; she had sent it to the *News*, which was only too glad to print it. Suzy had written: "Please let us keep Baby Eileen. She is the cutest tot. We all love her so much. We cannot give her up. Please let us keep Eileen. That is all we ask. Please." Now that fifteen hundred other orphans were about to come into our ken at Macy's, we still speculated about Eileen.

From nine o'clock in the morning on December 3rd, busloads of orphans started streaming into Macy's. They came from all over, urban and suburban localities alike. Helen and I arrived at the store at about ten and were taken to the third floor teeming with orphans who lugged giant shopping bags bulging with life-sized dolls, oversized mechanical toys, footballs, baseball bats, folding dollhouses, and construction sets.

The orphans were being ushered along in groups of a hundred. The first orphan I encountered personally was small, black, and handsome and he had a brand-new five-dollar bill attached to his shirt with a safety pin. I said, "Hello. What are you going to do with all that money?"

"I don't know," he answered. "It's a dollar."

I corrected him, trying to explain the difference between one and five. He didn't follow me. His mind wasn't set for that much expansion. "I wish I had a dime," he announced. Realizing that the orphanage hadn't yet taught him to regard green paper as a medium of exchange, I dug up a dime that made him both rich and happy.

As we began to get used to the confusion, we realized that every one of the orphans, boys and girls alike, had a five-dollar bill pinned to its chest or tucked into a pocket. We were told that the money was donated by the Jaycees (the Junior Chamber of Commerce of New York City).

Next we were ushered through droves of other orphans into the enormous Personnel Dining Room, where another batch were up to their ears in breakfast. The atmosphere suggested a sort of cozy pandemonium; it was comforting and, at the same time, it split one's eardrums. A rock combo was trying to drown out some country music of a group from Greenwich Village called "Your Father's Mustache." There were also a number of clowns milling about, producing squeals of joy. We soon found out that they were members of the Macy staff. Their routines appeared so professional that they must practice all year round. "It's probably the main attraction of working at Macy's," Helen remarked.

From cookies and juice we were guided to a backstage area— the shipping department, vacated for the time being to make room for a meeting of the orphans with Santa Claus. And what a Santa! A giant just plump enough for symmetry, pink-cheeked, hearty, and with a mellifluous voice. For the speech expert, Helen, this was the final touch: "I'll buy him without a quibble!" But he was unmasked as another member of the Macy staff. In fact, although now retired, he always comes back from his upstate home for this one big event of his year.

From Santa the orphans, and we along with them, were released upon the toy department to browse there for half an hour. This was the chance to spend that five dollars on something of one's own choice. "Funny," Helen observed, "but hardly anybody's buying." I couldn't help feeling that the children were so dazed by the overabundance of swag they'd already collected that they could no longer function. But a pessimistic representative from the Junior Chamber of Commerce had another explanation: "Actually it's because there isn't very much a kid can buy for five dollars any more. Next year we're going to up it to ten."

At this point, Helen spotted a small would-be purchaser. He was standing at a cage in the bird department, his longing gaze on a canary as he fumbled to remove the five-dollar bill from his jacket. We could tell from his anguished expression that, to him, the canary was worth so much more than that scrap of green paper that he had small chance of making a deal. But as Helen started a rush to the rescue, a clerk took the project in hand. The bird's price was just $4.95. "The look of joy on that orphan's face," I remarked, "is worth more than a million." (I was getting to talk just like Helen.)

But then, on December 24th, the spirit of Christmas really reached its climax. I had settled down with my *Daily News*, glanced at its front page, and leapt to the phone. I dialed Helen. Her line was busy. And busy. AND busy. Until suddenly I realized *she* might be trying to call *me*. I hung up and waited for her call.

It came. "Have you seen the *News*?" we asked each other in unison.

A full-page, front-cover picture of a baby sucking on a candy cane. Underneath it the caption read: "Eyes sparkling, six-month-old Eileen Scott sucks on candy cane in Brooklyn after she was given her best Christmas present—*a family*."

And a merry Christmas to the selfish, skeptical millions milling in Manhattan, Brooklyn, Queens, the Bronx, and Richmond—and all the dear, kind people like the Scotts among them.

READING BETWEEN THE LIONS

$\mathscr{W}$e might just as well have been entering a jungle one day except that it was at 42nd Street and Fifth Avenue and the lions on each side of the steps were of sculptured stone. Three hours later, when Helen and I left the Public Library, she could only exclaim, "Where has *this* been all our lives?"

"And to think that we don't even own library cards!" I exclaimed.

"Well, old dear, that just about puts us on the lowest level of inertia anyone can sink to in this town."

"And makes us sound like nonreaders."

"That's not exactly true," said Helen, leaping to our own defense.

The truth is, we are book buyers and cadgers. Writer friends keep us supplied with some of their output; so do publishers, sometimes asking for blurbs.

But that doesn't excuse our ignorance about the Public Library. Helen had thought we'd need a knowledgeable guide to show us around. "I have a book-reading friend who may be able to help. I'll try to contact her." Before long, Helen phoned to say she'd dug up her friend. "Her name is Bobsy Chapman and I asked her if she had a library card, which she does. She's volunteered to take us in charge."

Now, Helen has a great many unusual friends but I was totally unprepared for Bobsy. When she showed up to fetch us in her limousine, she wasn't in the least like a "Bobsy"; she looked more like a sort of intellectualized model for the cover of *Vogue*. Every time Helen addressed her by her nickname it gave me a shock.

As Bobsy led us into the Library's grand foyer it puzzled us vaguely that she was on close terms with the attendants, and this

197

continued as she led us about from one department to another. But, most surprisingly, it appeared that Bobsy had alerted the curators in all those departments to expect us and they had placed their special treasures out on display for our benefit.

At length, when we were actually allowed to *touch* the Gutenberg Bible, Helen took Bobsy aside and asked, "How did you manage to get us all this attention?"

"Well, you see," answered Bobsy, "for the past twelve years my husband has been President of the Library."

So the Guardian Spirit that looks after Helen and me was once again on the job. Bobsy, as I then found out, is the wife of the industrialist Gilbert Chapman. But not even Helen knew that her husband had any connection with the Library.

Later, commenting on her ignorance, Helen said, "The trouble with these rich who devote so much time to civic matters is that they rarely bother to let people know what they're up to. And the news media find that the worthy element in our society is unexciting, so we're only briefed on the annals of crime."

As Bobsy led us on through one category after another—art, architecture, literature, maps, manuscripts, theatre, movies, comic strips ("Good heavens!" murmured Helen), and foreign languages—our shared sense of ignorance made us feel pretty insignificant but it all added up to the thrill of discovery.

It was in the department that houses the Arents Collection that we first learned about "Books in Parts," which are novels as they were published in the nineteenth century—tantalizing bits handed out as they came hot from the author. Helen was enthralled by their illustrations.

"To look at these lovely Victorian people makes me visualize groups of fans in hoop skirts and swallowtails, waiting at the Battery for the latest installment of *Pickwick Papers, Vanity Fair*, or *Barchester Towers* to arrive by ship from London."

"The Arents Collection," said Bobsy, "has the distinction of being so heavily endowed that it's reached the saturation point; there's scarcely anything more for it to buy. And when we think

how poverty-stricken some of our other collections are, we long to
borrow from it. But we can't."

In the map department we found a precious antique so inde-
structible that we were allowed to handle it at will. It is the earliest
existing globe, made of copper, on which North America isn't rep-
resented at all, South America is a large island, but Cuba is there
(although it is labeled "Isabel" after the royal lady of that name).
That should please Fidel Castro!

However, as proof that North America does exist, we were
taken on to the manuscript department and shown the actual letter
written in quill and ink by Christopher Columbus to two royal
officials, Señors Santangel and Sanchez, announcing that he had
just discovered a piece of land he hadn't expected. One can realize
from Christopher's handwriting that he had never discovered a
very good teacher of penmanship; which goes to show that history
can be made by the illiterate.

And on the subject of letters, we got another thrill from one that
was written by Thomas Jefferson to George the Third, just before
the Boston Tea Party. It is co-signed by nearly all the patriots who
would soon sign the Declaration of Independence. That letter "respectfully" asks the King to consider the needs of "his most loyal
subjects" in the new colony.

"Does the Library own the King's answer?" I asked.

"No," said Bobsy, "because he never bothered to write one."

"Just to think!" exclaimed Helen. "If George had only had
some manners we'd all be speaking the King's English. But then,"
with a sigh, "there'd never have been Brooklynese."

In recognition of our standing as researchers we were permitted
actually to hold the final draft of the Declaration of Independence,
in Jefferson's own handwriting, and Helen, scanning the text,
exclaimed, "Listen to this, Anita!" And she quoted, " 'With
a *decent respect* for the opinions of mankind . . .' I've never before noticed that phrase the two or three times I've read the Declaration. Maybe it didn't seem so important to me then. But now I
can't even recall a period when we were all so vociferous in our

contempt for the opinions of mankind. I believe we ought to do what we can to circulate Mr. Jefferson's thought. How about sending cards at the holidays to all the writers and producers we know in theatre, movies, and TV: "A Very Merry Christmas and a Decent Respect for the Opinions of Mankind in the New Year"?

While Helen was lovingly bending over the past, I began to cast a jaundiced eye on the present. The Library is living proof of the tremendous speed with which the backward nations of the world are suddenly exploding into print, swamping one enormous area of the Library with books, pamphlets, and periodicals in their native tongues.

I went back to fetch Helen. "Just lay off Thomas Jefferson and George the Third," I told her irreverently. "Come get a load of these new exhibits from the black countries!" She joined me and together we viewed the crowded bookshelves and met the curator of that department, Dr. John Mish. He, however, turned out to be as apologetic as we were flabbergasted. "I'm sorry to confess," said Dr. Mish, "that we're still a little lacking in Kazakh, Uzbek, and Byelo-Russian. But we're building up extremely well on Azerbaijani!"

I was too spellbound to comment, but not Helen, who said, "Well, it's comforting to hear that about Azerbaijani."

I, anything but comforted, finally spoke my mind. "This explosion of black literature may well signify that we're plunging right into Spengler's Decline of the West!"

Helen was shocked. "Let's have no more of that kind of talk. The West is only just beginning!"

By this time we had reached the Armenian collection. "It's the largest in the entire world," declared Dr. Mish. And Helen, thinking of her cultured secretary-companion, who is of Armenian descent, said, "I can't wait to tell my blessed Vera about this. Why, Dr. Mish," she added, "the Library really touches every one of us in a vital area. Anita, here, just had a thrill when we were in the Berg Collection of rare first editions, and the librarian flashed its copy of *Gentlemen Prefer Blondes*."

We presently discovered a treasure trove of things that nobody else has ever bothered to collect.

"The trivial archives of today's life that will be precious research items tomorrow!" said Bobsy. "Not that they don't come in handy today, sometimes in the most dramatic manner."

And she told us of a fugitive international crook having been caught by a detective who found his name listed in a Moroccan telephone directory. The periodicals that deal with horse breeding come in handy for racetrack touts. There is one certain contingent that studies them every day with full co-operation from the Library. No librarian would ever suggest that gambling is an ignoble pursuit. That is a man's personal affair and his sacred right.

The map department deals with such intangibles as buried treasure. On a more practical side, the curator of maps told us that he had recently had a call from a woman who was lost in Brooklyn and phoned in for the location of an obscure back alley she couldn't find.

Well, it wasn't long after our day with Bobsy that Helen flew off to Cuernavaca. And there, in the peace and seclusion of her Mexican hideout, she wrote me a letter. It tells better than I can about her evolving relationship to our great Library.

Helen began with the confession that she actually had first gone to the Public Library as a teen-ager.

"I was new to New York and meeting people who impressed me so mightily that I didn't know what to talk to them about. I needed a gimmick to cloak the fact that I was shy and intellectually underdeveloped. I hit on the subject of Japanese prints as my ploy. I felt that, while they rated high as culture, they were dainty enough not to scare off the men. Then too, the subject was unusual; I wouldn't find too many rivals. I spent a whole winter coming back here to the library, perusing books on prints.

"But I soon learned that my hobby involved mentioning a lot of Japanese names. Now, name recalling is my least talent, even with good, simple American monickers. But Japanese—! So I gave the whole thing up. And the heck with Japanese prints."

Now, in return for Helen's confession, I can report that as a young girl I took a lazier method of impressing people. I was seated at dinner next to the brilliant piano virtuoso Artur Rubinstein. It was a tough spot for a girl whose favorite compositon was "Melancholy Baby." But as a conversational gambit I remember telling Mr. Rubinstein, "I've decided to save music for my old age, so that growing old has now become something to look forward to!" Mr. Rubinstein gave me a look I couldn't seem to translate.

But here I am, after all these years, living across from Carnegie Hall, next door to the Cami concert studio and a ten-minute walk from the Metropolitan Opera House, and I still get my greatest musical thrill from "Melancholy Baby."

"After deserting those Japanese prints," Helen's letter went on, "I didn't walk out on the Library completely because I'd learned that, for a girl in New York without any ties, that blessed Library was the best friend-in-need I knew. At that I didn't really know it beyond the great marble entrance and the vast, although somehow cozy reading room. The hours I spent in there!

"But my devotion didn't last very long because . . . well, I discovered Charlie. And, like Francesca when she met up with Paolo, I lost interest in reading a book.

"As time went on I still neglected the Library, but last week when I went back there after half a century, with Bobsy, like Cinderella's fairy godmother opening up worlds I never knew existed, I could have wept over lost opportunities."

In all the years I've known Helen, I've never heard her theorize about her profession. But our visit to the Library opened up new disclosures, and one day she came through with a confession about her trade.

"The hardest thing about taking on a new role is to feel your way into the character," Helen said. "Sometimes I move about vaguely for days trying to feel like the character I'm going to act, sensing that if I can project myself deeply enough into that other woman, I'll begin to think like her, speak and walk like her. It's a maddening time for an actor."

Helen's comment reminded me of the weeks I'd spent with Carol Channing when she was about to play that idiot blonde that gentlemen prefer. I recall sitting with Carol at lunch when she said, "Look! Is this the way Lorelei Lee would eat lobster Newburg?"

Getting back to Helen, she went on, "Actors should use this Library more to learn about the people they are playing. It shames and disturbs me to think of all the historical characters I've acted in my long career without having deepened my insight through research in the quiet rooms of that old Library. How much richer my performances might have been if I'd gotten closer to those women and their times!

"Only once did I find myself quite near to a character out of the past. I was preparing to play Mary Stuart and was taken by a friend to the Morgan Library. There I was allowed actually to hold in my hands and read, in her own writing, several letters that were written by Mary, Queen of Scots.

"One in particular had been sent to Queen Elizabeth shortly before Mary's execution. The letter began 'Dear Cousin' and it begged for a chance to speak face to face with Elizabeth. Throughout her long, unexplained imprisonment, Mary had been regularly pleading for that visit and now, near the end of her life, she was begging again.

"Reading that long letter, one can see the gradual deterioration of Mary's handwriting and, at its close, she apologized to her 'gracious cousin,' explaining that the prison was so cold her fingers couldn't get a proper grip on the pen.

"At every performance during the three-year run of the play, I saw that line in my mind's eye, and it somehow made me feel the poor Queen's suffering much more poignantly than all the dialogue in Maxwell Anderson's eloquent script."

There were days, when I was whiling away the time for Helen's return from Cuernavaca, that I found myself with a free hour or two. On one of them I went to the Library and took out a card. "I bet you'll never use it!" commented Gladys. But I actually have used it, although at the same time I keep well away from that exploding section of black literature and those disturbing thoughts that were generated by Professor Oswald Spengler.

THREE MEN OF MANHATTAN

*E*arly in March we had an engagement to go to the summer fashion show of Mainbocher, but Helen called me up the evening before. "I can't make it to Main's tomorrow," she said. She gave an uplifting excuse, something about a board meeting in Haverstraw for a rehabilitation hospital. "I'm sure Main will understand. I've often had to miss other showings."

I cut in to say that this might possibly be Main's last collection. Helen reacted to my argument in disbelief.

"What are you talking about?" she asked.

"I mean it, Helen. Main has just learned that the rent of his salon has been raised to ninety thousand dollars a year. And if he can't find another location he's got to quit."

There was a pause and then Helen said, "I'll come on in."

The next afternoon we set out for Main's salon, which occupied the eighth floor of an office building at 48th Street and Fifth Avenue. It was not a very elegant location, but wherever Main has shown his clothes, the surroundings are identical to those of his first salon that opened in Paris back in 1931.

The décor at Main's is light, bright, simple, and expensive with a sky-blue ceiling dotted by little white clouds. "I never come into this room," said Helen, "without feeling an aura of elegance glowing over me. Just the fact of being invited makes me feel that I belong to the elite."

As a matter of fact, neither Helen nor I had bought any of Main's dresses for several years. I remember a time long ago when an accountant was going over my bills and, coming to Mainbocher's, he blanched and said, "Young woman, you're going to be the best-dressed girl in the poorhouse!"

Looking about as we entered Main's salon that day, we saw the same expensive faces we'd been seeing at Main's practically from the beginning. Diana Vreeland was present, as usual, even though, being editor of *Vogue*, she had gone right along with the trend toward ugliness that entered fashion about five years ago.

Sitting in her regular corner was the most superbly turned out woman we know, who is, alas, not a New Yorker. She is Mrs. T. Charlton Henry, of Chestnut Hill, Pennsylvania. She is slender as a wraith, and Main's dresses fit her as if she was his skinniest mannequin. And she has been a steady client for more years than she would care to tell. But then very few of Main's customers are young. The young seldom control enough money to pay for his clothes. Not, alas, that they even want them any more.

I whispered a bit of fashion news to Helen. "There's a rumor that this year a Coty Fashion Award is going to Levi Strauss."

"Well, why not?" Helen commented. "Blue jeans have had a greater impact on fashion than anything since the bustle. We've just simply got to forget about elegance because it's gone and that's the end of it."

That day Main's collection seemed more masterly than ever; design, color, and workmanship were so subtly combined that they gave an effect of disarming simplicity. For his designs are classic, and they no more go out of fashion than the Venus of Milo. They could possibly last as long as she has. I wouldn't know, since I've never yet been able to wear out one of Main's dresses. He has never accepted any synthetic dress material. Now, the staunchest and most reliable fabric known to man is spun by little worms. And so, one of Main's silk dresses just goes on and on.

Main's mannequins are always ladylike. There were two new ones that day: an Oriental girl who moved with all the majesty of a young empress. The other model, blonde, tall, and sinuous, made a stunning contrast.

At the end of the show Main joined us and we lingered on for a while, being tactful not to bring up the fact that we might just have seen not only the end of his career but the end of an era.

"Where did you find those two exquisite new creatures who modeled the clothes?" Helen asked.

"The dark girl is from Korea, and I figure she must have left the rice paddies only a few weeks before she showed up here and applied for work. We've all tried to find out something about her, but she hides behind her ignorance of English and tells nothing. So this adds mystery to her other enticements."

Main sent for his new blonde model. "I want you to meet her," he said, "because she's possibly one of the most extraordinary beauties I've ever encountered." Presently the lovely young creature joined us, dressed in her linen smock, and we were introduced. Her name is Mary Ussery and we learned that she occupies a small apartment on West 80th Street where she scientifically breeds and studies the largest assortment of ants in New York.

"Her specimens are used by scientists from every school in the city," said Main.

Mary Ussery laughed when she told us, "My life is utterly ruled by ants. They require so much daily care that I can't even leave them alone for a weekend."

"Well," said Helen, "there's New York for you!"

When we left Main's, we strolled up Fifth Avenue, trying to hope that Main would find another location and carry on.

Talking about Main, Helen said, "Something that never fails to amaze me is that the genes which produce artistic genius sometimes seem to have nothing to do with either heredity or environment." I agreed, for Main's roots were in the soil of the American Midwest, Boone, Iowa, to be exact, where his grandpa was for a time its mayor. Yet from earliest youth Main had two unaccountably sophisticated interests: fashion and classical music.

He had a fine voice and, with training, could have made a career in concert, singing lieder. But as a boy Main was taken on a trip to Paris. "And there in 1914," says he, "I was born all over again."

Eventually Main gravitated to Chicago, where he went to work in the stockroom at Sears Roebuck and got a first, rough idea of the fashion world. "But in time I earned and saved enough to get back to Paris, the place of my second birth," said Main.

While his interest in music never waned, Main's voice was not sufficiently trained for a career. But his sense of fashion was inborn and it led to a job on the Paris edition of *Vogue* magazine. Ultimately Main became its editor.

At that time it seemed the height of presumption for an American to open a *maison de couture* in Paris. But Main had three American friends who lived in Paris and believed he could make the grade there. One of them was the Countess de Vallombrosa, who as Ruth Dubonnet now decorates the New York world where fashion is mixed with philanthropy. Main's two other backers were Kitty, the wife of the international theatre impresario Gilbert Miller, and a socialite, Grace de Mun. The three elegant young women got together and raised forty thousand dollars, which in those days was sufficient to decorate a stylish salon with a sky-blue ceiling and little white clouds.

Main's first collection found the Parisian fashion world apathetic and was a failure. But in '32 along came the second collection, and with it Boone, Iowa, vanquished Paris, France. The initial investment of forty thousand dollars was recouped sixteen times over in a matter of weeks. From then on Main made the Paris fashion world his own. It became the essence of French snobbism for a Parisienne to buy her dresses from the American Mainbocher.

That day when Helen and I were strolling up Fifth Avenue, she stopped me as we were passing the windows of Saks Fifth Avenue.

"Look, Anita, that evening dress is an absolute steal from one you got from Main way back when."

It was indeed. The same little cape of white organdy banded by sable.

"How did Main ever think of introducing organdy to sable?" I asked.

"But that was nothing," Helen said. "He made a court robe for a royal presentation out of checked calico."

"In memory of Boone, Iowa!" I observed.

Proceeding up the Avenue, Helen reminisced about her first introduction to Main.

"It came about through Charlie's Chicago brother, Telfer MacArthur, who was married to a middle-class, Middle Western clubwoman and civic leader. She spoke pure Chicago. It came right through the nose and with plenty of rrr sounds. And she dressed to match. If she had gone into a chic New York restaurant, a pained maître d'hôtel would have led her to its least conspicuous table.

"Well," continued Helen, "one day in the late Forties, my sister-in-law was visiting New York and I invited her to lunch. She turned me down because she had a date with a friend from high school days. His name was Main Bocker (which was the way she pronounced it), so I never dreamed she was talking about the famous Mainbocher whose label had become a status symbol for well-dressed women all over the world. That is, I never dreamed who Ruth was maundering on about until she mentioned that, after lunch, her old friend was going to take her to see a dressmaking shop he'd just opened on East 57th Street. Ruth was casually bandying about a name that struck awe into the likes of me. But I'm sure that Ruth never bought a Mainbocher dress. Too plain.

"But, good Lord, Anita, Main isn't the only example of that high degree of sophistication that has sprung up in the plains of our American Midwest. Remember the last time we had dinner with Cole Porter in that fourteen-room apartment of his at the Waldorf Towers? Remember the exquisite dining room with its *chinoiserie* wallpaper, and the Chippendale dining table and the sparkling crystal and the priceless Georgian silver? And there, confronting us, in the middle of the table, were two Lowestoft bonbon dishes filled with homemade fudge from Peru, Iowa.

"Cole explained to us that a box of it came regularly from his first girl friend. She'd never forgotten how he had loved the fudge she used to make when they were fifteen. And now they were both in their sixties.

"Do you suppose a lingering touch of small-town innocence gave Main and Cole their staying power? It seems to me that too many creative people—especially our writers—mistake their self-indulgence for talent and take off like Tinker Bell for their own Never-Never Land, where nobody cares to follow them."

We dropped in at the King Cole Room of the St. Regis, ordered tea and cinnamon toast, and further indulged our nostalgia for the past. There was a period just before World War II when Helen and I were far separated. I was in Hollywood writing movies, she in New York doing plays. She proceeded to bring me up to date on one of her activities of those days that concerned Main.

"Gilbert and Kitty Miller had taken me to Paris to get clothes for the play I was doing in the fall for Gilbert—it was *Ladies and Gentlemen* by Ben Hecht and Charles MacArthur and was the only play by those two I ever got a whack at."

I had to remind Helen that she had played in a revival of *The Front Page*, that classic farce of Ben and Charlie's in which she stole the show in a bit part that was based on her Mamma, Brownie. Helen chuckled in reminiscence.

"That's true," she said. "Lucky Brownie never realized she was the inspiration for that pesky woman. She'd have lit into her son-in-law for sure!

"Well, at any rate, in *Ladies and Gentlemen* I was to play a secretary who was on jury duty. Kitty very cleverly decided that the simple, attractive wardrobe required for my role could only be found at Mainbocher's. Quite right, too. Gimbel's or Macy's would have come across too high style. So, mid-August, 1939, found us in Paris, housed at the Plaza Athénée Hôtel and having a lovely time. Charlie had remained in New York to work on script revisions with Ben.

"That was the year when Main went Edwardian—brought back the old laced corset and *hips*. I was so happy that for once my hips could be an asset that I also ordered a wardrobe for me. I remember particularly a pale blue satin Lillie Langtry ball gown sprinkled with velvet roses in deep pink and moss green.

"I had my first fittings with Main and was to go back for another in a week. But somewhere in the time between fittings, the Big Blowup came. Hitler began with awful precision to do everything he'd been telling us he intended to do, starting with Danzig and the march on Poland.

"We woke up one morning in the Plaza Athénée to the sound of marching men, the rumble of gun carriages and army trucks. France was mobilizing. All that day I wandered around the city alone, painfully aware that it would be my last look at Paris for Lord knew how long. Notices of mobilization were tacked on every public building. Clusters of solemn-faced people gathered to read them. I remember one woman, all in black—not too old, really, around about forty—who pushed her way through the crowd. She read the notice carefully, every word, top to bottom, then turned and slowly worked her way through the crowd, staring straight ahead with the most pitiful, vacant expression I've ever seen. I'm sure she had been widowed—maybe while she was still a bride—less than a quarter of a century ago in that other war when France was overrun. Now it was beginning all over again. Another generation of young men would be decimated. Maybe she had a son who'd be among them. And now she must be wondering if her life had all gone for nothing!

"I wandered into the Bois. There were the usual lovers on the benches, but that day they weren't smooching; every last pair had an open newspaper and was devouring the news, unabashedly agonized. It was terrible. I've never seen Americans take war that violently—not until this present Vietnam disaster. I could still remember 1917 with the bands and the cheering crowds and the cocky A.E.F. marching off to make the world safe for democracy. And later in '41, the mood would be grim and angry—not at our own leaders, as today, but at the enemy. And everybody would feel righteous and ever so determined. A miasma of despair hung over Paris that day, but it didn't stop Kitty from dragging me off to

211

Mainbocher in the afternoon to find out about my clothes. With our Kitty, war came second to fashion.

"But by then we knew we had to get out of France, at once—orders from the Embassy. Next morning we would be off to London in a commercial plane, Gilbert's plane having been instantly commandeered by the French. They were commandeering everything in sight: taxis, station wagons, and delivery trucks.

"Even so, Main had a solution to our problem. He would send to my hotel for my big Vuitton trunk, and as soon as the clothes were finished they'd be packed and sent on to New York in same. I don't know what conveyance Main found to pick up the trunk, but miraculously it all went according to plan as things sometimes do in time of chaos. And when my clothes arrived in New York, they were perfect although I'd only had one fitting.

"We left Paris for London after a four-hour delay at Orly while a mystery plane circled the airport. It turned out not to be a Boche bomber, but a privately owned Belgian plane, for God's sake!

"Later I heard that Main had waited until all his orders were delivered and had then walked out of his salon, his Paris apartment, and his great career in France, forever. He left his establishment—worth, I think, $125,000—to his staff and carried away just what he had brought there so many years before: a suitcase. And that's how New York came to acquire the best couturier in Paris."

On all weekdays at one o'clock two gentlemen who typify everything of culture, graciousness, and high fashion in our town are at La Grenouille Restaurant on 52nd Street just east of Fifth Avenue. They are Main Bocher, who goes there for lunch, and Charles Masson, who provides it; for La Grenouille is the creation of Monsieur Masson. Here, in a world which is rapidly changing and, in the opinion of La Grenouille's clientele, sinking right into the gutter, Main can feel very much at home. He glances about the room, smiling at ladies who have been his clients for years; whose mothers, and in a few cases, grandmothers, have been his clients; whose coming-out gowns and wedding dresses he designed; and for whose babies he made christening robes as gifts.

Helen and I sat there at lunch with our friend of many years, Henry Sell, who also belongs to the world of Main Bocher and Charles Masson. The restaurant was crowded as usual, mostly with women who were as beautifully turned out as the flower arrangements that decorate every possible niche and corner of the restaurant.

La Grenouille, in this day and age, is an anomaly. Elegant restaurants have been closing all over the East Side on account of the recession.

"How does it happen that this place can prosper when so many others are going under?" I asked Henry Sell.

"It can be answered in one word," said he; "the word is 'service.' If people can afford the amenities which are important to them, they'll gladly pay the price.

"But service is a very subtle commodity," Henry continued. "It goes without saying that here the cuisine and wines are superb and most of Charles' clients feel that those two things are the raison d'être of the place. They seldom realize how extensive Charles' service is.

"He has, of course, the assistance of John Benjamin, a great maître d'hôtel, who's been here from the day the restaurant opened. But Charles pays enormous attention to even more basic matters. Every day at dawn the sidewalk in front of the entrance is scrubbed with soap and water. Now there's no visible difference between a swept sidewalk and a scrubbed one; the difference is psychological and aesthetic. It starts to create an ambiance that continues to unfold as one enters inside."

Henry gestured toward a large floral arrangement that faced us. "It would be easy for Charles to have a florist attend to the flowers. But no florist could provide Charles' own personal touch, so he does the arrangements himself."

"All of them? Every day?" Helen gasped. "Why, it must take hours!"

213

"It certainly does, my dear! A large part of Charles' time is spent with flowers. Not only arranging them but painting them too. I can ask him to show you his studio if you'd like."

We certainly would.

Naturally, Henry couldn't make the appointment during that lunch hour. Charles was too busy judiciously seating clients at tables, supervising menus, helping choose wines, and, quite naturally, seeing that people of wealth but undistinguished worth were politely escorted to the doghouse at the rear of the back room.

Helen, who had only that day met Monsieur Masson, watched him with special interest. "What a handsome man!" she exclaimed. "So healthy, fit, and vital. He doesn't look like an indoor type. He might be a tennis pro!"

Our appointment with Monsieur Masson was made for 10 A.M. on a future day. We met him in his empty restaurant, just as he was putting the finishing touches to his flowers, and were led up a flight of stairs to an area on the second floor. It consists of a vast room, so French in spirit that it looks like the background for a Toulouse-Lautrec painting. It harbors a mishmash of luxurious objects which bear no relation to each other. First off, one wall of the lofty cavern is lined, from floor to ceiling, with wine racks. Most wine caves are underground; Charles' is high up above the restaurant and there a permanent temperature is created for its special benefit. The room is lighted by enormous studio windows and contains an easel and some workmanlike paintboxes, for it is here that Charles paints the portraits of his friends, the flowers. Many of his paintings hang on the walls. There is nothing dilettantish about them but, at the same time, they have none of the professional adherence to any one art style. They are merely flower arrangements made perpetual.

At the rear of the room a flight of stairs leads to a platform with a long worktable, where Charles attends to the business matters of the day. And seated at his table, I mentioned an incident that had brought Charles and me together some twenty years ago. At that time Charles was the headwaiter at the elegant Pavillon Restaurant. While he was there, however, Charles had been seduced by the American Steamship Line to become maître d'hôtel on the old *Independence*. Now that the American Line no longer exists, it may not be too disloyal to state that the *Independence* was not the last word in comfort. It was always full to overflowing with family trade, Americans who took all the kids along on their holidays. Service in the dining room varied between being slipshod and impertinent. Before we boarded ship in Naples, we'd heard rumors of what to expect. But when we entered the dining room for our first meal, we were overjoyed to be greeted by our elegant friend Charles Masson. Charles, however, didn't seem to share our pleasure in the encounter. He was embarrassed, in fact, and as he led us to a table he suggested a diet which eschewed anything in the way of vegetables. "They're all out of a can," said Charles, and at his suggestion we entered into a diet of steaks, chops, and three-minute eggs.

When time for going ashore arrived, Charles looked us up and said, "Please, when you go back to the Pavillon don't tell anyone about the cuisine on this ship."

"Why do you stay here?" I asked.

A flicker of humiliation crossed his features. "The salary," said Charles, "is colossal."

Sitting in Charles' atelier that day, Helen and I heard from him the real reason why he had plied the seas on that inglorious old tub. "All the while," he said, "I was saving every penny for the day when I could put to use the knowledge I'd learned about fine living. At times I dreamed of a restaurant in Paris. But no. There's only one place in the world where people have a chance to begin at the bottom and grow: New York."

Madame Masson had established herself in New York to search for a location. The day finally arrived when there was money enough to launch a business, but still Gisèle Masson had found no suitable building.

"One night I was sitting in the salon of the *Independence* with my friends Florence and Fredric March," said Charles, "when a cable from Gisèle said she'd found our location. Freddy March ordered champagne and the three of us drank to the birth of La Grenouille."

At that point I interrupted to ask Charles why he had picked on a name that few Americans can pronounce, of which many Americans didn't know the definition, and one which might embarrass a young man inviting his date to lunch and not knowing what to call the place.

"The Marches and I sat up half the night pondering that very subject," Charles reminisced. "We thought of any number of names that seemed so banal we dismissed them." Finally, prompted by gratitude to his devoted Gisèle, it entered Charles' mind to suggest the nickname he'd given her when they were courting. "Little Frog" he used to call her. "Not that she looks like a frog," he was quick to advise us, "because she's a great beauty. But the moment I mentioned 'La Grenouille,' Freddy March spoke up and said, 'That's it! Don't go any further!' "

(But the end of Charles' servitude on the *Independence* didn't separate him from the sea, for which he truly has a passion. He satisfies it today by turning chef and supplying gourmet food to the American crew of one of the International Yacht Race entrants.)

On that day when the *Independence* docked in New York Harbor, Charles came face to face with a grave disappointment. The premises Madame had found were quite adequate except for the kitchen area. Too much had to be done there with too little capital. "We did the best we could," said Charles wryly, "but the day we opened my balance at the bank was thirty dollars."

And so it came about in this era, when taxes are exorbitant, expense accounts in question, the future dubious for everybody, that a spirit of opulence proudly raises its head every day at La Grenouille. As long as Charles Masson can carry on, elegance has not yet departed from the city.

216

And now I'm thinking of another luncheon at La Grenouille, at which the host was another outstanding man of Manhattan whose rags-to-riches rise is so typical of our town.

Late in January I had a phone call from this friend whom I like and respect tremendously. He is Irving Rosenthal, one of the few celebrities whose profile in the *New Yorker* magazine ran into three installments. "You know Oliver Smith, don't you?" Irving asked. I did indeed. Oliver is a leading designer of stage décor and elegant interiors. "I'd like you to ask Oliver Smith if he'll decorate my place for next season."

I was a little staggered when I realized what Irving meant by "my place." He was not referring to his Fifth Avenue apartment but to Palisades Park, that gaudy, glittering pleasure park which beckoned us, all summer long, to "come on over" to the Jersey side of the Hudson River. Its huge sign, long a fixture on the historic Palisades bluffs, was visible for miles to residents of Riverside Drive and to everyone driving along the West Side Highway and across George Washington Bridge.

Now, seeing that Oliver's field of work is more pertinent to jobs like the Waldorf Astoria ballroom, I wasn't too sure of his interest, but I told Irving I'd pass on his request.

It turned out that I'd been completely wrong. Oliver was enthralled. "I've decorated everything except a pleasure park," said Oliver. "I can't wait."

And so Irving, being a gourmet, asked us for lunch at La Grenouille to talk things over.

En route there, I tried to explain Irving's extraordinary life story to Oliver. He began his career as a little boy peddling pail-and-shovel sets at Coney Island for a dime. Now in his seventies, he owns Palisades Park and not long ago was offered millions of dollars for just the ground it stands on. Irving wouldn't sell. Irving knows and loves every inch of the Park. It is run much more immaculately than the homes of most people who frequent it. When Irving walks about the Park, he carries one of those canes with a nail at the tip to spear cigarette butts and scraps of paper.

Oliver was fascinated. "Tell me more!" he said.

I was on a favorite subject, so I told him: Irving doesn't allow frozen food to be served at any of his concessions. And a testing crew goes the rounds every day examining food for purity. To test a hot dog, the investigator breaks it apart, puts a drop of iodine on it, and if the contents turn black it means the beef is mixed with cereal. Out it goes!

Irving believes in advertising the way a Muslim believes in Allah. Luckily, he is married to exactly the right sort of helpmate. She is a slender, pretty blonde who has for years been one of ASCAP's highest-ranking song writers. It is she who composed the words and music of Irving's theme song:

> Palisades has the rides,
> Palisades has the fun,
> Come-on-over.
> Shows and dancing are free,
> So's the parking, so, gee,
> Come-on-over.
> Palisades, known coast to coast,
> Where a dime buys the most,
> Palisades Amusement Park
> Swings all day and after dark.
> Ride the coaster, get cool
> In the waves in the pool.
> You'll have fun—so come on over.

For any ordinary peace-loving mortal to run a pleasure park would be anything but pleasure. Such a spot is always a hangout for rowdies. And even more dangerously, the Park has always been looked on by "the mob" as a place to muscle in on. Now, Irving is only a little taller than me and I am under five feet. Yet he'll go up against a gang of mobsters as if he were Superman; he is invincible through sheer hypnotic righteousness.

218

Irving's acts of kindness are legion and regardless of race or religion. During many years the Catholic Chapel in Fort Lee was presided over by a certain Monsignor Morrison. At least twice a month the Monsignor visited with Irving. But there came a time when he was too old and ill to function and his Church sent the Monsignor to a sanatorium in Lakewood. Now the Monsignor had spent many years within sight and sound of Palisades Park and he missed them sorely. He applied to the Church for permission to go home, but the mills of the Church grind slowly and nothing happened. Moreover, the Monsignor knew his time was getting short. Finally he phoned his fears to Irving, to whom a solution was simple. He merely got into his Cadillac, drove to Lakewood, picked up the Monsignor, and took him home. And there he died in peace amid the sights and sounds of Palisades Park.

Noisy though it is, the Park is noted for its decorum. As a stickler for morals, Irving keeps a special eye on the bumpier type of rides, knowing full well that they are sometimes used by ladies who are distressed by unwanted pregnancies. He is alerted by any attendant who notes a young creature with an outsize middle and a look of grim determination taking ride after ride on the Cyclone. Irving knows darn well what she's up to, so the ticket seller is alerted not to sell her any more tickets.

There is also a rule that any unaccompanied kid seen flashing as much as five dollars must be brought to Irving's office, where he himself phones Junior's home to find out if he came by his wealth legitimately. If it turns out to be stolen money, Junior is held incommunicado until a parent arrives to take him and his ill-gotten cash in charge.

Numbers of Irving's patrons have visited the Park for generations. People have met there, married, had children, and continued their attendance to the third generation.

There was a time when Irving used to preside over marriage ceremonies and give the pair their household furnishings in exchange for the advertisement of being married on the roller coaster. But Monsignor Morrison didn't approve and when he asked Irving to desist, Irving obliged.

Many famous careers began in the Park. As a young man, Arthur Godfrey managed the roller coaster. Buster Crabbe taught swimming at the pool. John, the maître d' at La Grenouille, began as a waiter in the Park. It was at the Park that color television was tested for four years before it was put on the market. The reason, naturally, was that the Park provided the most colorful environment in the entire New York area.

I told Oliver of an emergency when Irving's initiative was put to a sore test. "During a night last July one of the Park's attendants pushed a wrong button in the booth which housed the flea circus, and next morning Irving arrived at the Park to find his entire troupe of performing fleas burned to a crisp. But never yet had Irving failed that ancient ruling that 'the show must go on.' Now the best performing fleas are bred in Brussels, Belgium. Irving got their trainer on the long-distance phone and ordered a troupe to be organized immediately and delivered to the pilot of a Belgian commercial plane. As a result, by eventide the flea circus was in full operation. It had never missed a single evening's performance."

The more I told Oliver about Irving, the more he was intrigued. And, as we sat with Irving at lunch that day, Oliver fell completely under his spell. They were two perfectionists with the same ideals, speaking the same language, Oliver as a member of the National Arts Council and Irving as an aristocrat in the world of Carny.

"Every year since I opened the Park," said Irving, "I've repainted it and changed the color scheme. Up to now, it's been designed by a carnival specialist I bring on from San Diego. But the specialist died. I'm never satisfied with anything but the best, and that's why I want you to decorate my Park, Mr. Smith."

After lunch, Irving took us over to the Palisades in his limousine. It was still winter and the outlook was bleak. As we drove about the lanes, they were deserted except for caretakers, electricians, and carpenters busy making repairs.

"Everyone's on the job except the painters," said Irving. "They're waiting for the new color scheme."

But when we came to the end of our tour, Oliver could only dismiss his temptation to tackle that mighty job.

"If I were you, Mr. Rosenthal, I wouldn't change the color of a single trash can. Everything's so clean, it doesn't even need a paint job. Just as it stands, the Park is absolute perfection."

Irving, however, ordered a duplicate paint job for its already sparkling façade, so that Palisades Park finally turned out to be better than perfection.

UNITED WE STAND

FOR ALMOST ANYTHING

*H*elen happened to have an "in" at the United Nations. Many years ago in Hollywood she was sometimes linked with Shirley Temple by film critics who called the two of them the best (and the more scurvy critics said the only) actresses in motion pictures. "Shirley wouldn't remember meeting me then," said Helen, "she having been only four at the time, but now that she's been appointed a Special Delegate at the UN, I'll call on her to get us in."

Shirley most graciously made an appointment to meet us in the lobby of the Secretariat Building the following Thursday at two.

The day turned out to be sunny and mild, so we started early in order to take a stroll in the neighborhood. Gazing around at the grand and stately United Nations Plaza, Helen got off one of her favorite dicta: "How typical it is of New Yorkers to harp on our run-down neighborhoods and give no credit to those that have been made modern and beautiful."

It's true, of course, that our City Fathers haven't always appreciated the unique fact that three wide rivers run through, or by, New York. When the UN first began to search for a headquarters, Manhattan wasn't even considered; there had been talk of building it in Philadelphia, Boston, or San Francisco. Obviously, our town was too crowded and, even if it weren't, who would ever have chosen that filthy neighborhood facing the East River, between 42nd and 48th Streets? For generations it had been a jumble of slaughterhouses, breweries, cold-storage bins, and a rickety old railroad barge landing. The district was an affront to the eyes,

222

ears, and even noses of the cultured neighbors at Turtle Bay, around the corner.

But then John D. Rockefeller, Jr., had a vision of the beauty of the riverfront through all its trash. Moreover, he had a practical reason why the site would be ideal. There is a schist of solid rock running underneath the area that extends more than sixty feet below sea level. "Isn't it about time the Prudential Insurance Company stops plugging the Rock of Gibraltar," I thought, "when the rock of Manhattan outweighs it by several billion tons?"

At any rate, in December of '46, Rockefeller bought that squalid property for eight and a half million dollars and offered it as a site for the United Nations. Surely the best Christmas present our city ever got! And the United Nations Plaza emerged in beauty on the site of those ancient eyesores.

At the same time, none of the good old things was destroyed. The fine brownstone residences of Turtle Bay may have been thrown into low relief by the tall buildings, but they're all the more colorful for that. One entire block of houses borders on a central garden where children can play in safety, a community baby-sitter does duty for the lot, and neighbors can hold longer chats than in an elevator.

Helen and I are familiar with two of those old houses: Katharine Hepburn's and the Garson (Ruth Gordon) Kanins'. When Ruth deserted Turtle Bay for Hollywood, she leased her house to Walter Reade, the entrepreneur who is responsible for most of the sophisticated neighborhood movie theatres that dot New York. (One may be affronted by the product on a Walter Reade screen, but by the surroundings never.)

Dominating the UN Plaza is the Secretariat Building, that dramatic slab of green-tinted glass, aluminum, steel, and white marble. "I'm sure," Helen commented, "that tourists look on it as the symbol of New York just as the Eiffel Tower is of Paris."

Much of the architecture surrounding the Secretariat Building has been inspired by it. To the north on the river is the grand apartment house of amber-tinted glass which once housed Robert Kennedy, and shelters other tenants whose wealth happens to match their fame. "Truman Capote lives there too," I commented, and Helen remarked, "On *Cold Blood* money, no doubt!"

We wandered about inspecting other buildings on the Plaza; peered into the windows of the World Trade Corporation of I.B.M. and there discovered four large, white, angular works of modern sculpture. Looking for the name of their creator, we learned from a note on the window that it was nothing more or less than an I.B.M. computer. The "statues" had been turned out by a machine which could supply hundreds of designs in a matter of seconds by the simple means of pushing a button. Actually, those objects were examples of origami, the ancient Japanese art of folding any flat material into an infinite number of variations.

This opened up a chance for me to air one of my pet opinions on art. "It seems to me that when a computer can design these things in a few seconds, it sure makes monkeys out of a lot of modern sculptors." Helen's eye, however, was now on more substantial structures: the Institute of International Education, the U.S. Trade Mission to the UN, the Boys' Club of America, in an impressive row. And a few steps farther, unknown to that day by both of us, an ornate flight of stairs led to a French restaurant, La Bibliothèque, perched high and picturesque on a cliff.

The Spirit of the New, mostly encased in glass, extends beyond the Plaza in all directions. Approaching the Ford Foundation on East 42nd Street, we could see through the glass front a garden with trees and exotic vines that drip from the ceiling four stories above.

All these edifices, as we were to learn shortly after, overshadow and obscure one of the most outstanding areas in all New York. It was when Helen suggested, "Let's stroll down toward the river," that we two discovered the United Nations Park.

Helen's reaction to greenery comes close to her passion for the theatre. "Isn't it beguiling," she continued, "to see how completely man can conquer nature if he puts up a stiff enough fight?

Except for me. I don't know just how long it will be before I have to hack my way with a machete down to my swimming pool." We gazed at long stretches of lawn. "Not a blade of grass is out of line. Not an empty bottle in sight. Not a rumpled page of newspaper. No battered tin cans. No vandalized benches. Just sheer harmony."

We entered the main gate on First Avenue near 47th Street and were stopped in our tracks by the view. "Look, Anita, at these beautiful proportions!" exclaimed Helen. "Everything so cunningly laid out that you have the feeling of a great English garden. And what a startlement to see the broad sweep of the East River with a wide esplanade just like the one along the Thames in London."

I had to compare its international spotlessness with my usual hangout, Central Park, where grass and trees are in constant conflict with empty pop bottles, tin cans, and assorted garbage. It's true that Central Park has an alibi: visitors are not admonished to please *"ne pas marcher sur le gazon."* We saw no infraction of that rule other than a young student on a shady bench busily writing in a notebook; his shoes were off, and his bare feet brushed the grass, just for the feel of it.

We started down the path beside a wide greensward. A small boy with a shovel and pail was scooping up dirt. A baby was asleep in its carriage under a tree. The black mamma was chattering to a companion in a very strange tongue. She wore a long robe of exotic fabric (from Ghana?). We passed an Oriental pair so beautiful that Helen spotted them as Koreans—"the most handsome of all the Asiatics," she said.

Helen was fascinated by the clipped hedges lining the walks, so firm and smooth that you could safely set a tea tray on them. She picked off a leaf to sniff. "Good Lord! It's nothing but just plain privet!"

Now we came on a secret sort of place, hidden by trees and shrubs which obscure an enormous semicircular granite bench long enough to accommodate the several assorted readers, think-

225

ers, and dozers who were occupying it. At the back of the bench is engraved a name: "Anna Eleanor Roosevelt." Helen remarked: "I'll bet that some of these people come to this spot every fine afternoon and possibly think of Eleanor Roosevelt as their own."

Feeling like trespassers, we started to leave, but stopped when we were faced with a big stone stele that serves to separate this intimate hiding place from the rest of the Park. And here we read: "She would rather light a candle than curse the darkness, and her glow has warmed the world."

Back in a rush came our memories of that fabulous woman. Helen as a fellow do-gooder knew her very well; I as a do-no-gooder could only admire her from a distance, as a magnificent, uninhibited creature so lacking in vanity that she dared to be her own homespun self. She usually wore the sensible shirtwaists and skirts that could have been afforded by any modest housewife. But it was rumored that in the matter of housekeeping she was as slap-happy as an East Village hippie. The cuisine at the White House when Eleanor presided there was only saved from being dull by being awful. But her spirit was so radiant that it turned every fault-finder into a smart aleck.

She had a totally disarming winsomeness, too, that won her male admirers whose feelings bordered on calf love. One of them was John Golden, a prominent figure in show business who had produced a succession of hits which made him rich. But he was best known as composer of that wonderful old standby, "Poor Butterfly." John and Eleanor frequently lunched together, and I was once privileged to join them. The table talk that day concerned some sort of humanitarian project on which Eleanor wanted John's aid. I expected to hear glowing generalities related to national pride, civic virtue, and such; I couldn't have been more wrong. Eleanor spoke in strictly practical terms, mentioning ward heelers by their nicknames, and being quite open about the Machiavellian conniving by which she planned to bring about that particular good deed. Eleanor was no idle dreamer; she was a real pro—a unique mixture of hard-core common sense and soaring altruism.

Helen had a story of her own about Eleanor. "When little Mary was about ten, we sent her to an exclusive private school in Englewood, a half hour's drive from Nyack. She was going to make some charming, well-bred friends there, we hoped. Then about midterm Mary began to return in the afternoons wearing 'campaign' buttons—different ones every day—all aimed at insulting our President's wife: 'No Soap, Eleanor!' (Mrs. Roosevelt was doing a radio commentary sponsored by a soap company); 'Teeth for Two,' which was a nasty, personal gibe. When we asked Mary not to wear those buttons any more she was alarmed. The leader of her crowd distributed them. Mary would look 'just terrible' if she didn't wear them.

"Well, Charlie and I yanked Mary from that school and those charming young companions, and sent her to the public school in Nyack, where, blissfully, there was no 'smart set.'

"Two years later Mary met Mrs. Roosevelt in my dressing room in Washington at an opening. That night Eleanor singled Mary out and forgot all about Charlie and me in her earnest conversation with our child.

"As our family was walking back to the hotel later, Mary spoke up thoughtfully: 'Why do people say that Mrs. Roosevelt's plain? I think she's beautiful.' And any person of discernment always felt the same."

We reached a pathway parallel to the river and entered an avenue bordered by trees that formed a graceful arch. Suddenly Helen stopped. "Do you realize what these trees are?" she asked. I didn't. "They are flowering Japanese cherries! Every springtime, around the first of May, I begin to think about getting down to Washington to see the cherry trees in bloom. And several times I've gone through all sort of inconveniences and managed to get there, only to find that I'm too early or too late. And now I find that the blissful experience can be had right here at 47th Street and the East River. Makes me feel I don't deserve my eyesight!"

Sometimes I have a peculiar reaction to pure beauty, as if it were almost too much to endure. Looking around for something commonplace to break the spell, I sure found it on the far side of the river: the monstrous Pepsi-Cola sign that glares right at the United Nations from the shore of Queens and is ugly enough to take the edge off all the cherry blossoms in Nippon.

With a special fondness I have for kitsch, I promptly pointed out a pure example of it: the statue presented to the UN by Soviet Russia. A laborer with a double set of muscles illustrates this bit of naïve hypocrisy graven on the socle: "Let Us Beat Our Swords Into Plowshares."

Helen made her own discovery; over against a windowless wall were fruit trees trained in amazing patterns, crisscross and diagonal, and at one of them Helen stopped to exclaim: "I'd swear that's the pattern of the MacArthur plaid!"

At this point luck brought into our ken the head gardener, tending to the irrigation system. Of course, Helen accosted him. "These are the most remarkable patterns of espalier I've seen in a good many travels around the world," she said glowingly. The gardener, delighted, left off work to show us around. Having exchanged our identities, Helen tackled a problem that's ever foremost on her mind. "Tell me, Mr. Blaney, how many workers do you have on your staff?"

"Twenty-eight."

"And where do you get such highly trained men?"

"Off farms, out of schools," he told us, "and sometimes they come without any knowledge of horticulture at all. So we take them on and train them. Then when they're offered better jobs, we lose them." He shrugged and then summed it up: "What are you going to do? You wouldn't want to keep them from bettering themselves."

"Oh, wouldn't I now!" declared Helen. "The last full-time gardener I had was ten years ago. He saved enough to buy himself a nursery in Vermont. When he came to tell me good-by, I wished him luck. But in my wicked heart I was wishing him aphis, gypsy moths, and powdery mildew."

Mr. Blaney then took us around to the acre of rose garden, the star turn of the Park through all its blossoming season. "The rose growers of the U.S. gave them to the UN," he said. "They keep track of their condition and renew them every year."

Helen made a political observation. In the center of the rose garden, one row of bushes rises tall above the others. They are labeled "Mister Lincoln" and were flaunting their blossoms right into the teeth of that statue from the U.S.S.R.

Our time with Mr. Blaney was now up, as we had to report at the Information Desk of the Visitors' Lobby. There we were met by a lively young brunette who introduced herself as Joan Bel Geddes. She had been sent to tell us that Shirley was held up in a committee meeting but would be able to join us a little later. In the meanwhile, Joan was to take us in charge and show us about.

Now, anyone whose name is Bel Geddes is pretty certain to be related to anyone else whose name is Bel Geddes. Sure enough, Joan turned out to be the sister of the Broadway star, Barbara Bel Geddes. Moreover, the girls' father was Norman Bel Geddes, the avant-garde designer of stage décor who had created a revolution in the New York theatre. Norman was a close friend of both Helen's and mine and when we talked to Joan about her father, sparks began to fly.

In the Twenties Norman had been chosen by Max Reinhardt to design the American production of *The Miracle*, for which he proceeded to convert the entire Century Theatre into a medieval cathedral.

Helen regaled Joan with a story that was typical of her dynamic daddy. At one point in *The Miracle* a staggering sound effect was required, one that might seem to come from a world far beyond our own. So Norman had caused a thick steel cable of the type used on suspension bridges to be stretched from the highest point in the theatre's ceiling to the lowest depth of its cellar, after which Norman looped a big hemp rope about the cable and it was to be pulled as far as it would go and then released like a guitar string. Norman said, "It would have produced the damnedest noise ever heard by the ears of man."

It was unfortunate for auricular history that someone informed the city authorities of Norman's project and they canceled out a sound effect that would possibly have caused the Century Theatre to collapse.

The last time I had seen Norman was shortly before he died. We lunched together, and he told me an idea he had for increasing the number of New York playhouses. In those old days there were many more shows than theatres, and Norman's scheme was to make use of the empty spaces existing in large New York hotels, areas where luggage was stored and other rooms that were infrequently used. Why not convert those spaces into theatres? At that time people called it "just another crazy idea of Norman Bel Geddes'." But now several such theatres exist and skyscrapers are being designed to have theatres inside them.

Well, off we went on a tour of the UN with Joan to tell us what we were looking at. As we proceeded, Helen and I felt most deeply affected when some single incident or character emerged above the awesome display and became quite personal and human. Instead of being involved with nations, we were meeting up with *men*. How frequently we were reminded that when Dag Hammarskjöld was Secretary General he must have been as greatly loved as he was respected. Throughout the UN complex there are five different monuments to his memory. The most affecting to us was the stained-glass panel by Marc Chagall that was financed by Dag's fellow staff members after he was killed in a plane crash in 1961.

"Among the most precious memories of my life," said Helen, "are those that concern Dag Hammarskjöld. He sometimes invited Charlie and me to lunch at his quarters in the UN. He was, as far as I know, the only member who had his own kitchen and staff. His small lunches were a delight. One would meet all manner of people there: Leonard Bernstein, Thornton Wilder, American and European statesmen. I'm proud to report that Dag Hammarskjöld was an admirer of my acting. He tried for several years to interest me in doing Strindberg's *Dream Play*. He especially loved this most mystical of Strindberg's works. I have a deep and enduring regret that I never caught fire at his idea. I did not feel equal to the role. Had I been able to bring Strindberg's play to New York, I might have repaid Dag Hammarskjöld for a service he did our own American genius, Eugene O'Neill. For at a time when O'Neill was discredited by drama critics in America, Hammarskjöld brought him to the attention of Dr. Gierow, the Director of Sweden's National Theatre.

"And that's how it came about that O'Neill's last and greatest masterpieces had their premieres in Swedish, far from the land where they were conceived. I bless Dag Hammarskjöld for his recognition of our greatest playwright when our native critics had tried so hard to annihilate him.

"Aside from his intellectual pre-eminence, Dag Hammarskjöld was *the* greatest humanitarian I ever knew. I never had the wonder and joy of meeting Schweitzer, but Hammarskjöld, like Schweitzer, was in love with people, all people—poor, rich, artists, pretty ladies, the successful, the despairing. The last time I heard him speak was at a banquet for rich and powerful New Yorkers. It was shortly before his death and he was making an impassioned plea for the infant nations of Africa. He needed our financial aid for his new 'family.' I don't think we will see his like again in my time."

We were greatly awed, too, by the small meditation room off the lobby of the General Assembly Building where, under a spotlight, a massive block of iron ore takes the place of an altar, chosen because it represents the earth itself and the people thereof. A more sophisticated tribute to our earth is a pendulum, the gift of the Netherlands, which swings from the ceiling and gives visual proof that the earth is in rotation.

It is always affecting when public spirit is exhibited by the very young, and this we experienced at the fountain for which American children had collected fifty thousand dollars. On the floor of the pool a pattern is formed by alternating bands of crushed white marble and black pebbles.

"After the fountain was designed," Joan told us, "the architect discovered there was no place he could buy black pebbles. They exist in profusion on the beaches of the Greek island of Rhodes, but how to collect them was a problem. Word was then sent out by the Greek delegation to the children of Rhodes, who went down to the beaches and collected the black pebbles for the UN fountain."

Helen recalled having seen those black pebbles in Rhodes. "They literally covered the beach and shone so dramatically in the sunlight that I longed for some reason to collect them. If I'd only thought of something like this, I'd have lugged some pebbles back home to decorate my small fountain in Nyack."

Our next stop was the elegant V.I.P. lounge, a spot which only the privileged may enter. A number of ladies belonging to delegations from Oriental countries passed by with a swish of silk and jingle of gold. "It's like being transported into the Arabian nights," Helen remarked. "I feel like a sparrow among peacocks." I, however, was riveted by some dramatically handsome Oriental men, mysterious and alluring.

While waiting for Shirley, we quizzed Joan about her job with UNICEF—the United Nations International Children's Emergency Fund. A major part of her duty is to answer masses of mail from irate citizens who have "bought" the propaganda that UNICEF is a part of the Communist conspiracy to destroy our nation. Every letter must be answered and the charges carefully refuted in detail. "As if people who write those letters would even bother to read my replies," sighed Joan.

Helen could well understand what Joan was up against. "I did a couple of radio appeals for the UN Children's Fund, and dozens of people accused me of playing right into Kosygin's hands."

Presently there was a stir in the whole vast chamber. Mrs. Shirley Temple Black was making her entrance, escorted by a male chorus line of delegates.

Neither of us had seen Shirley in years, and there she was in her thirties almost as rosy, dimpled, and curly as in the days of *The Good Ship Lollipop*. Taking over as guide, she proceeded to escort us through the inner mysteries of the UN. Following Shirley was like a royal progression. "She is our princess," remarked a Lebanese delegate. "When things go wrong she lights up the whole establishment and makes it seem worth while."

Shirley showed us the General Assembly Hall, which is decorated in blue, green, and gold. Here each delegate has his own leather-covered table facing the speaker's rostrum, equipped with earphones so that the delegate can listen to a speech as spoken on the floor, or translated into any of the five official languages: Chinese, English, French, Russian, and Spanish. "The African nations don't require their own language," said Shirley. "They're so civilized that they speak several tongues."

In that august atmosphere Helen mentioned a speech I had once perpetrated, which was delivered there and created a minor sensation back in the Forties. "Tell Shirley about it," Helen urged. So I did.

"When Selwyn Lloyd was British delegate to the UN, I met him at Fleur Cowles' one day at lunch. His Excellency discoursed about the atrocious behavior of the Russian delegate who was repeating the same violent attack on the U. S. A. day after day ad nauseam. 'I wish I had the proper words to tell him off,' His Excellency said. Then turning to me, he added, 'You're a writer. Tell me something to say.'

" 'Like what?' I inquired.

" 'Something terse. And preferably in American slang.'

" 'Why don't you merely rise and say to the Assembly, "Dig that broken record!" ' I had to translate the vernacular for His Excellency, but he thought it was precisely what he needed. And the next day he spoke my speech at the General Assembly.

"Neither of us could believe the scandal it created. The General

233

Assembly, after listening to insults by the hour from the Russian delegate, was shocked to the bone by the language used by the United Kingdom's representative. Selwyn Lloyd must have bitterly regretted taking a lesson in diplomacy from an American flapper."

Shirley, too, had recently been present during a vituperative attack on the U. S. A. by the woman delegate from Cuba and made particularly sizzling because she spoke in American slang. "How often I've thought," said Shirley, "that if enemy nations could only make a breakthrough, talk to each other face to face, perhaps we might be getting somewhere. But the Cuban Government forbids its delegates to have personal contact with our UN representatives. And they're ordered to pour out insults on the floor as the Russians do, in volley after volley of scathing lies.

"The things that woman said made my face flush red-hot in anger. Then, when the session ended, I made my way to the ladies' room to pull myself together. When I entered, there stood the señorita from Cuba at the mirror, calmly applying lipstick." The two delegates locked eyes in the mirror for a moment, and then Mr. Castro's representative began to hum very softly as if to herself, "It Had to Be You, It Had to Be You."

"It took me a moment or two to figure out my strategy," said Shirley, "but when I did, I started to sing, quite audibly, 'I'll Be Glad When You're Dead, You Rascal You.' Then I flounced into a cubicle. I don't know which nation won that day but I felt smug and quite satisfied. Because the next week when I talked to President Nixon, I could report that the United States and Cuban representatives had made a breakthrough in communication." Then she added, "But isn't it sad that the only sure meeting ground for members of the human race is the loo?"

There are many who think that the UN as a political arbiter and influence for peace among nations is about done. But there are others who feel that UNICEF is the greatest international humanitarian force ever devised. "Is it too much to hope," asked Helen, "that honest human feelings can enter into world affairs and start to weed out evil?"

Trying to reassure Helen, I quoted from Benjamin Franklin, who said in effect: "If rascals could only learn all the advantages of virtue, they'd become honest through sheer rascality."

THE BRONX THAT CHEERS

$\mathcal{T}$he dreary old injunction, "If at first you don't succeed, try, try again," came vividly to mind in two experiences Helen and I had at the Bronx Zoo. The first time we went there together, it was a cold day in November; the sky was overcast, even the foliage looked gray and drab. Furthermore, our venture started with an incident that could have ruined even a sunny day for any female.

Vera was driving us in Helen's station wagon and, on reaching the entrance, we were stopped by a silly-looking old gate attendant. Indicating Vera and me, he said, "It'll be a dollar each for you two." Then, turning to Helen, he added, "But you get in for free." Thinking she was getting V.I.P. treatment, Helen beamed and thanked him. "Don't thank *me*," he spoke up. "Everybody gets in free who's over sixty-five."

Helen, knowing that it was many long years since I'd been sixty-five, stiffened in affront. I tried to ease the tension by advising the old boy that I was a lot older than Helen. "Okay, then, you get in free, too," he said amiably.

Helen remarked rather tartly, "Anita, dear, this incident could well mark the end of our beautiful friendship." But then she grinned and our friendship survived.

Vera parked the car and we proceeded on foot, not knowing what direction to take. We were aware that the Zoo had done away with cages, that animals are surrounded by moats which protect them from the public and allow them to wander free in large out-door spaces. We passed several such areas, but all the animals had disappeared, evidently into shelters. "They've decided it's no fit day for man or beast," said Helen.

Presently we came upon a dreary-looking structure labeled "The World of Darkness." Stopping to read a sign, we learned it

236

was an exhibit of creatures who are active only at night. We stumbled down a murky corridor in the dark, when suddenly we encountered a dubious-looking male standing beside an exhibit in which we could barely make out two shadowy owls. He seemed to be a little too much at home in that Stygian interior, so Helen clutched me and exclaimed, "I'm scared! Let's get out of here." We escaped but, on returning to daylight, were met by a gust of rain, so we gave the whole thing up and departed from the Zoo, possibly forever. I shudder now to think how near we came to not going back to that magical place.

But a little later our Guiding Spirit, as usual, caught up with us. It had so happened that on the day we were touring the United Nations with Joan Bel Geddes one of us mentioned the Bronx Zoo and told of our disappointment in it.

Joan stiffened with a resentment that made us feel like personal enemies of the Bronx. At any rate, she made us promise to return to the Zoo. "Why," said Joan, "it has an exhibit called The World of Darkness that's the envy of every zoo in the country. I pay periodic visits there to see the night animals, the ones who roam about when the rest of us are asleep. But just promise you won't go to The World of Darkness without me." We promised. Joan had to go off to India on UNICEF business, however, and six months passed before she was able to organize our return trip to the Bronx.

By now it was spring. The weather was superb. Both Helen and I felt more like sixteen than over sixty-five. Joan was accompanied by a teen-age son and daughter. Their getups of identical faded blue jeans suggested a generation gap but it never evolved. Perhaps the wild animals we saw that day helped to bridge it.

Again, Vera drove the station wagon, but this time everything was great. It is pleasing to report that the road signs to the Zoo are quite explicit because most of the road signs in our city could take the place of crossword puzzles.

We arrived at the side entrance, where Joan had arranged for us to pass straight through as guests of the Bronx. Our old friend the gatekeeper waved us on our way without interrupting a conversation with his co-worker at the next booth. "So up comes this here lady and she's all pregnant and everything else from California." (Now, Helen and I, who know California, realized the lady was victim of a lot of awful things.)

We were met just inside the gate by a staff member of the Zoo, Mr. William Conway, who looked ever so much like a handsome, successful New York businessman. He wore a gray summer suit that suggested Brooks Brothers and his necktie had a restrained design of little animals. (What else?) Mr. Conway ushered us onto one of the Zoo's minibuses and we proceeded on a tour.

And may I here pause to remark on the fact that, once in a while, Helen and I run across a New Yorker who becomes our special candidate for sainthood. William Conway is like that.

Now, any saint worthy of his title has got to be capable of wrath. And when William Conway speaks about his charges, he quite often smolders with rage over what mankind is doing to animal life. At one such moment, he stopped at a cage where he gestured off to a magnificent, stately crane. "That is a specimen of the rare African wattled crane," said Mr. Conway. "We were able to breed it here in the Zoo. But one single example doesn't help now that it's too late to save the species."

"And what about the disappearance of the American Bald Eagle?" spoke up Helen.

On which subject our friend was nearly speechless with rage. "It seems as if we never see the writing on the wall until our backs are against it."

Mr. Conway was unaware of Helen's theory that no animal can be happy in a zoo, but just the same he proceeded to scotch it. "Forests are so full of disease germs," he informed us, "that every wild specimen has to be disinfected before it can join our healthy colonies." As an example, he explained that the life of a bird in its native habitat is less than two years, while the birds in the Bronx Zoo live for an average of twelve.

238

At which point I felt impelled to speak a kind word for the human race. "Then it seems," said I, "that Nature can sometimes be a little bit more vile than we are."

"Ah," Helen countered briskly, "but Nature is vile in a natural way."

In Helen's long experience with zoos, she has found that each has its specialty. "What's special about your zoo, besides its being biggest and best?" she asked Mr. Conway.

"It's possibly the fact that, from the beginning, we've specialized on propagating the various species," he replied. "Each year we're able to breed and sell animals to other zoos throughout the world." To illustrate which point he made a detour that brought us to a vast field in which a pair of baby buffalo emerged into view.

"What utterly improbable creatures!" Helen exclaimed. "All scraggly head and big humid eyes. Only God and Walt Disney can make a baby buffalo!"

Our guide disagreed. "I'm afraid you'll have to add the Bronx Zoo to that list, Miss Hayes, because it's due to this place alone that the American buffalo has been saved from extinction."

At that point I nudged Helen and indicated Mr. Conway's tie with the little animals on it. It seemed an extension of the mania he entertains for his charges. Helen spoke up quite boldly and said, "We've been admiring your necktie, Mr. Conway!"

He smiled and said, "Thanks. You see, I collect them. I've got over forty."

He went on to expand his information about the buffalo. "As the railroads carried our population deeper into bison country, it took less than fifty years of slaughter for the herds to be reduced from sixty million specimens to around eight hundred. But in 1905 a group of animal lovers met right here in our Lion House and founded the American Bison Society. It gathered enough animals from far and wide to begin breeding in captivity, and in due time the Bronx Zoo was able to stock government preserves in

Oklahoma and South Dakota. There's now a total of about thirty thousand bison in the country. Forty of the best specimens are right here!

"Incidentally," he continued, "the sculptor who designed the American nickel worked on it with a Bronx buffalo as his model." But with a bitter smile he added, "We were quite ready to preserve the buffalo on our money. We just didn't give it the same protection in flesh and blood!"

In a secluded corner of the park we encountered three small, scruffy specimens of homo sapiens who had caught a bullfrog in a pond. The ensuing drama went like this:

Mr. Conway (in a firm smoldering voice): "Put the frog back in the pond before you hurt it."

Small Homo Sapiens: Absolute silence.

Mr. Conway (voice quieter but getting deadly): "Go on, put it back—*now.*"

Small H. S.: More silence.

Mr. Conway: "If you don't put it back, it will die. You don't want that—do you?"

Small H. S.: "We *caught* him!"

Mr. Conway: "You shouldn't have done that. You must put it back in the pond at once."

H. S.: A string of noises that shouldn't be heard in a zoo— only in barrooms and theatres.

But, all the same, the frog was tossed back into the water.

We then heard an almost incredible fact: that the most dangerous situations in any zoo are brought about by the common, ordinary house dog. Mr. Conway explained, "The wild animals see creatures they've never before met, darting about and barking, and they become panicky. They dash into trees or fence posts, sometimes at such great speed that they are actually killed. At any rate, they can easily be maimed."

We continued past a small stream that tries to wend its way through the northern section of Bronx Park. However, it is almost totally choked with paper bags, empty cans, and even more disgusting trash. "We're planning to leave this just as it stands and label it as a special exhibit of pollution."

"What do you bet that as soon as you do," said Helen, "the ornery cusses will stop using the river for a garbage dump and you'll lose your exhibit?"

"We wouldn't mind," answered Mr. Conway.

We passed the enormous antlered elk known to the world of science as the Roosevelt Wapiti. Mr. Conway was reminded of a time in the Forties when an elderly member of the violently anti-F.D.R. Establishment pleaded, "Couldn't you label that masterful creature the *Theodore* Roosevelt Wapiti?"

Past the African Veldt teeming with addax, gnu, eland, dik-dik, and emu—"My dear old crossword-puzzle friends," exclaimed Helen.

Past a fat blonde with whom we had a nasty confrontation. She was leading a four-pound Yorkshire terrier on a leash. Our minibus advanced on them at top speed (six miles per hour) and Great White Hunter Conway led the attack on the one animal in the world he does not love. "Don't you know you can't bring a dog into this Zoo?"

"But she's so tiny!" simpered the blonde.

"She's big enough to scare the animals," he declared. "Get her out of here!"

Abashed, the blonde stuffed her Yorkie into a tote bag and made for the exit.

Past the giant bird cages, beloved of Helen because they are of early Victorian design and remind her of her favorite role. Mr. Conway dismissed them coldly. "Eagles are uncomfortable there!" said he.

Past the coral flamingos. "Is it true they have to eat orange-colored food for their complexion?" asked Helen. But even as she posed the question, she grinned at its absurdity.

Mr. Conway set her right. "But of course it's true," said he. "We feed them quarts of carrot juice every day!"

"Well, we *are* getting a course in zoology!" remarked young Miss Bel Geddes.

Past an open field where Princess, the lioness, and her mate, Charlie, were at play with their twin cubs. "Three books have been written about this family's home life," Mr. Conway reported with pride.

Helen, her emotion matching his, exclaimed, "No wonder they call it a 'pride' of lions."

We stopped to watch the comedy antics of a polar bear juggling a beer keg. "He wears out one metal keg every month," Mr. Conway told us.

"Well," remarked Helen, "I'll never again say that animals are sad in captivity."

"Ah," Mr. Conway corrected her, "but here you see them in an ideal situation. There are a great many zoos not fit for animals to live in." And he named one in particular which, out of our loyalty to Manhattan, shall be nameless.

In time we arrived at The World of Darkness from which we had previously fled in such revulsion. Even in bright sunshine the building looks rather forbidding, its outer walls being made of coal-black pebbles that glisten eerily. As we followed our leader into total night, Mr. Conway issued a warning, "Don't expect to see anything at first. Just relax for about a minute and a half, and your eyes will get used to darkness." We stood and waited until, peering through a glass darkly, we could make out the vague forms of some little night creatures darting about in the gloom. A special lighting in the cages gives the night creatures the security of darkness but also makes them dimly visible to our eyes. There were a number of beautiful owls wide awake and winking at us.

We wandered on to examine a flock of bats flying in V-shape formation, making a sound which Mr. Conway said "is exclusive to the flight of bats." It produces a sort of clacking effect as if their wings were made of dry bones; the sort of racket one might hear in a wind tunnel of the nether regions of Hades.

If Mr. Conway is a candidate for sainthood, as Helen and I believe, we now met an assistant candidate in the curator of The World of Darkness. We were studying some creatures that looked like rats, except their hind legs were extraordinarily long and they hopped about like little kangaroos. "How repulsive!" Helen exclaimed, at which that assistant candidate suddenly loomed out of the dark.

He might have resembled Santa Claus except that, being much younger, his beard is a rich, luxurious brown. He was in a state of deep hurt over Helen's insult to his ratty charges. "I'm sorry, Miss Hayes," said he, "but I find them very loving little creatures."

Trying to justify herself, Helen gestured toward an illuminated glass slide of one of the rodents that showed his tiny, malevolent eyes, sharp, jutting teeth, and moth-eaten fur. "Do you honestly see anything lovable about that?" asked Helen.

"I love all animals," he replied, with a simple dignity that left her with nothing more to say.

Asking us to wait there, Santa disappeared, presently opened a small door at the rear of the cage, and switched on an electric bulb. The tiny creatures were unable to see in the bright light, but they heard their friend's voice and hopped toward him with great affection. As they played cozily together in full view of our all-seeing eyes, Helen exclaimed, "How adorable!" (Then, in an aside to me, "I might faint. They look like rats.") But, good actress that she is, she got back into the good graces of our second candidate for sainthood.

As we left there, Helen and I were surprised to learn from Mr. Conway that The World of Darkness was a gift to the city from a long-time friend of ours, Brooke Astor.

And we were soon to see another gift from yet another philanthropist friend, "The Lila Acheson Wallace World of Birds." Now, a large part of the fortune earned by the *Reader's Digest* magazine, which belongs to the Wallaces, has been spent on New York. Lila herself is responsible for the mountains of cut flowers that decorate the lobby and halls at the Metropolitan Museum and, among other treasures, the large collection of Egyptian jewelry there. "But," explained Mr. Conway, "The World of Birds is Mrs. Wallace's special pride, the only one of all her countless public gifts on which she has placed her name."

Its structure is modern in the best sense, with curves, circles, and ramps leading up to the various entrances. (No stairs.) When I asked the name of the architect, Helen said, "That's my girl, Anita! Most of us, including me, overlook the designers of the new buildings we delight in." The architect in this case is Morris Ketchum.

From this thoroughly modern exterior we were ushered indoors to a reproduction of Nature itself: shrubbery and trees which are much too old-fashioned to be in Mr. Ketchum's category. But we found the exhibits there in an unfinished state. A few of the areas, however, are complete; some are glassed in and others wide open so that birds can fly about and join their public if they wish. "They seldom do," Mr. Conway commented. "Which shows what wise birds *they* are!"

On we went to an enclosure where the mating instincts of different species are explained. There is a showcase called "The Whippoorwill Theatre" where one can watch those birds acting out their life stories. Another exhibit is dedicated to the Satin Bowerbird from Australia, which, when building its nest, will use only articles that are blue in color. Our saintly Mr. Conway permitted himself a bit of levity on the subject, something about an assistant having been relieved of a blue glass eye. A likely story! But Joan made a penetrating comment when she said, "All birds are clowns; no matter how beautiful a bird is, it is also comic."

We were shown one lofty area with a waterfall of forty feet, where a tropical rain forest has been planted. Fascinated, we watched the birds luxuriating in their native moisty air. "After we open," said Mr. Conway, "there'll be rain three times a day and four rainstorms on Sunday." The enclosure is three stories high, making it possible to watch the birds at ground level and then, by mounting a circular ramp, see them disporting themselves in the treetops. Bravo, Mr. Ketchum!

The last room in Mrs. Wallace's exhibit is a chromium and white-tiled diet kitchen, large enough to feed fifty or more members of the human race. But from that concession to hygiene, we were transported to its opposite: the apehouse.

It was getting along toward suppertime and the occupants, having spent the day entertaining visitors outdoors, were due to come inside to their "bedrooms" (Mr. Conway refuses to use the word "cage"). He stationed us at the bedroom of a favorite gorilla and departed to summon him.

Helen began to reminisce about the monkeys in her life. "We have a lot in common, being in the same profession," said she. "I used to have a string of monkey pals across the country, friends I'd made on tour. They'd remember me when I returned after an absence, climb into my arms, and I'd be moistly kissed in welcome. In St. Louis I had an orangutan friend named Brody who was a cigarette addict. The zoo's director, Mr. Vierhaller, was himself a smoker and he always gave Brody a cigarette when we visited him together. In the light of the disclosures of the past decade, I hate to think of the damage to the life, breath, and lungs of Brody.

"Then there were the two young lady chimps in Cincinnati who were always brought to the theatre to visit my dressing room. They wore very pretty dresses, but they ran amok in my make-up and ended with lipstick all over them and me too. It was glorious!

"There was a chimp named Sailor, who was my darling until he reached adolescence and was sitting on my lap one day when he picked up my skirt and peeked. It was most embarrassing to one and all and I never felt the same toward him again."

By this time, Mr. Conway was ushering a purposeful, bustling gorilla into its bedroom. Worn out from the monkeyshines he'd performed all day and wearing the perpetually worried expression of his kind, he made straight for a pile of supper on the floor. In one loose-jointed sweep of an arm, he brushed everything helter-skelter to the right; another sweep and it all went to the left. Then he surveyed the spread of lettuce, fruit, and vegetables as if to say, "Oh God, not this again!" But he finally accepted his menu; ate an apple, peeled a couple of bananas with finesse, and on to a bunch of grapes. We began to feel rude staring at him and left him to dine in resignation.

In the minibus on our way to the car, Helen mentioned a trip she'd made in the Thirties. "I'd been reading about three reptiles that were on exhibit here, the only ones of their kind in captivity. They had a lot of publicity as the last known dragons on earth. They were a type of lizard that grew as long as ten feet and weighed as much as three hundred pounds. And they actually looked like storybook dragons."

Mr. Conway knew all about that breed. "It's called the Dragon of Komodo, and it only exists on some small islands of Indonesia."

"Naturally, I made my way to the Bronx for a look at those dragons," said Helen. "But when I got here I learned they were ailing. Well, I talked my way into the infirmary and stood looking down on three sad, comatose creatures. Finally, the orderly who was my escort spoke up. 'You know what's the matter with them dragons? They've been photographed to death. That's what's the matter with them. Too many flashlight pictures for the papers.'

"Suddenly, I knew just how they felt. I'd been in the same situation, time after time. I never thought I'd feel a kinship with a dragon."

When we parted from Mr. Conway at the exit, I said I hoped we'd soon come back. And Helen added, "One of our reasons for being here today is to advise our fellow citizens to get out to the Bronx Zoo, for Heaven's sake!"

A few days later, when I was shopping at Bonwit Teller's, I wandered through the men's department and noticed a necktie that had a design of little animals. It reminded me of Mr. Conway, so I bought it to add to his collection as a gift from Helen and me. But later when I showed it to Helen, she was appalled. The design on that necktie was not only a dog, but the sworn enemy of wild animals, a beagle. May Mr. Conway and all his fellow saints forgive me!

THE PLEASURE OF OUR COMPANY

*D*uring the winter season Helen had a rollicking party life. Mine was very satisfactory, for there had been the usual flu epidemic which, to a party hater like me, served as an excuse to get out of a number of festivities. I'd also had a real and lengthy flu attack, as if Fate made me pay for my snide behavior. One day I told Helen, "I wish I had the integrity to decline an invitation in the way our friend John Golden used to do." He'd send out his formal regrets in this manner:

> Mr. John Golden
> sincerely regrets
> that he has no desire to accept
> your kind invitation.

This is a period in history when the lowliest social climber can easily attain a high plateau of snobbism. There's no need to be in the Social Register, the Jet Set, or the mishmash of Bohemia; for, in this age of the uneasy conscience, 99 per cent of the great parties are given for a Cause. All it takes to get invited is a king's ransom to pay for the tickets.

But an occasion arrived when Helen worked me in on a party that was given for fun, with no financial strings attached. She assured me I'd find it absolutely painless. The party in honor of Joseph Papp's birthday would be at his Public Theatre on Lafayette Street in the heart of Greenwich Village.

Joe's theatre is much more than one mere theatre. It is the ancient Astor Library which he, backed up by generous theatre lovers, has converted into a theatrical complex. (One of Joe's most liberal patrons was the late Bert Martinson, whose fortune came from the brand of coffee bearing his name. So millions of coffee drinkers have made a modest contribution to Joe's theatre.)

On the evening of any large supper party in New York, the custom is for guests to attend small private dinners before the main event. Our dinner before the Papp party was really small. There were four of us: Helen and me with our escorts, Mort Gottlieb (the successful Broadway producer, taking a look at how off-Broadway lives) and our host, Guy Monypenny, who is editor of a stylish magazine of interior decorating.

Now Guy, as a true connoisseur of Greenwich Village, elected to give his dinner at a restaurant which, for both ambiance and menu, might have been hidden away in an old quarter of Dublin. It is called McBell's Restaurant and there we found cock-a-leekie soup and Irish prawns and Irish soda bread and Irish stew, and Helen took on an Irish brogue.

"Sure and I never expected Anita to approve this bit of old Erin," said she, "even though she's playing it safe with a hamburger!"

We left before dessert to follow Guy to a coffeehouse on West Fourth Street called The Peacock. Once inside, we realized the place should have had an Italian name, for we seemed to be in a cozy quarter of Naples that was all the more fascinating for being on the wrong side of the tracks. We were served with delicious concoctions such as cappuccino (coffee with steamed milk and cinnamon) plus a dessert with much, much whipped cream flavored with almond extract.

After that we strolled in true Italian contentment along West Fourth to Lafayette Street and there came upon the Public Theatre, ablaze with floodlights. Helen stopped us to view it from afar. "Look! Just look at this truly great example of turn-of-the-century elegance!"

Once inside the theatre complex, we made a little tour en route to Joe's party and examined the ultra-modern recreation and rehearsal rooms. We also investigated an Art Cinema where deep

249

winged seats completely isolate the occupant from his neighbors. "Anita would adore seeing a movie from a seat like this! She, with her antisocial tendencies.

"Do you want to know how we got to this party?" asked Helen. "A long time ago I had an opportunity to befriend Joe Papp. At the time he was a lowly stage manager with a Broadway show. But he was a stage manager with a difference. He had a dream. He spent his off hours trying to promote free Shakespeare in Central Park. He had already achieved one short summer season on a makeshift stage near the lake. It had subsisted on a small grant from the city and a few private donations. But now it was time to prepare for the next season, with not a penny of backing in sight.

"Joe called me, a scared, young voice on the phone. I had never met him. He introduced himself and further explained that his wife had been a classmate of Mary's at the Academy of Dramatic Arts. That, of course, melted me! And now came the reason for his call.

"It seemed that Joe had incurred the suspicion of a New York City Councilman that he was a Commie, intent on undermining our city's morale by means of that subversive old rascal Shakespeare. Whatever the reason, Joe anticipated a rebuff when he had to appear before the Board of Estimate to appeal for city funds. Would I help by going down to City Hall and standing at his side as a character witness? Joe would do all the talking; I hadn't to say a word. That clinched it—I'd go. It would give me a chance to vent my disgust at all the mindless attacks on Art as a danger-ous weapon in suspect hands, and do it merely by my presence.

"Joe came for me, way out in Nyack, in a hired car that looked like a big hole in his week's salary. During the more than an hour ride to City Hall, he briefed me on the procedures. No words from me . . . well, maybe after Joe had appeared before the Board we would be interviewed and I could make a brief statement to the press and television news. 'Then for Heaven's sake,' I pleaded, 'tell me what to say. If I sound as uninformed as I really am, I'll wreck your whole deal for sure.' Joe decided the quickest way to get the information across was for him to read me his presentation. He had worked on it at length to keep it clear and succinct. I listened with all the concentration I'd learned memorizing roles in the theatre, and when he was through I had the major points fixed in my mind."

Now Helen shuddered. "Tell me, Anita, have you ever seen the Council Chamber of New York City Hall? It reminded me a bit of the Supreme Court in Washington, or could it have been the Grand Conference Hall of Versailles? The Mayor sits stage center on an elaborately carved throne surrounded by Borough Presidents and other Councilmen in slightly less grand and lower chairs. At one side is the petitioner's stand, looking rather like the dock in an English courtroom drama.

"We had plenty of time to get familiar with the procedures, because there was an endless parade of appeals being heard alphabetically. We were 'P' for Papp and 'P' for Park, to say nothing of 'S' for poor old Shakespeare, *in absentia*.

"Joe was tense. 'This could go on for hours,' he whispered. 'It's even possible they won't reach us today. You couldn't come tomorrow, could you?'

" 'Right! I *couldn't* come tomorrow.'

"Then and there Joe decided to approach the Board at the first recess and explain that I wasn't able to wait much longer—could they please put his case forward? Came the recess—he went forth. He returned triumphant. 'We're next!' said Joe. 'It was a cinch!'

"The Mayor and the Board filed back and took their regal seats. His Honor rose, rapped with his gavel, and silence *fell*. He spoke. 'We're going to interrupt our normal order at this point to accommodate a lady *who has come down here to address the Board* but must leave shortly. Our next speaker will be Miss Helen Hayes.'

"There I was, wide awake and open-eyed, living the actor's nightmare of being on stage without knowing my lines. Joe turned paper white and sort of croaked, 'Go up there! Say anything! Recite a poem!'

251

"I know despair when I see it, and I saw it in Joe's face. With a blank mind, I rose and started up that long, long trail to the dock. At one moment I turned and looked back at Joe—he was barely conscious. All his dreams of free Shakespeare for New York hung on the reputation that I could make for him that day.

"I reached the podium and without a moment's hesitation I miraculously began to speak. Words poured from me like 'Alice Ben Bolt' from Trilby under the spell of Svengali. For a few moments I couldn't believe those well-ordered thoughts I was spouting. And then I realized that the quick study I'd developed in years of theatre work had caused me to assimilate Joe's entire presentation in one hearing—I was declaiming Joe's speech word for word.

"When I finished, there was a round of applause; a few compliments from the Mayor, after which I was escorted out a side doorway leaving Joe alone to figure out what in tarnation he could say when his turn came. He must have ad-libbed a good speech, because free Shakespeare in the Park survived."

We presently learned Joe's party had already begun in the largest of the four playhouses which comprise the Public Theatre. It had once been the main hall of the old Astor Library and is still crowned with a great domed ceiling of stained glass. This is, moreover, the historic location where *Hair* began—minus its silly nude scene. And the future of the Public Theatre is secure because, largely through Joe's efforts, the building has been declared a City Landmark.

Tonight the great auditorium had become a Viennese cabaret, with tiny candle-lit tables spotted among the rows of red plush theatre seats.

When we entered there, the party was in full swing and Joe was stationed at the door. Ebullient and dynamic, he hugged everyone indiscriminately in true theatre style. The arena stage had become a dance floor, and a band was performing lustily, not playing the Viennese waltzes that would have suited its décor, for the band was Greek and it was playing dance tunes of its native land. Once

again, as so often in the Village, one had the feeling of long ago
and far away.

Somebody started a hora; ladies kicked off their shoes and got
into it. Joe's small children were scooped up into the circle. The
dance whirled merrily around us, and the laughter was con-
tinuous and loud. There wasn't one sensational celebrity of the
sort that make headlines. This was a party of friends and its spirit
was rather like a church sociable in a small town of the Midwest.
"So this is the joyful aftermath of that fearsome morning at City
Hall about twelve years ago," chuckled Helen.

Another party of that year was a much more arty event.

It started as a charming idea cooked up by the Special Events
Department of the Metropolitan Museum. The invitation called it
"An Annual Midsummer Fête" at the Cloisters, in Fort Tryon
Park. It was to be, in effect, a sort of highbrow picnic.

The details had been worked out lovingly but in a manner that
would have come off better during the year 1200 A.D. For one
thing, the world has grown too big for some of its gracious old
customs; better leave them to memory.

Thousands of Museum members were intrigued, however, by
one item mentioned in the invitation: "a cold bird" and "a bottle"
which could be enjoyed al fresco among the ancient Cloisters and
to the accompaniment of medieval music. Together with the other
guests, we stormed those historic ramparts on a June night of
1970 A.D. We were quite a crush. By the time our car arrived,
there was no parking space left, so Vera, the friend who drives us
where we cannot walk, shamelessly called out our names to the
policeman in charge of traffic. It worked!

Invitations had instructed guests to be on the lookout for "The
White Unicorn" who would be there to welcome us. And there it
was, an actor suffocating inside a fur suit and mask. The White
Unicorn, hoping to impress Helen, persuaded the officer to let us
park with the press cars. "Sometimes I really do relish fame, don't
you, Anita?"

The night was warm and the temperature got to us as we slowly made our way up the enclosed stone steps to the main lobby of the museum above. We midsummer revelers were packed body-to-body for half an hour on that airless staircase, emerging into the lobby at last, pink in the face and perspiring. From there we were led to a crawling line that was headed toward food. It took an added half hour to reach it, but at least we could see where we were and we found interest in our fellow breadliners. Naturally, there were some other Establishmentarians like us in smart linen dresses or seersucker suits, but most of the revelers wore sprigged calico from Liberty's in London or slimsy tie-dye silk that came way down to their artistic sandals. If they wore any jewelry, it was extremely forgettable. The gentlemen mostly had Sir Galahad hairdos, beards, or sweeping mustaches. "They look as if they should remain a part of the permanent exhibit," Helen remarked.

We finally reached a long refreshment stand where a white cardboard box was thrust at each of us as we passed: our picnic feast. Farther on, a sweating and flustered waiter deposited a tiny plastic glass of bubbly pink wine into our free hands, and we were on our way.

We had read in a program that "Supper may be eaten on the ramparts overlooking the Hudson; or in the Cuxa, Bonnefont, or Trie Cloisters facing the gardens." So, warily protecting our wineglasses, we set out in search of a picnic spot.

We first made for the Cuxa Cloister, it being Helen's favorite section because of the variety of its exquisite columns. Besides, it was the nearest stopping place and we were starving. A few paces on, Helen's elbows were joggled and she spilled part of her wine down the front of her yellow linen. A few more paces and it happened again. But she overcame that hazard by gulping down what was left of her wine, by which time she sorely needed it for encouragement.

Finally we made it to the Cuxa Cloister—guided there by the sounds of a fragile *moyen-âge* song which was all but lost in the rugged hum that's made by large masses in transit. We squeezed through the arched entryway and paused inside to look for a place to alight. There wasn't an inch of free space. People were packed everywhere; the luckier had found camp stools where they perched, lunch boxes in laps, wineglasses jiggling. A group called the Sine Nomine Singers were struggling in vain to make themselves heard. We could see them in quick peeks between the merrymakers in front of us. Behind us a sharp voice rasped, "You're interfering with my view!" Turning, we confronted a lady munching a medieval apple. I apologized and tried to move out of her way—an impossibility unless I wanted to walk over a pathway that was paved with human insteps. So we got out of there.

Each cloister in turn was the same. Then we tried the terrace overlooking the Hudson and Helen's beloved George Washington Bridge. The terrace was packed with people squatting on the stone floor, which at least was cool. We stepped gingerly over them (and their boxes) and made for the ramparts. Finally, in a state of half starvation, we came to rest there. True, there was no place to sit and there was no place to put our boxes, but we could imitate those who, with great ingenuity, were using the stone balustrade for a lunch counter, overcoming the fact that it rose to a point by depositing their lunch boxes on the slant side and holding them in place with their chests. This gave us two hands for opening our picnic box, and we did so like ravening wolves— nearly two hours after dinnertime.

Inside our boxes, a surprise. All our food was tightly sealed in nonmedieval plastic coverings. I have no gift for opening these things even under normal circumstances and I realized that Helen was in the same fix. We finally settled for some Camembert which was merely wrapped in old-fashioned tinfoil and a big hunk of French bread that made a shamble of our diets.

As we neared the end of that hit-or-miss repast, two ladies approached, carrying camp stools. "We've been watching your struggles from over there," one of them said, "and we'd like to offer you our camp stools."

255

While we gratefully unfolded them, the lady remarked, "We came all the way from Brooklyn for this shindig and it will give us some return for our trouble to know you're enjoying our stools." No sooner were we seated than two quite elderly ladies came up, juggling their boxes, and one asked, "Do you mind if we wait here while you finish your supper? We'd like to have your places when you're through." We finished very shortly after because we hadn't steady enough nerves to stick it out for long under the steady gaze of their hungry eyes.

On we went to the terrace garden. It is unique for having been planted with every one of the hundreds of flowers scattered throughout the White Unicorn tapestries. "Isn't it comforting," remarked Helen, "to see that flowers haven't changed at all in nearly five hundred years?"

We next passed the Trie Cloister and were intrigued by the sounds of strictly modern laughter and applause coming from within. We wormed our way through the crush and finally achieved a clear view of the best magician we had seen since the great Thurston; a tall, handsome black man named Frank Brents, in impeccable twentieth-century tails and top hat, from which he produced all manner of things, including a huge, very noisy white goose. "Bless dear Frank Brents," said Helen, "he saved our midsummer eve for us!"

WHERE PIE IN THE SKY IS PIZZA

The next party on our agenda was an even bigger crush, but with what a difference!

To get invited to the outdoor fête of San Gennaro nobody has to have any culture. All you need is subway fare to Mulberry Street, the price of as much Italian delicatessen as you can consume, and a Neapolitan stomach lined with lava from Mount Vesuvius.

Helen thought it best to take a few friends along. "We'll need some gourmets who'll appreciate the cuisine!" she declared.

"And," I suggested, "some gourmandizers who won't mind eating it off pushcarts."

Helen, who has no shame on the subject of her greediness, grinned and replied, "That's right!"

Our list of friends included pretty and stylish Ruth Obre Goldbeck de Vallombrosa Dubonnet, who is a connoisseur of the foodstuffs of every country she ever married into. Then came Danny Apolinar, the brilliant young composer of "Your Own Thing" who would appreciate the music. Our friend John Britton would do anything for a laugh. And there was one of Helen's favorite sidekicks, Guy Monypenny, editor of *1001 Decorating Ideas*, who could appreciate the Mulberry Street décor.

The festa begins toward the end of September and goes on for a week. Long before our cabs reached the Italian district we could hear sounds of the celebration: arias of Verdi, "O Sole Mio," mingling with "Ciribiribin" and "Santa Lucia." They were all being warbled at the same time, but Danny, whose music is rather avant-garde, approved because the melodies were lost in the din. We gradually got used to that and nobody tried to talk anyway. At the Feast of San Gennaro mouths are only used for eating.

Guy approved the decorations, which were real party boosters. For about ten blocks, Mulberry Street was spanned by glittering metal arches in a lacy pattern of curlicues studded with colored lights. The arches went on so far that we couldn't even see the end of them. And in every direction there were colored lights in festoons, swatches of bunting in red, white, and green, and plastic flowers in vivid shades that nature wouldn't dare attempt.

Milling about among the Italians were Chinese from adjacent Mott Street, denizens of nearby Greenwich Village, and blacks in elegant Afro hairdos. As a gesture of hospitality, many of the Italians wore large buttons that read: "Kiss me, I'm Italian."

Along the sidewalks, in close formation, were stands of Italian

257

food specialties. "Dear God, what marvels!" exclaimed Helen.
"One could almost be sustained by the mere aroma." Their
aroma, as a matter of fact, was all I required. "You and your
skinny figure!" said Helen. "Will you break down for once in
your life and *eat*?" No, I wouldn't.

Meanwhile, Helen, Ruth, and the boys were sampling everything, and, since the counters were lined up without any regard
for a menu, they were eating their supper backwards. I remember,
as in a nightmare, that they began on Sicilian cream puffs, went
on through *fritto misto*, Milanese sausage with hot sauce on a
hard roll, pizza, various odd pastas, biscuit tortoni, and they
ended with clams on the half shell.

At one moment in our progress Helen was recognized by the
lady behind a pizza counter. She called out above the racket in a
loud sun-kissed Italian voice, "Hey! Looka here, everybody;
looka who's here!" Helen was subsequently enveloped in a number of ample bosoms, and before she could manage to protect her
slab of pizza it was squashed on her green and white outfit and
added the note of red that gave it the tricolors of Italy.

By this time we had been separated from our escorts, who had
succumbed to gambling fever. One could throw balls at things or
squirt water at other things or spin wheels for prizes that were
valuable or repulsive according to taste. There were games where
you could win a bottle of chianti or, if very lucky, a fifth of Scotch
or vodka. At one wheel of fortune there was a sign "Get lucky and
get drunk."

Our boys got lucky to the extent of a pint of chianti which had
set them back seven dollars. And then, with everybody except me
still eating, we fought our way out of the mainstream to a side
street where anyone with an impulse to be heard in song was encouraged to mount an improvised stage and enjoy his moment in
the spotlight, to the accompaniment of a right good orchestra.
There we listened to a basso profundo who could easily have made
the Met but had evidently had other fish to fry.

Getting back into the mass movement, we heard a brass band

blasting out a hymn and the crowd parted to make room for a parade. It was led by a parish priest in miter and vestments of sparkling gold lamé who was flinging holy water in all directions, en route to the shrine of San Gennaro at the entrance of the neighborhood chapel.

Carried along in the wake of the parade, we reached the shrine where the patron saint's effigy, in colored plaster, sat enthroned. From our vantage point, San Gennaro's robe seemed to be fashioned of myriads of long green leaves that were fluttering in the breeze. We were informed that the good saint would grant one wish to everybody who came through with a dollar bill. This explained his fluttery green robe; it was a solid mass of dollar bills attached to his saintly vestment with pins (of which there was a plentiful supply for free). Nothing would do but that Helen, doughty Catholic that she is, would fight her way through that mob, make a wish, and pin a dollar on San Gennaro.

It was now getting time to leave, but on our way out Helen was tempted again, this time by something squashy made of puff pastry, stuffed with a greenish sort of custard and frosted in shocking pink. She made one last attempt to proselytize me into joining her and when I refused she put it down to my dreary, cast-iron will power, vanity, and cowardly fear of adventure.

The next morning I felt a few bad effects from our night of dissipation, so I couldn't resist phoning Helen to ask her in poisoned tones, "How do *you* feel today?"

"Simply great!" she replied in a matter-of-fact voice and then went on to another subject.

I couldn't listen to Helen. I was too stupefied. If she felt "simply great," it could only be a miracle. And then it came over me that most likely Helen had prayed to San Gennaro, "Please, San Gennaro, let me survive all these Italian delicatessen and live to toss the fact right into my skinny girl friend's teeth!"

259

WEST IS EAST

Mott Street, the main stem of New York's Chinatown, is just one block east of Mulberry, the main stem of Little Italy.

Indeed, south of Canal on Mulberry, Chinese storefronts mingle with the Italian—the neighborhoods have merged. Also, they seem to have formed a habit of jumping aboard each other's celebrations whenever possible.

Thus, during the San Gennaro festa, a big banner at Canal and Mott Streets proclaimed the advent of the "Great Chinese Pushcart Derby" at noon on a certain day the following week. Now, to Helen, pushcart means a vendor's wagon and the vendors of Mott Street meant glorious Chinese goodies such as egg roll and sweet-sour spareribs and chop suey burgers. I pictured Helen eating her way along the full length of Mott Street just as she'd done on Mulberry.

Well, it wasn't like that at all. Those "Pushcarts" had nothing to do with food. They were an Oriental version of the old soapbox racers of some years back: a soapbox on roller-skate wheels. These were painted to simulate racing cars, and in each of the eighteen or twenty of them sat a small boy of Oriental extraction—every one very beautiful, as Oriental children are.

The cars were drawn up in two lines at the end of Mott Street under an unusually hot September sun. We arrived on the dot of noon, but Heaven knows how long those patient little tykes had been frying under their racing helmets. Beside each car was an older boy to propel it down a steep hill. It looked very alarming. We joined the watchers along the curb near the starting line and we waited. And we waited. For an hour we waited. Nobody seemed to be doing anything to get the show off the ground.

We took a stroll because walking is easier on the feet than standing. Having skipped breakfast in order to make room for all those "pushcart" goodies, we were getting hungry. (Had we consulted an expert, we'd have found out that the Chinese never, but *never*, eat off pushcarts.)

We strolled the whole length of Mott Street, looking for an American interloper with a hot dog or hamburger stand. But in all Chinatown there seemed to be nothing but elaborate restaurants that require time to serve their fare properly. "This neighborhood is stuck with the old Chinese custom of sitting down to eat!" Helen grumbled. "I'd even settle for a bag of fortune cookies!" But obviously the Chinese haven't advanced far enough in Westernization to have mastered eating on the run.

It would be foolish, to say the least, to miss the race after we'd come all the way down there. So we decided to forget about lunch and settle for a packet of life savers which Helen dug out of her purse. We returned to our vigil on the curb and took our places at the starting line. Absolutely nothing had happened since we'd left there. We asked a couple of young Chinese aficionados nearby, "What about that twelve noon starting time?"

They asked *us*, "What time is it now?"

"Two."

"Oh, we *are* late, aren't we?" They settled back into immobility.

Helen was raging. She gets cross when she's hungry. Then came a ray of hope—actually, two rays, in the persons of a pair of beautiful, big, easygoing New York cops. They unobtrusively took the whole project over and got things moving. A tall judges' stand was put in place, white lines were painted down the middle of the street, the participants were got into place—all inside of a half hour. Now, now, it would happen! Only two hours and forty-five minutes late!

But then came the crusher. A small girl was led forth and after a lot of palaver was crowned queen of the day with a gold paper crown. She was then joined by a group of people—family, we guessed—and after much chatter and giggle they arranged themselves in a line behind the toddler queen. Off they started down the street, the racers crawling behind. They intended to parade the whole length of Chinatown and back at this pace. It would take another hour. We were hot and tired and hungry and frustrated. We were also leaving, going back to our Western world of rush and turmoil where, anyway, we will know where we *are*.

En route back to Occidental Manhattan, Helen recalled another visit to Mott Street, a banquet way back in the Thirties. "Harold Ross, the creator of the *New Yorker*, was host. The place was 21 Mott Street—Chinatown's answer to the Twenty-One Club of West 52nd Street for superlative cuisine.

"The menu had been selected by Ross's friend Anna May Wong. It included, as I remember, bird's-nest soup—a very strange sort of gelatinous substance, ancient eggs which tasted to our Western palates like nothing at all, but have the sturdy texture of rubber. There were other weirdies which I won't try to list.

"The guests included Harpo Marx who, as we left, muttered a comment in my ear. It wasn't pretty, but as long as I've got this far I'll go right on. Harpo said, 'Now for a good vomit.'

SOUTH IS NORTH

There is nothing like fine Latin food, too. In our town one can eat Latin, Greek, Armenian, and every other kind of cuisine as if one were on foreign soil. And outdoor markets sell all sorts of exotic products. Colorful comestibles are heaped on stalls and pushcarts, giving streets a gay, festival air. No matter how disadvantaged our minorities are, somehow they are able to obtain their own native foodstuffs.

Puerto Ricans, the newest arrivals, have their own market up in Spanish Harlem. It stretches for six blocks from Park Avenue and 111th Street, under the Penn Central's elevated tracks.

We ventured up to Spanish Harlem one day, first fortifying ourselves with a hearty lunch to supply energy for walking. In honor of the occasion we set out to eat Latin food, and our old friend Lillian Gish gave us the pleasure of her company.

"Say what you like," I told them on our way to lunch. "The best chili con carne is not in Mexico or Texas or even San Francisco, which always claims the best of anything. It's right where we're going on East 60th Street."

But Lillian had another interest in our destination, for she is Vice-President of the Ice Cream Appreciators of America, a league organized to ferret out obscure localities where ice cream attains perfection. The place we were going to was not obscure.

Reaching Serendipity, we headed for the dining area in back, but only after dragging Helen away from eye-catchers in the front store. In this city version of a country store there was a lot to look at, such as Tarot cards of the Art Deco period, toilet tissue printed with fake hundred-dollar bills, and an antique suit of red flannel underwear dangling from a wall hook.

When hunting for unusual gifts for foreign friends, I usually shop at Serendipity. And it is a favorite haunt of theirs on visits to New York.

The dining area looks, with its glittering Tiffany lamps, and old ice-cream-parlor tables and chairs, like a perpetual Christmas party. The waiters look Edwardian, and the cuisine stems from old New Orleans. Best to leave your calorie counter at home. Everything is heaped with the thickest cream this side of Devonshire, and that even goes for the chili con carne. But it's well worth a month's starvation on Melba toast and grapefruit juice to let yourself go at Serendipity.

As Calvin, our host, seated us, he said, "We've just installed a second kitchen with a Japanese chef who specializes in macrobiotic food. All his ingredients are organically grown."

The three of us opted for a health lunch but learned it is served upstairs in the "Zen Hashery." We hated to leave our Tiffany-lit table, so Calvin had our lunch brought from above.

Then we lit into our organic macrobiotic lunch. Lillian and I

263

had ordered yogurt gazpacho followed by curry with alfalfa sprouts and lemon curd for dessert. Helen had an open-faced vegetable sandwich garnished with lotus root. She took it apart to steal the receipt for a ladies' luncheon of her Nyack bridge club.

It may sound weird, but try it: On a slice of homemade wholewheat bread spread a thick mixture of crushed walnuts and mayonnaise. Add alternate slices of cucumber, apple, and raw mushrooms and top with melted ricotta cheese.

For dessert Helen reverted to a caloric dish (not that her tasty sandwich wasn't). After indulging in "Miss Milton's Lovely Fudge Pie," straight from New Orleans, she vowed that she'd count calories the rest of the week.

The clientele was as fascinating as the food. They ranged from a zany pair of old females who looked like *The Madwoman of Chaillot* and a romantic twosome of boys as decorative as the banana splits they ate, to a group of square executive types— "They're executives from Bloomingdale's, on the corner," Lillian whispered.

After lunch we parted from Lillian on our way to Spanish Harlem. She gave us a final warning: "I hope you're taking along an interpreter." To make her feel helpful Helen fibbed, "Why, of course." But, let's face it, we *were* headed for a crime belt, so we'd hired a limousine with a driver who could stand by for protection.

Like most of New York's danger zones, the streets looked harmless enough under a flawless sunny sky. "A friend of mine lives in San Juan," I remarked, "and he says the crime rate among Puerto Ricans is practically zero. It's only when they reach New York that some of them develop a tendency toward crime."

At this point our driver spoke up. "I was born and raised in this neighborhood, and we kids sure gave the Puerto Ricans a rugged time. A lot of those poor folks were hungry and in the winter they were always cold. I can't blame them now for being resentful."

This was a cue for Helen the moralist. "I feel a personal shame," she sighed, "for what New York has done to these people. Of course they weren't *forced* to leave their lovely island and live ten to a room in our Harlem slums. But I suppose that when they first arrived and learned the truth, they were lonely for their own kind. So they encouraged others to come up here too. Hope is sometimes a dirty trickster."

We entered the closed-in area under the elevated tracks. It was teeming with market people, both buyers and sellers, and in spite of Helen's gloom I saw evidence of pleasure in bargain hunting. Puerto Rican shoppers were milling through artfully arranged heaps of strange vegetables and fruit. We didn't even know what they were called, but easily got their names when we inquired. For all Lillian's warning, everyone but the very aged spoke English.

There were plantains, chayotes, papaya, breadfruit, giant yams, and great hunks of raw ginger root. There was also every kind of meat, fish, sausage, native cheese, and items we'd never before encountered.

Presently Helen exclaimed, "Heavens above! Love potions!" On a stall stood small bottles of aphrodisiacs, probably guaranteed to work on such hard-to-hook types as Tom Jones or Engelbert Humperdinck.

"Have you also got hate potions?" I asked the vendor. She had indeed. "Made of rattlesnakes' blood, dried and powdered." She also had a supply of water from the River Jordan in tiny vials and little glassine envelopes containing a spoonful of veritable earth from the Holy Land.

Wandering on, we came to dry-goods stalls displaying items that horrified Helen because of their bad taste. "Dear God!" she cried. "Look at these awful ersatz satin negligées. And these vulgar plastic religious symbols." She was even more shocked by the see-through bikinis in blatant colors, embroidered with slogans like "Dig Me Man, I'm Groovy" and "Baby, Light My Fire."

Having always placed human happiness ahead of good taste, I remarked, "Why should Puerto Rican teen-agers be denied the permissiveness granted to Park Avenue debutantes? Why shouldn't a Puerto Rican girl indulge in bright-colored panties inscribed with American folk sayings?"

"But, Anita, if American purveyors didn't supply this trash, these people couldn't buy it, could they?"

Just then I was able to single out another culprit. For I'd found a pair of panties in shocking pink with a legend reading "Eeny Meeny Miney Mo—This Is As Far As You Can Go." And on it was a tiny sticker marked "Made in Japan."

GEORGE SPELVIN, WHERE ARE YOU?

*M*any years ago a custom was established in the American theatre that when an actor played two different characters in a play, his program credit for the lesser role would read "George Spelvin." It was, so to speak, a *nom de jambon*. George Spelvin got no salary, but actors so love to act that they are more than happy to play two parts for the price of one.

Now, George Spelvin's name hasn't been on a Broadway program for lo these many years because Actors Equity no longer allows him to work for free. But George has a champion who is hell-bent on bringing him back: that staunch New York theatre lover Leo Lerman.

About a year ago Leo organized a series of luncheons to be given in honor of George Spelvin. There were to be about thirty guests, half of whom would be from show business and the other half from the world of industry: the type of successful people who love the theatre, buy tickets, and sometimes even put money into plays. During lunch these businessmen and women would be asked for advice on how to combat the sorry state of the theatre; the exorbitant cost of producing plays; the high crime rate in the city after dark; the rivalry of TV as a cheap home diversion; the economic recession and the hampering rules of theatrical unions like the one which sent George Spelvin into limbo.

Leo had invited Helen and me to his final luncheon of the season at the Algonquin Hotel, that caravansery for show folk where, from the early Twenties, the wisdom, wit, and wisecracks of Broadway have crackled like an electric circus.

Well, at lunch that day we encountered some of the wit and wisdom of the Seventies. Leo has scholarly qualities which are rare in our modern world. A man of letters, a connoisseur of fine

267

living, and a wit, he is chiefly distinguished as author of the history of the Metropolitan Museum titled *Museum*. He is also editor of *Playbill*, that racy little magazine which is handed out as a program in all Broadway theatres.

Leo sat in a place of authority at the center of the table, looking like a twentieth-century version of Jupiter, very sturdy and expansive in his opulent beard, Leo having grown one long before the male population followed suit. In Leo's case, a beard veils his quite sensuous mouth, which is a giveaway that, along with other attractive weaknesses, he loves food.

Helen occupied a place of honor between Leo and Robert Whitehead, the producer, whose wife Zoe Caldwell sparkles equally either on or off Broadway. (She was sparkling at home that day playing Mamma to their two-year-old son.)

My luncheon partners were Clive Barnes, the dance and drama critic of the *New York Times*, and Morton Gottlieb, the youthful producer of *Sleuth*. The two couldn't be more different.

Mortie's hair is short, black, and curly, and his garb suggests the Establishment with snazzy overtones from Bond Street. Clive Barnes, for those who have never seen him, comes on as a surprise. Boyish and plump, in the manner of Lord Byron; his pale brown tresses are so long they might have earned him a featured role in *Hair*. He has a mild sort of old-world look, a Dickenslike ingenuousness. One wonders how such a harmless soul could slap down even a bad play. Yet Mr. Barnes has been known to slap down a number of good ones.

Others of the theatre were Mary McCarty (one of the stars of *Follies*), Emory Lewis, Frank Segers of *Variety*, and the entire staff of *Playbill*.

At the beginning of lunch, Leo turned to Helen. "What do *you* think we're doing on Broadway that's wrong?" he asked.

Helen was startled. "Oh dear," she said, "I thought I was here to learn. I'm not prepared to talk."

"Then just skim the top of your mind," urged Leo.

Helen hesitated, thought a moment, and then said, "Well,

268

offhand, Leo, I think we've become too earnest. We've forgotten that the main function of a player is to *play*. I wish we'd all relax and put on some gay, glamorous shows with actors wearing beautiful romantic clothes."

"Hear! Hear!" spoke up several guests. Clive remained silent because his best reviews go to plays of the kitchen-sink genre, where the clothes must, perforce, be deplorable.

"That's a very good hunch, Helen," said Leo. "And what else?"

Helen was flustered. "But, Leo, I'm such a slow thinker! I can't be glib about something I feel very deeply about."

"Go on! Be as emotional as you like."

Taking a deep breath, Helen continued. "All right, you asked for it.

"I think Broadway started to slip when we began to take ourselves seriously as Artists, and spelled it out in capital letters. We strained for what we called 'artistic integrity.' The trouble was that too many of us mistook pretensions for integrity. We've been sold on the idea that truth has got to be ugly, depressing, and vulgar. In recent years we've tried so hard to strip the theatre of beauty that we've stripped some actors of their costumes. Let's see what can be done to put clothes back on our actors."

Helen got a round of applause that startled her. She turned to Leo. "Oh, dear, you mustn't let me babble on like this."

"Go on," said Leo.

Helen braced herself. "Well—I'd like to see our commercial theatre relieved of its phony pretensions to Art. In all the years I've been in the theatre, I can count the number of great artists I've encountered on the fingers of one hand. But I've worked with plenty of real pros like me. We adored our jobs, developed and used what talents we had to the limit of our capabilities. If we fell short of greatness we weren't undone by that so long as audiences liked and appreciated us.

"That was the time when we only hoped to please the public who paid to see us. But now they are the last thing we ever think about. We only aim to please ourselves and to impress other actors or the critics, whom we pretend to despise." (Clive masochistically appeared to like *that*!)

"Time was when there was a love affair between the theatre and the public, and because love creates a magical illusion we loved ones behind the footlights—those dear, kind footlights!—walked in beauty. People came to the theatre to see us enacting lives of vivid color, in elegant speech and in gorgeous clothes—all in an aura of Du Barry Pink light. It was not Art, it was not Truth, but it sure was comforting. I'd love to see a matinee idol again, suave, impeccably tailored, breaking hearts with a light touch. Or an improbably chic Ina Claire changing Chanel creations eight times a performance and never being caught with her wit down.

"Yes, I'd like to see the commercial theatre relieved of the burden of 'Art' and free to caper.

"In the name of George Spelvin's devotion to the theatre, let's revive our love affair with the public." There was more and louder applause, which Helen gratefully took as an excuse to sit down.

Mortie, always on the qui vive to put in a plug for *Sleuth,* now saw his chance. "When a playwright is *really* an artist he doesn't have to be a bore. Tony Shaffer crammed *Sleuth* so full of rowdy laughs that the audience never detects his peerless prose style."

"Right-o!" interpolated Clive Barnes, not trying to disguise the fact that he, like Shaffer, is English.

Mr. Griffin, an advertising expert, now put in his American oar: "Anyway, I'm tired of authors who parade their private hangups across the stage. I don't care to know that a Southern author hated his Southern Mamma or that the old lady had a drug habit and the entire family loathed each other."

Mr. Begleiter, the Vice President of a wine and spirits company, next spoke his mind against the type of play in which two drab characters in one grubby stage set grumble about why they were born. "In other words," with a glance toward Clive Barnes, "the sort of entertainment which wins accolades from *you*!"

That gave Helen another cue: "Yes, you agree with me *here*

270

that glamour should be brought back to the theatre, but you slap it down in print every time it shows its lovely face on a stage. How should we newspaper readers accept your reviews?" she asked Clive.

"With absolute skepticism," was his answer, but he spoke with the smile of a cat as it licks some little yellow feathers from its jaw.

"Well, in the final analysis, it shouldn't matter how you critics react," Helen said with her own kind of smile, "or who wins Tonys, or what new gimmicks we invent to attract the public, such as theatre clubs and the reduced-rate previews. If people really care, they'll find their way back to us. If only we can start people caring again, Broadway will come back."

The upshot of the session was theoretical rather than practical, a theme of uplift: for the theatre to be successful once again, actors and playwrights must love their audience and not their ego. And in every play there should be at least one character whom the audience itself can love.

At the same time, I grant that hate can sometimes be successful, as in the shows of that unsophisticated Broadway producer who is Pollyanna-in-reverse. His two musicals, *Company* and *Follies*, have both been motivated by hatred for humanity, which has been sugar-coated with lovable costumes and scenic effects. So it appears that at least costume designers and scenic artists sometimes love their audiences.

At the end of lunch, Leo proposed a toast. "Here's to George Spelvin, that actor who so loves the theatre that he'll work for nothing. To George Spelvin, who makes feasible the big casts in which the audience gets its money's worth. And to the day when George Spelvin makes his comeback and LOVE returns to Broadway."

On our way back from the Algonquin, Helen announced moodily, "I'm beginning to feel guilty over what I said about our loving the public." I asked her what she meant. "In the past we didn't always use the poor theatre public very well. I've sometimes

271

been in a bad play that would fail on Broadway because it was unacceptable and then be sent on tour, trading on a star's name to make up any loss to the producer. I went on such a tour once under the most distinguished auspices; the producer was Charles Frohman, the star John Drew. We played one-night stands in towns I've never heard of since; we presented our awful show in nickelodeons, movie houses, and Knights of Pythias halls. Whenever possible we'd get out of town before the morning reviews. But we felt very noble about those hardships, never recognizing they were caused by the *ig*noble reason that Mr. Drew's self-esteem wouldn't allow him to lose money for his dear friend Charlie Frohman. How about all those dear, trusting 'friends,' his public, who had paid their money at the box office?

"I did the same thing many years later; cheated my loyal public in order to recompense the Theatre Guild for a bad play I'd wished on them. It was called *Candle in the Wind* and when we opened on Broadway everyone was trounced, including me. The decent thing would have been to close the play on the first night. However, feeling very righteous, I agreed to go on a five months' tour, so that the Guild could get back its production cost.

"Though we never admitted it, even to ourselves, we were using the public instead of serving it. And what happened? Well, the inferior offerings of those Good Old Days lost us a lot of our public in the hinterlands. Then, when those folks came to New York as tourists they'd gotten out of the habit of theatregoing. Broadway needs tourists to survive. But they, just like many New Yorkers, have deserted it for off-Broadway shows we can love, like *You're a Good Man, Charlie Brown* and *Story Theatre*.

"Let's take a look at off-Broadway, Anita!" To which suggestion, I squirmingly agreed.

STEPPING OFF BROADWAY

"Of course," said Helen, on examining the list of off-Broadway shows, "things aren't all sweetness and light in these plays, either. There are a lot of ugly shows and violent protest shows, and there are some pretty dirty shows for insecure people who need to prove their sophistication."

She then ran across an item that caused her face to light up. "But here's a rave review for a new rock musical based on the Gospel according to St. Matthew. It's title is *Godspell*, which is long for Gospel. Shall we see it?"

That title worried me as being pretty coy, but I didn't say so and off we went to the Cherry Lane Theatre in Greenwich Village for a Sunday matinee. It was a mild June day, and we were early enough to loiter a bit before show time.

Well, on Bedford Street, around the corner from the Cherry Lane, Helen stopped me and gestured toward a ridiculously tiny house. "It's the very narrowest in the entire city. It only measures ten feet at its widest point! And yet that innocent-looking doll's house had been occupied, in succession, by two sex-potted characters who burned up Manhattan with their wild goings on. One tenant of the place was Edna St. Vincent Millay, whose poem about those two-way candles that burned brightly at both ends might have been applied to John Barrymore, who followed her into the premises as a tenant."

Helen went on to inform me of an incident concerning Jack Barrymore and the young actress who was playing the lead in my play *Gentlemen Prefer Blondes*. "He nearly closed your show one night during a session in this very house, by kicking your Lorelei Lee downstairs as a signal that their romance was over. The poor child pulled herself together and managed to get through her next performance, but it was with an aching back that would have been more suitable to Whistler's Mother. And poor protected poke

273

that I was, I felt a twinge of envy about that kick downstairs. 'That,' thought I, 'was *living*!' "

Matinee time brought an end to our gossip, and we proceeded to the theatre.

I must now confess that those young "Jesus actors," dressed to look like Tarot cards and just as devoid of any human dimensions, left me cold. In my mind, to use the Bible for inspiration requires a genius commensurate with the subject matter. I once heard Duke Ellington conduct a service in the Cathedral of St. John the Divine where a tap dance was performed in front of the altar and the holiness of the Duke's message came through clear and strong. But I found that the Bible, as dished up by those jejune talents, produced nothing more than noise and amateurish horseplay. So at the first intermission I told Helen I'd see her at the end of the show and went for a stroll, fully aware that I'd soon be in for a curtain lecture.

I later picked Helen up in the lobby and, possibly to sweeten the trouncing that lay ahead, she suggested that we look for some ice cream. We found it on the terrace of a cozy café that had fancy iron tables and ice-cream-parlor chairs. The ice cream was served in old-timy bell-shaped sundae glasses and, fortified by all that early Americana, Helen proceeded to let me have it.

"You see, Anita, I've grown accustomed to the high volume of today's sound, thank heaven, or else my hearing has dulled—still thank heaven. And I'm learning to know one rock song from another. I can tell if I admire the score—I did this one. I adored the lovely song 'Day by Day.' And that last exuberant procession up the aisle as they belted out their rock march, 'Long Live God.'

"There was a little boy sitting behind me and I wondered how a child would respond to the Bible stripped of its smothering holiness and presented like a fresh new idea. Well, after you deserted me, I couldn't resist asking him, 'How do you like the show?' My young neighbor told me emphatically that he *loved* it.

"I was especially grateful when those dazzling young performers took the mystery out of some of those awful parables and turned them into comedy routines. I long ago gave up trying to understand the story of the Wise Steward, for instance, and decided that Jesus must have told that one to amuse his audience. I say this in all respect because I'm sure that great teachers like good TV announcers warm up their listeners with a few jokes. Of course sometimes those young actors in *Godspell* do gag it up. But Jesus' Sermon on the Mount was delivered with such beauty that the words went straight to my heart as they have rarely done when I've heard them from a pulpit.

"And in spite of your opinion about youth, Anita, I'm perfectly content to leave the future of our theatre in its hands. I feel this most strongly when I'm at the rough-and-tumble eaterie called Joe Allen's, far west on 46th Street. That's where the young and mostly unarrived can eat well and cheaply and stick together. They may look like hippies, but they're integrated, energetic— they talk, they laugh easily, and they love what they're doing. I've been told that they're carried by the management when things are slow and jobs are scarce. That's what's nice about our city. Joe's hamburgers are great; so are his coffee and pretty special pie. And the decorations—a collection of posters of flops!

"So what I should have said at Leo's lunch party for George Spelvin is that if poor old Broadway can be put into the hands of youth, it will again have vitality and strength."

"Helen, darling," I admonished her, "you're off on one of your flights of fancy again! The stars who've been providing Broadway with strength and vitality today have been Kate Hepburn, Ruby Keeler, Patsy Kelly, Alexis Smith, Lauren Bacall, Yvonne de Carlo, Mary McCarty, Danny Kaye, Dorothy Collins, Jimmy Stewart, and, may I add, Helen Hayes."

It took Helen almost as long to concede as a defeated Presidential candidate. At last she said in her non-Broadway verbiage, "By cracky, perhaps you're right!"

But then her face brightened as she suddenly thought of a way

275

to put me down. "What about those two creative youngsters in *Purlie Victorious*? What about Melba Moore and Cleavon Little?" she asked triumphantly. It was now my turn to concede.

Our next venture off-Broadway was to see Sada Thompson in the Pulitzer Prize play, *The Effect of Gamma Rays on Man-in-the-Moon Marigolds*, and I'm glad to say we both highly approved it. I, in particular, got a great lesson in playwriting from the author. He has invented a trick of creating a dreadful female whose every move scares the living daylights out of you. And, while you're sitting breathless with terror of what she'll do next, it turns out to be something quite banal and you experience the joy of sudden relief. A double set of emotions for the price of one.

And, incidentally, that experience gave us a clue to one of the things that's wrong with Broadway: its lack of discernment—for here is a play that had been disregarded, rejected, and kicked around for more than seven years by every producer in New York, before Orin Lehman recognized its wallop and ventured to produce it.

BROADWAY NOW AND THEN

One afternoon we were taking a customary promenade, this time along Broadway, strolling past those numberless bazaars that feature pornographic posters and blatantly suggestive lingerie. "Can you visualize the sort of female who would wear such things?" Helen asked, as if I were an expert. Well—I was. Research had led me to the fact that those see-through nightgowns, sketchy bras, and fringed bikinis are largely manufactured for boys, those desperate and incomplete souls for whom 42nd Street is now a haven.

The block between Broadway and Eighth Avenue, which was once lined with legitimate theatres, is now taken over by pornographic movies. And here again I was able to act as mentor for Helen. The 42nd Street brand of filth, I could assure her, is more innocuous than it seems. The marquee may feature *Go-Go Girls at*

276

Play and all it amounts to is an old-fashioned pillow fight among girls who are not even topless.

"Just think of the offerings of our friendly neighborhood cinema where stars who used to be respected as household favorites are now exhibited in the buff, playing scenes that attain the ultimate in communication."

Then what makes the comparatively mild pornography of 42nd Street survive that formidable competition? The answer seems to be that these theatres are largely homes-away-from-home for transients such as sailors, for panhandlers and those deviates whose search for satisfaction must always end in the briefest of encounters. For the price of a ticket, those oddballs can find shelter day or night, with warmth or coolness according to season. So alluring are these seedy emporiums of joy that they are even frequented by the opulent from stylish neighborhoods of our town who, lacking emotional roots, become drifters.

This being the sociological reason for 42nd Street, how can one explain it materially? Putting our minds to the problem, Helen and I give most of the discredit to a dear old friend we both adored named Harry Brandt. Harry was a real-estate tycoon, who over forty years ago began to buy up, one by one, the legitimate theatres that lined both sides of the block. He converted elegant spots like the New Amsterdam, which had been the home of the *Ziegfeld Follies*, into these present-day honky-tonks.

Saddened by the disappearance of so much glamour, I once asked Harry why he didn't turn them back into the legitimate theatres they once had been. "It would surely be more profitable to sell tickets for a live show," said I, "than the mere price you're getting for a movie." At which Harry argued that a legitimate theatre can be empty for long periods and, even when occupied, it functions for only about three hours a day. Whereas Harry's cinemas sold tickets twenty-four hours a day, three hundred and sixty-five days of the year.

But Harry, in addition to his holdings on 42nd Street, did own a string of legitimate theatres along upper Broadway. They were

277

grouped under the name of "The Subway Circuit," and after a play finished its season downtown it would go on a short tour for Harry Brandt. It was while Helen was playing the Subway Circuit in *Coquette* that she met Harry and, because we always share any goody we discover, she couldn't wait to introduce me to him.

Harry's unique mixture of crass Broadway cynicism and blue-eyed innocence made him the hero of some very endearing episodes. The most priceless one I remember concerned a certain play that was about to open on his circuit and was suddenly hit by a double catastrophe: the star and his understudy were both incapacitated. But in the tradition that "the show must go on," Harry jumped into the breach and addressed his first-night audience. "Looka here, folks," he said, "youse and me are in trouble. The star of this play has took sick with flu, along with ditto his understudy. So either you can get your money back, or I'll poisonally read the star's part from the scrip. But I gotta be honest and say I never set foot on any stage before in my entire, goddam life. So it's up to you to make your cherce."

Harry's face lit up with pride as he continued. "Do you know what? Not one single customer walked out!"

"And *you* read the part?" Helen gasped.

"Every woid of it!" said Harry.

I ventured to ask what the play was.

"The Barretts of Wimpole Street," answered Harry, "and the part I interperated was a fag poet by the name of Browning."

"Did you get any . . . laughs?" Helen asked gingerly.

"Are you kidding? Why, I gotta belly laugh on every line! I toined that nance poet into such a genuine, square-shooting guy that at the finish of the show, they give me a standing ovation."

"I'd have paid ten times the box-office price," exclaimed Helen, "to have seen your interpretation!" At which Harry beamed and took one more bow.

"When I think," Helen said, "that dear, sentimental Harry Brandt, whom I was constantly meeting on do-good theatre committees, had a hand in dimming the magic of Broadway it makes me sad. How could he do it? Maybe it wasn't Harry's fault, after all. Maybe neighborhoods, like some people, lose grace naturally when they grow old.

"Times Square!" Helen sighed nostalgically. "When I think of what that old place meant to me in the magical days when I had no memories, only hopes. All the most meaningful events of my youth took place here," Helen needlessly reminded me. "And sometimes when I fill out an application that requires my place of birth, I feel I ought to put it down as Times Square."

Helen was eight years old when she started as a professional on Broadway. It had only just been dubbed "The Gay White Way," which inspired the British writer G. K. Chesterton, dazzled by the electric signs, to comment, "What a fairyland this would be for anyone fortunate enough to be unable to read."

"I was able to read all those plugs for Chalmers Underwear and Melachrino cigarettes," Helen said glowingly, "and it was still fairyland to me!"

As Helen remembers Broadway, it was a parade ground for all the theatre greats. George M. Cohan would march along as if leading a parade. "He was our poet laureate! 'Tell all the boys on 42nd Street that I will soon be there.' " Or she might have had to step aside for Flo Ziegfeld, so elegant, so awesome to the likes of her as he strolled from his Pierce Arrow limousine into his theatre, The New Amsterdam. What memories that façade conjured up to Helen—Marilyn Miller in *Sunny* intoxicating her worshipers with her small voice singing "Look for the Silver Lining," or Fanny Brice reducing them to weakness with laughter at "I'm an Indian," or thrilling them with "My Man"; that lone figure, stage center, with only a lamppost for company is burned for all time in the memories of those who saw her. And right beside that vision is Bert Williams, eyes rolling, playing his poker hand close to the chest, and W. C. Fields shooting a game of billiards such as never was before or since, or bewildering the eye with his juggling act and splitting the sides with laughter at his patter; Will Rogers taking pot shots at Presidents and other natural targets with a gay good humor that seems to have got lost somewhere along the way.

"I saw them all for free," Helen reminisced. "It was the custom to have professional cards printed. Mine read, 'Miss Helen Hayes, management Lew Fields.' Then, when I was at liberty, Mother would present my card at the box office, being careful to choose an off night or a Wednesday matinee, and we'd get seats somewhere, if only in the back of a box. I well remember standing beside Mother trying to look my smallest so the box-office man would give us seats down front. A few years later I'd become a featured ingénue acting in some of those very theatres where I used to sit and gape at the stage from the other side of the footlights.

"Even now, as I gaze up at the curved window above the stone arch of the Amsterdam Theatre entrance, my heart gives a little jump, although it's fifty years since I used to take that iron cage of an elevator up to my producer, the man who made me a star, George C. Tyler. His office was small and at its end was the arched window you see from the street. A huge old roll-top desk almost hid him from view, though he could be traced by a column of smoke from the cigar that perpetually jutted above his rock-hard chin.

"Covering the office walls were photos of the stars Tyler had created, Laurette Taylor, George Arliss, Jeanne Eagels, Lynn Fontanne, Alfred Lunt, Mrs. Fiske, Emily Stevens, and, in his eyes, the star of stars, Eleanor Robson—she who had deserted him and the theatre at the peak of her career, to become Mrs. August Belmont.

"Surrounded by such luster, Tyler won every battle with me! I approached his desk, as I've been told prize fighters used to go into the ring with Cassius Clay, feeling doomed. It would have taken more grit than I had at the time or, I guess, have since developed, to stand my ground in a disagreement over the merits of a play while those illustrious eyes in the photos gazed down at me making me feel insignificant. I acted in terrible plays, *Loney*

280

Lee, Golden Days, The Wren, and several more, after having loathed them at first sight. I learned too early and too well the dubious virtue—in the theatre, at least—of humility. To this day I find it nearly impossible to turn down a bad play.

"When I think of the torture and strain I went through in my youth for those inconsequential plays! A parade of masseuses, osteopaths, voice trainers, and throat doctors were needed to get me through an opening night of such bombs as *Golden Days* or *Loney Lee* or *On the Hiring Line.* But don't ever think I'm ungrateful for those early failures. All plays, even terrible ones, were my education—even though it wasn't Mr. Tyler's reason for producing them. I learned, too, from the plays I saw when I was at the receptive age. Comedies were my first choice; I early formed the ambition to become a comedienne. I don't know how I got sidetracked for so long into tear-jerkers and tragedies. In my adolescence I loved sexy problem plays. I remember one by Cosmo Hamilton titled *Scandal* which starred Francine Larrimore. Lord knows what pretense of a plot it had. I only remember Miss Larrimore's fascinating struggle between marriage and sin. It stirred me deeply.

"We had nudity too—remember? But our nudity was beautiful! And how inspiring when Mr. Ziegfeld was its producer. Those gorgeous show girls forever descending staircases, balancing huge headdresses and manipulating yards of train which originated at the waistline in back; in front the strategic areas were chastely concealed by jewels or rosebuds."

On the subject of the *Follies* I could join my memories to Helen's, because there came a time when on vacations from Hollywood I was able to be a regular visitor to New York. And I didn't come here as a rank outsider, either. I was on the staff of Douglas Fairbanks, so a holiday for him was a holiday for his entire troupe. We would all check into the Algonquin Hotel, where we'd be in the thick of the best that Broadway had to offer: all the Barrymores (Ethel, Jack, and Lionel), Jeanne Eagels, Tallulah

281

(Tallulah Who?), and Elsie Janis; the lot. I found myself knee-deep in Broadway without having had to serve any apprenticeship.

"And do you remember, Anita, that it was on account of censorship that nudity was allowed on Broadway? There used to be a city ordinance that an actress could appear in the buff only if the pose was 'artistic' and she never moved. So Ziegfeld engaged a bona-fide painter, Ben Ali Haggin, to arrange tableaux in which some girls wore sketchy costumes, while those at center stage were stripped. No one dared to budge. Accompanying those delights was a tenor as handsome as an Arrow collar ad, who intoned such ballads as 'A Pretty Girl Is Like a Melody,' in a milk-chocolate voice.

"I remember thirty years ago when Ruby Keeler was married to the great Al Jolson and made her movie debut in Warner Brothers' *Forty-Second Street*. How innocent it all was; only a few gangsters thrown in for thrills and, at that, they had sex appeal. We girls were all in love with Humphrey Bogart."

The most elegant theatre of them all was the Empire, and that was where Helen was rehearsing her teen-age role in *Dear Brutus* on November 11, 1918, when the glorious news erupted all along Broadway: World War I was over. "Everything paper and tearable started raining down on our heads," Helen remembered. "Many a manuscript must have been shredded, never to be read again."

Rushing from the theatre, Helen started to make her way through the dense crowd to get to St. Patrick's Cathedral, where she might kneel at the altar and give thanks. But at 42nd Street the mob had been brought to a standstill by the sound of a glorious voice reverberating along Broadway. Enrico Caruso was at his sixth-floor window in the Knickerbocker Hotel booming out George M. Cohan's hymn to patriotism, "Over There."

"When the song ended, a hush descended on the crowd; the moment was too solemn for applause," Helen reminisced. "Crying like a baby, I elbowed my way toward Fifth Avenue, wanting to be among the first to reach the altar at St. Patrick's. But when I got there it was already jammed to the doors and I could only kneel on the steps outside along with thousands of others."

We could both recall the first signs that elegance was beginning to desert Broadway. "I knew we were in for it when I heard that the old Empire Theatre was to be torn down." Then Helen asked if I'd ever noticed a little pincushion covered with red brocade that she keeps on her make-up table in her dressing room. I hadn't, but I nodded noncommittally. "It's my good-luck emblem," she said, "made out of a scrap of the curtain I bought at the auction of the Empire fixtures. And then, of course, there's a piece of the balcony railing that became our bar at Nyack, the railing Brownie and I had hung over in our days of glorious poverty."

During the Forties, history once again caught up with Helen on Broadway. It was in the heyday of radio and she had a show called *The Helen Hayes Theatre of the Air*. Helen loved the excitement of radio, the immediacy of live broadcasting, the get-togethers with pals during the lunch hour at Lindy's. Irving Berlin would generally be there on a kosher diet (remembering Hester Street, maybe?). A couple of Marx Brothers would be rocking the joint, and Sophie Tucker, while looking like a Grand Duchess, would sit there exuding sexiness.

Every Sunday Helen's broadcast was presented from the Mark Hellinger Theatre. But on December 7, 1941, it was abruptly cut short by a tragic news bulletin. Pearl Harbor had been attacked.

"The next day," said Helen, "while we were still in a state of shock, we were hit by a repercussion that was only a tiny splinter from that terrible bombardment, but it killed our beloved show because our sponsor was Lipton, the importer of Oriental tea."

All the while that Helen's innocent young eyes were being dazzled by the fairy-tale aspect of show business, I was involved in its earthier realities. Stars of whom Helen only saw the glitter were my ordinary girl friends: Marion Davies, Mary Pickford, Nita

Naldi, and Marilyn Miller. I was mixing into their private lives, knew their secrets and their scandals, and later on would put some of them into a book.

The Flo Ziegfeld little Helen Hayes stood watching as he crossed the sidewalk seemed stately, authoritative, and majestic. But I saw him from the viewpoint of my friend Marilyn Miller, with whom he had the most tortured relationship. For that connoisseur of women, with the world's largest collection of full-blown American beauties, was helplessly in love with childish little Marilyn. She, with the impudence of a Lolita, could see him only as her middle-aged boss and rather a dodo. It made the most titillating gossip when Marilyn passed Ziggy up to marry the imp brother of Mary Pickford.

We girls were all involved in another fascinating love affair that had a basis of heartbreak. Fanny Brice's great hit song was "My Man," but Fanny's Man in real life was serving a prison sentence for larceny of a very grand degree.

There was one classic occasion when Nicky managed to break out of jail. He hitchhiked down to the city and when trying to cross Fifth Avenue was blocked by a parade of cops. For half an hour Nicky stood on the curb with a devilishly attractive smirk as he watched New York's finest proudly file past him. It's small wonder that Fanny loved him with the anguish and passion that only a rascal like Nicky Arnstein could evoke.

In those days Fanny burned with aspirations that I doubt Helen knew about. As a side line to her job in the *Follies,* she ran a dress shop at her apartment in the West Forties. There she designed clothes in the fashion of the expensive couturière who dressed all the best-kept ladies, Madame Frances. Any time I'd run into Fanny, she used to say, "Look, kid, why don't you come over and do a little shopping? I steal all my designs from Madame Frances and the price is right."

Fanny also carried on business as an interior decorator, for which her price was more than right, because she never charged anybody a cent. When she decorated my apartment she went even further and gave me a valuable present, a Spanish antique that had started out as a high-rise dining table. Fanny sawed a few inches off the legs and it still faces a couch in my living room.

On the day that Fanny finished my apartment, she tremulously asked, "D'you like it, baby?"

"It's just simply smashing!" I replied.

At which Fanny gasped, "I think I'm going to faint!" And she collapsed on the couch in an actual catharsis of artistic fulfillment. The achievements that made Fanny a great star seemed to her only a side line. Her real enthusiasm lay in fooling around with chintz and sewing fringe on lamp shades.

I've always been fond of certain denizens of Broadway who are only vaguely connected with show biz, fascinating oddballs of which the old street still has its quota. Today we have a magnificent example in the gentleman called Moondog who stands for hours on street corners wearing the garb of a Viking, with a helmet complete with horns, and wrapped in woolen shawls on the hottest days of summer or getting soaked by winter rains. Moondog rates himself as a songwriter, which gives no hint of a reason for his way of dressing.

And back in the Twenties there was the most adorable character named Dave Clark. Dave was fortyish, graying, handsome, and a jaunty dresser with an artificial carnation in his buttonhole. He had been a fairly successful Tin-Pan Alley songsmith until he contracted a case of premature senility and took to penning lyrics the like of which have never been written before or since, even on Tin-Pan Alley. One song that still runs through my mind was titled "When It's Peaches Time in Georgia, Was the Name He Knew the Place." Dave's habitat was Broadway, which he prowled during the night, stopping people on street corners to sing his ditties to them. He also had the lyrics printed on cards which he would pass out to all and sundry.

If I adored John Barrymore, which I did, it wasn't because of his superb Hamlet but because he, too, was ardently addicted to Dave Clark. How often I joined Jack and others of Dave's adherents spending the sweet hours of the night in Lindy's, listening to Dave recite his poems. I keep copies of them among my most precious archives. Dave was an optimist, highly religious and always at his best during the Christmas season. One of his lyrics was titled "There Is No Cruel Tide When Yuletide" and it went:

> Of all the Human Beings,
>   In any foreign sod,
> Should feel the touch for Christmas,
>   Of all the Gifts from God,
> No matter what the nation,
>   The Tears comes from your heart,
> And all their self-confessions,
>   The sound from the Church—HARK!

Dave Clark's upkeep was paid by ASCAP and by special gifts from Irving Berlin, who used to say, "No matter how hard I tried, I could never match that little guy's lyrics!"

When at length the Grim Reaper put an end to Dave's composing, all Broadway turned out for his funeral and joined in one of his own numbers:

> When you hear an ancient hymn,
>   Most infatuated,
> If you even start a rhyme,
>   You'll be saturated,
> Just try to write the lyric,
>   "Thought!" Almighty and mine,
> From the Gospel of St. Luke,
>   And take it from the line.

Those are the memories of Broadway which touch *me* to the quick.

Well, so much for the *then* and *now* of Broadway. But we still had to speculate about its future. And we ultimately got around to doing it one day when we were having lunch at Sardi's.

This has been a favorite restaurant of ours from the time we were girls. As teen-agers we went there with much the same spirit that Broadway kids go to Joe Allen's today. It was more expensive than Joe's, but Helen and I were prosperous and felt ourselves the peers of all the celebrities—the Barrymores, the Fairbanks, the Drews, and the Pickfords—who hung out there. Vincent Sardi's heritage comes to the fore in the specialties of his Italian ancestry. As we reveled in spaghetti it became evident that Helen had been doing some thinking. Now she opened up her batteries and let me in on it.

"D'you know, Anita, I think I've figured out what's the matter with our theatre. It suffers from a self-depreciation that's all too typical of New York; a sort of antichauvinism.

"I trace this attitude to a highfalutin critic of the Twenties, George Jean Nathan, who used to tell us that great theatre existed only in Middle Europe and that we could never hope to match it. I now think George chose Middle Europe because Americans didn't know much about it and couldn't contradict him. But a few years ago I went on a tour for our State Department that took us to Hamburg. There our company was addressed by its Mayor in the venerable City Hall and, referring to New York, he called it 'the fountainhead of all the arts for the entire world.' From anyone else I'd have taken this as arrant flattery, but not from an earnest, scholarly German. We've just got to begin to believe we're as good as Europeans think we are.

"And as to Broadway, the old street is *bursting* with signs that its period of shoddiness may be near an end."

Now let no one think that this last statement was merely another of the Hayes flights of fancy. It has an uncommonly solid base in fact.

One of our brightest young contractors told us that plans are being discussed to make 42nd Street a broad avenue of arcades stretching west from Broadway, something like the Rue de Rivoli in Paris. And traffic would be barred except for strolling pleasure seekers.

Helen's optimism had had further corroboration when we

learned of the playhouse now under construction in a high-rise office building at 46th Street and the Avenue of the Americas. It will be the new home of the American Place Theatre, an organization that has put into practice an entirely new concept in theatregoing. Tickets are available only to subscribers; there is no box-office sale. And all the plays are by American writers of consequence who are not yet accepted by the commercial theatre.

During the past the American Place Company has produced some enormously important works in makeshift quarters: plays that proved their worth by their long runs, several of them ultimately being done all over the world. Among performers who were first given recognition at the American Place are Dustin Hoffman, Faye Dunaway, and Sandy Duncan.

So now the organization will have a fine new home, an intimate theatre of only 299 seats, every one of which will have a perfect view of the stage. Advance bookings have already assured its first season of full houses at every performance. There will be a café where good food will be cheap, a cabaret for political and social satire, and frequent conferences will be held in which the theatre staff will exchange views with the audiences.

"How inspiring, Anita! An intellectual center for the theatre lovers of our town!"

"But, Helen, with all those highbrows milling around Sixth Avenue, think of the streetwalkers who'll be dislodged."

"*You* think of them, love!" replied Helen.

The American Place Theatre is only one of five splendid new Broadway playhouses, all of which will be open by the fall of '72. We already knew of the two theatres in the Astor Plaza building on the site of the old Astor Hotel. But there would be two more new playhouses of which we were ignorant until one afternoon when our friend Earl Blackwell dropped in at my place for a visit.

Earl conducts a deluxe public-relations bureau that keeps track of the activities and whereabouts of international society. Its center of course is in New York.

Earl came to tell us of a new project of which we were unaware. The Uris Buildings Corporation is in the process of finishing a high-rise office building on Broadway between 50th and 51st Streets. The structure includes two theatres, one of which is the largest in America (which most likely means in the world).

Helen and I have been passing that sixty-story building for over a year without being aware of its existence, possibly because the structure sits back from the sidewalk from which it is separated by a deep plaza.

Turning to me, Helen exclaimed, "Just think, Anita, with five magnificent new theatres in the Times Square area, all its human litter will automatically disappear. Prostitutes and bums aren't happy in a clean environment. I feel it in my heart that Broadway is due for a glorious renaissance!"

At which I spoke up like a killjoy. "Sometimes beautiful playhouses can result in downright trashy productions. Just look what happened with the Lincoln Center Repertory troupe!" Even that example of crass ineptitude couldn't dim Helen's euphoria. "Don't forget that even in its present dingy surroundings, Broadway has produced great theatre, like *1776* and *Fiddler on the Roof*."

Earl had yet another surprise. "Included in the Uris complex will be a Broadway Hall of Fame to record all the great theatrical talents, from the time of Edwin Booth, Joseph Jefferson, and the Christy Minstrels on down to the present.

"But," said Earl, "there won't be a quick or easy way to get in there. A star will need twenty-five years of Broadway exposure to be eligible. Even Carol Channing doesn't yet qualify. It's only twenty-four years since she first played on Broadway in *Lend an Ear*."

I thought of somebody else who's a cinch to make the grade. "I'd like to be out front some night when Jonelle Allen is tearing into the smash song hit of 1995, or reviving some of Tin-Pan Alley's old cornballs."

"That would be fine for you," said Helen, "but my eye will be trained on those young people I see all over the country working with such dedication to learn about theatre in the only training grounds left us—universities and community theatres. So many of those kids have talent. Please God, we'll welcome them!"

Take it from there, Broadway!

SUDS IN OUR EYES

*I*n spite of having contemplated Broadway, on, off, past, present, and future, we had still overlooked the one element of our theatre that has its greatest impact on the nation at large. Helen and I were on the way to round out our investigation.

At 57th Street and Eleventh Avenue Helen stopped me to exclaim, "How it overwhelms me, Anita, that out of this one corner of our town come sound waves that influence the thinking of the entire world!"

Even I was impressed, for here it is that Walter Cronkite daily broadcasts "The Evening News" and at night the "Eleven O'Clock News" is covered by Jim Jensen.

But there are other programs emanating from the many C.B.S. studios—broadcasts which affect things more vital than thought: the heartbeats and the libidos of our land. These are the eight major TV soap operas which have caused the big building to be baptized, in a sort of affectionate derision, as "The Soap Factory."

It seemed to be the hour for new shifts to arrive, and, while waiting, we watched employees stroll in. Everyone looked slick with prosperity, for they belong to an essential industry and were as sure of their jobs as one can be in uncertain times like these.

"The girls are so pretty and well turned out it's hard to tell whether they're actresses or secretaries," Helen observed.

"On the other hand," I remarked, "it's easy to spot the actors; they always walk as if their hips are important."

"How did you ever come by that observation?" Helen asked.

It dated back to the days when I was a child-bride and frequently had to wait in our car on West 44th Street while my bridegroom spent an hour or more inside The Lambs club. "It was

291

such a deadly bore that to pass the time I used to play a game with Joe, our chauffeur. We called it 'Ham.' We'd watch pedestrians as they came down the street, and when we spotted one who was headed for The Lambs, the first to say 'Ham!' won ten points. I became such an expert through watching those pedestrians' hips that I seldom lost a trick."

Helen grinned. "I remember now what a pesky mind you had in those days! And, may I add, still do!"

At which point, a C.B.S. guide appeared to take us in charge. We were first escorted to the news department. Its main room looks for all the world like the office of a big newspaper. At least thirty people sat at typewriters pounding out radio and TV items, to be handed on to the broadcasters. "What a triumph of personality these different newscasters manage to send out over the airwaves," Helen remarked, "just by sitting quietly at a desk and reading news. Have you a particular idol?"

Figuratively blushing and digging my toe into the carpet, I revealed that Walter Cronkite sends me the most. On hearing which, our friendly studio guide led us off toward a rendezvous with Walter.

After all the brouhaha of the wholesale news departments, the scene of Walter Cronkite's broadcasts was a surprise. It's about the size of a modest anteroom and contains a smallish desk above which hangs the map so familiar to Helen and me, as Cronkite fans. Behind his chair to the left is the screen on which films that illustrate his reportage are flashed. Cameras and lights are permanently fixed to walls and ceiling; a really simple setup. "Just move the one-man cast onto the set," said Helen, "press the button for silence, lights, camera, and presto—Cronkite's Evening News is on the airwaves!"

Facing the stage is a cubbyhole of an office, the front of which is of glass so that, seated at his desk, Cronkite can view the entire area. We could see a man writing at the desk, but he didn't look like Cronkite. It turned out to be Charles Collingwood, substituting for our hero, who was off in the Middle East, where the action happened to be that day. We were not let down for, with apologies to Mr. Cronkite, Charles Collingwood was all right with us. We three have been friends for many years.

Charles presently glanced up from his work, saw us, and strode manfully out to say hello. (Although as handsome as any film star, Charles has never walked like an actor.)

"Charles!" Helen exclaimed. "What a surprise to see you. I never know where you are."

"Neither do I!" said Charles.

"What were you doing just now? Answering fan mail? Starting another novel?"

But it turned out that Charles had been trying to work out the quickest way to get to Saigon, where he was due two days later. "I'm trying to decide whether to go via Japan and Hong Kong or head in the other direction and go by way of Paris, Greece, and Colombo."

"We think we have problems trying to get around in New York!" Helen observed.

"At any rate," Charles said, "whatever route I choose, I'm going to lose a whole day, thanks to the international date line." At which point Charles lost me. I was suddenly fascinated by a sign on the nearby wall. It read:

DON'T TELL 'EM NOTHING!!!!

"Now what do you make of that?" I asked.

"Could the 'em' in that phrase mean N.B.C.?"

It seemed to figure.

And then, still beset with that puzzlement, we were suddenly brought face to face with another. We passed a monitor on which *N.B.C.'s* Chet Huntley *was doing a newscast*! Now the TV world had long since said a regretful good-by to Chet, whose future, said he, would be far from the broadcasting studios. He'd be leading the life of a farmer, breathing the pure air of the Midwest countryside.

I inquired of our guide, "What *is* all this?"

"Oh," said he, "Chet does some sort of a local newscast out there where he lives. He just hires C.B.S. to process it for him."

"So," I told Helen with malice aforethought, "Chet Huntley can no more retire from TV than you can retire from the theatre."

"You're being pesky again," Helen grinned. "Shut up!"

Came the magic moment when we were to plunge into the suds. En route to the sound stages, Helen voiced her appreciation of them. "What a blessing those 'soaps' are to the world! I've heard recently that, during the last quarter century, mental illness among farm wives has been on a sharp decline. I'll bet it's because their deadly frustrations have been relieved by soap operas!" While Helen's concern was for farm wives, I was thinking of sophisticates like Cole Porter and Tallulah Bankhead who were hooked on soaps.

On reaching the first set we found everything going smoothly—no tensions, no nerves or tantrums. "One has the feeling of being in the presence of contented actors. That's rare in the theatre!" said Helen, the seasoned pro. "What a luxury to have the joy of creating added to all the comforts of privacy."

"*And*," I added, "no critics." Helen nodded, grimaced, and crossed herself.

Presently we were led onto the set where they were filming *Search for Tomorrow.* Helen joyfully found that an old friend, Richard Dunlap, was its director, and we settled down for a spell.

We watched a kitchen scene in which a sexy young housewife was stuffing a Thanksgiving turkey and, at the same time, carrying on a flirtation with an equally sexy young neighbor. But, in bald reality, we watched both the housewife and her swain contenting themselves, between takes, with hot dogs that must have gotten cold and cokes in paper cups that had probably gotten warm. All the others on the set, from actors down to the lowliest prop boy, were occupied with identical snacks. To me, the great miracle of television is that, living on that soggy diet, all those characters managed to look like normal, healthy citizens of the type that are nourished on the home-cooked food they produce in those phony kitchens.

Listening to the dialogue that day, I was reminded of Aldous Huxley, who was an enthusiastic fan of the soaps. "I'm constantly amazed at the fine quality of the dialogue," he once said to me. "The characters talk exactly as they would in real life. It is realism at its best."

"I have my own private theory about TV drama," I told Helen. "When so many of our citizens are content to sit in front of TV sets and hold still for all those goings on, our Ship of State is never going to rock, roll, or turn over. Just as the soaps are relieving housewives from ennui, they may yet save us from revolution."

Next we were taken to the master control room, where all the "takes" are given a final checking. Fascinated, we watched the monitor where programs are projected on eight or ten screens at the same time.

After a while Helen nudged me. "Look," she said, "every one of those sets is either a kitchen, a courtroom, or a hospital."

"That seems fair enough," said I. "Food can be poisoned in a kitchen, rapists may be brought to justice in a courtroom, and heroines can have illegitimate babies in a hospital. What other locale is more in key with the soap opera mystique?"

Suddenly a climax developed on one of the TV screens. In the close shot of a grieving husband who had just received proof of his young wife's infidelity, a fly lighted on his bald head.

Although exasperated that the close-up would have to be reshot, the film inspector seemed to take the matter fatalistically. And we then learned of a curse that plagues the entire institution, one that is even more peculiar than any in the TV plots themselves.

The C.B.S. studios occupy a converted building that was once a dairy depot. And now, after more than a decade, the building is still haunted by flies whose ancestors date back to the milky days when cows held sway there. They are a constant menace because one single fly that happens to alight on an actor's nose in a close-up could mean the death of romance, tragedy, or even tenderness. During filming special attendants have to be on duty with swatters to safeguard the product. But even so, the fly may not be visible until it shows up on a screen in the control room.

"The repercussions of this plague are so widespread," our guide remarked, "that they reach as far as Hammacher Schlemmer's hardware store at the other end of 57th Street. Yesterday I sent an employee to purchase a gross of fly swatters and he was immediately asked by the clerk, 'You must work at C.B.S., don't you?'"

At lunchtime one of the young executive producers took us to the cafeteria. His name is Chuck Weiss. He seemed ebullient enough to withstand the grief of all those serials. "Our whole product," said Chuck, "is based on the theme of domesticated sex. And judging by the awful snarls our characters get into, we're subtly brainwashing the public into an impression that sex is a low-down, dirty deal."

"Ah!" I exclaimed, "that's what makes all those neglected farm wives feel so content!"

When time came to depart C.B.S. Helen was summoned to the telephone on our way through the lobby. Long-distance phone calls are to Helen what flies are to C.B.S. But she dutifully obeyed the summons.

Left alone, a sensation of vast unfulfillment began to overwhelm me. I wondered why there couldn't be as many heart throbs in our own existence as we'd just viewed. "Why can't love be more the way it is on TV?" I thought.

Presently a troop of teen-agers dressed in tatty, unisex garments started to stream into the lobby from all the elevators. Inquiring at the reception desk, I learned they were students from a high school in Riverdale, on a quest for culture.

They were in the charge of a guide who looked like a teen-ager himself but, far from being tatty, wore the slick outfit of C.B.S. officialdom. He rounded the kids up and proceeded to give them a few parting statistics about what they'd just seen—propaganda slanted toward the glorification of C.B.S.

At length another young studio official showed up and approached to ask me, "You're waiting for Miss Helen Hayes, aren't you?" I nodded. "She says to tell you her call's having difficulty getting through, but please don't despair."

At which point, from out of the group of bored-looking youngsters there emerged one bright alert face. It belonged to a small brunette who could scarcely have been more than fifteen. Her miniskirt stood out neatly in contrast to the droopy wrappers worn by the other girls.

It appeared that her sharp ears had picked up Helen's name, for she bounced over, grabbed both my hands impulsively, and gasped, "Are you in show business?" Learning that I was, she exclaimed, "Then you must know Fred Astaire!" I had known Fred for years, and the fact almost threw her into a frenzy. "I love him!" she suddenly declared. "I've loved him all my life! From the very first day I ever . . ." She interrupted herself. "Wait! Just wait. I want to show you something." With trembling hands she removed a wallet from her purse, opened it, and took out at least a dozen pictures of Fred cut from magazines, tattered, torn, and smeared with lipstick. "I've collected his pictures for years," she babbled on, "and I've read everything I could ever find about him. Tell me, is he . . ." Again she interrupted herself. "No! Don't tell *me*. I'll tell *you*. And let me know if I'm right. . . . He's shy; he's very religious; he goes to church every Sunday; he loves his mother. He's shocked by his sister Adèle's language. *Am I right?*"

"You've practically told the story of his life, in depth."

At this point, Miss Quicksilver grasped my arm.

"Do you know his address? Where can I send him a letter?" I suggested that just "Beverly Hills" would be sufficient.

Before we could go any further into the life and times of Fred Astaire, we were interrupted by the teacher in charge of the tour. He started to round up the group and head them out to a bus.

Miss Quicksilver was last to leave but, as she was being pulled away, she called back to me, "Next time you see him, will you tell him about me? Will you ask if he'll answer my letter? Send me a *real* picture? With an autograph? And will you tell him that I'll . . ." By this time, the teacher had jerked her through the revolving door and removed forever her one contact with her Dream Prince.

I hope that when Fred gets Miss Quicksilver's letter he appreciates it; in case he doesn't, I can tip him off to the fact that its writer looks a lot like Audrey Hepburn, when Fred played with her in *Funny Face* and adored her.

When Helen joined me, I told her about the episode and, sentimentalist that she is, Helen beamed. Then, paraphrasing a historic anecdote about the time when a little girl named Virginia questioned the existence of Santa Claus, Helen said, "Yes, Virginia! Life *can* be a soap opera."

HOMES WERE NEVER LIKE THESE

*O*n shorter outings Helen and I often traveled by bus. One day we sat beside a tourist couple, and eavesdropped on their comments. Holding forth like a housing authority, the lady said, "These New York apartments are just like beehives. *I'd* never want to lead such a regimented existence."

We were then passing through the Grand Concourse, where, it must be admitted, the brick buildings are more or less alike. But Helen was indignant. "What would that woman know about the insides of those apartments? Their décor might be anything from gilded Louis XIV fakes on down to Museum of Modern Art oddities."

"Like my flat? No fakes, but it's full of oddities."

"Yes, I know," said Helen. "And it's got charm and individuality."

"Thanks. But some of our friends have far more individual homes. Homes as eccentric as their owners, like no others anywhere else."

SEA NYMPHS FOR NEIGHBORS

Our friend Michael Myerberg, the theatrical producer, is an individualist who knows what he wants when he sees it. He is so intelligent that sometimes even show folks call him an eccentric.

Some years ago, Michael was on an ocean liner returning to New York. As his ship approached the Narrows he looked toward the shore and saw a sight that started his mind to spin. It was a row of eleven small houses, unremarkable for anything except that their front yards took in the Atlantic Ocean.

Standing at the rail with an acquaintance, he pointed toward the shore. "See that block of houses?" he said. "That's where I'm going to move tomorrow."

"What section of the city is it in?" asked his companion.

"I haven't the foggiest notion," Michael replied. "I never saw it before."

The next morning he got in his car and started out to find the house he planned to occupy that afternoon. The shortest route to the ocean was by way of Brooklyn. Reaching the shoreline, he followed it for several miles, passed the Narrows, came upon the Atlantic, and there they were: eleven two-story houses hugging the shore in a row.

Studying them, he decided that the three in the center were the most attractive, so he pushed on in search of a real-estate office. The nearest town turned out to be Far Rockaway, where Michael was informed by a realtor that those three houses belonged to the families of a prominent firm of Fifth Avenue jewelers, Black, Starr and Frost.

A series of phone calls established that neither Black, Starr, nor Frost had the slightest intention of selling. Undaunted, Michael got the realtor to dig up a furnished apartment in Rockaway, which he moved into that afternoon, and he began to wait.

As time went on he put into practice the unfailing law of mind-over-matter. Finally, Mr. Frost's resistance broke down and he agreed to sell.

One fine Sunday, Helen and I drove out to lunch with Michael. His pink stucco house, solid enough to withstand the wear and tear of salt air, had wide verandas and a front lawn enclosed by a sea wall almost hidden by a hedge of hydrangeas.

Sybarite that Michael is, he gave us a gourmet lunch prepared by his chef, Wong. A master of Chinese cuisine, Wong was desolate because we'd come on short notice and he needs three days to prepare a decent meal. But had the menu been "decent" we'd have had to despair of our capacity.

There was a co-guest that day who was as unusual as the food,

300

Michael's grandson, Garry. He takes after Grandpa and, at nine, was qualified to talk expansively on any subject that happened to come up.

He informed us that his Grandpa's weather is ten degrees cooler than Manhattan's in summer and just as much warmer in winter and the ocean is practically unpolluted. "You see, pollution only begins at the Narrows. And it takes Grandpa less time to get to his office on Broadway than when he lived on Park Avenue and had to drive through midtown traffic."

When table talk began to veer into the past, Garry was rather out of it, but he listened avidly to what was evidently new information about his Grandpa. Michael had been the producer of Thornton Wilder's *Skin of Our Teeth* at a time when every other Broadway manager had tried to dissuade him; had warned that the play was a lot of garbled nonsense without a beginning, a middle, or an end. "I was sure the critics would feel the same," said Michael, "and the fact that Wilder's theme was the survival of the human race would go totally unrecognized. So I took the precaution of sending a typed manuscript to each of the critics and, be it said to their credit, they read the play and had some realization of its quality before they came to that triumphant first night."

I spoke of the excitement that Helen had engendered as Mrs. Antrobus in Thornton's play when it was done at the Théâtre Sarah Bernhardt in Paris. "In French, Miss Hayes?" asked Garry.

"No, darling. It was in English."

"Oh, a cultural exchange," said little Garry. "I get it!"

"Yes," Helen exclaimed. "You've certainly got it!"

After lunch we took a stroll along the beach, which was deserted except for two elderly neighbors dozing in canvas chairs. Looking off, we could see the Ferris wheel and other torture machines that tower above Coney Island. They seemed to have no influence on Michael's retreat. "I don't even have to worry about my hideout being invaded," he said. "Not even a realtor could crowd another

301

house into this corner of New York. And there's a restriction against high-rise apartments."

As we strolled the beach, Manhattan seemed so far away that Helen began to worry. "Oh dear, our book's supposed to be about New York! We surely must be outside the city limits."

"Just read that sign," said Michael, gesturing off toward a breakwater. It read: "Curb Your Dog. Help Keep *New York* Clean."

"Thank heaven," Helen sighed in relief. "But how *do* you keep this beach so spick and span?"

"No problem; the New York Sanitation Department."

When it came time to start for home, Michael and Garry drove ahead to guide us as far as Coney Island, there to meet Michael's favorite neighbors. They occupy the New York City Aquarium, and we shall always envy Michael for them. The most exciting are three fat, snow-white whales. They are housed in outdoor tanks that extend down beneath a terrace into an enclosed area. There we stood and studied them from every angle as they swam, snoozed in comfort, or opened their small, ridiculously round, baby-blue eyes to wink at us. It seemed incredible to me that such enormous hulks could be so cute!

While on the subject of cuteness, we went on to visit the Aquarium's sixty or more penguins, and later watched a vaudeville show that's given by dolphins every afternoon at four.

"How lucky you are, Michael," I said on the way back to our cars. "Any time you're fed up with the show-biz characters of Broadway, you can just slip over to the Aquarium and get back your esteem for the living."

That remark earned me a black look from Helen and a grin of assent from Michael. "You could be right about show folks, Miss Loos," Garry said, "if you'd just leave out my Grandpa."

OUR FRIEND WHO THINKS LIKE A FISH

By far the kookiest of all New York pads belongs to Luther Greene. At one time Luther was an actor, married to an actress friend of ours, Judith Anderson. He also produced plays, among them several of Judith's. "If he still produced them," Helen commented, "he'd never have allowed her to stub her toe last year trying to play Hamlet."

Be that as it may, Luther has given up the theatre and turned an extraordinary talent for gardening into a new profession; he is the designer for many of the penthouse gardens of New York.

"If you'll excuse the pun," said Helen, as we wended our way toward the Greene ménage, "Luther must also have green thumbs." His fruit crops are so plentiful that some of his clients have founded the Sutton Place Jelly Company, Inc., which puts up enough apple, mint, and grape jelly from their own roof trees to supply their families and provide gifts for Christmas.

"When I talked to Luther on the phone this morning," said Helen, "he remarked, 'This has been a bumper year for grapes! One of my best vines has climbed all over a water tower on East 57th Street. They'll have to harvest those grapes pretty soon or their weight will pull the water tower down.'"

Unique as Luther's profession is, it pales into insignificance in the light of his home, a residence which is nothing less than a grotto, complete with stalactites, stalagmites, a waterfall, and an indoor brook.

Luther's apartment was originally the cellar of a brownstone. It occupies a utility section that was once the kitchen, laundry, boiler room, and whatever else goes on in the bowels of a grand old house. Now they have all become a somewhat dank living room, bedroom, dressing room and bath, a minuscule kitchen and a dining room, which boasts a waterfall and a fish pool. In every room the walls are covered with thousands of sea shells in all colors, shapes, and sizes, arranged by Luther himself in intricate designs. The big round dining table, where we sat for tea, is encrusted with shells. So are the chairs, which, alas, can cause snags in one's pantyhose.

Knowing that Luther doesn't mind being kidded, I told him, "We rather expected you'd serve us ocean water for tea."

"And," added Helen, "toasted sea urchins could be much more to the point than muffins."

At any rate, the over-all effect is staggering, not to say improbable. The only reason for it seems to be that Luther was born under the sign of Aquarius, which makes him as near as any human can be to a fish.

Later, on our way home, Helen remarked, "When I stood in the doorway of that shell-covered living space, I was swept back to a moment of my childhood when I was taken to Captain Young's home at the end of his Million-Dollar Pier in Atlantic City. Its walls were one solid scab of sea shells and at the age of nine I thought it the most beautiful sight I would ever witness. But even Captain Young's place didn't boast a waterfall."

An unspoken thought I'd been holding back now surfaced. "Don't you think that the misty air at Luther's place might give him arthritis?"

"If fish don't get arthritis, why should he?" asked Helen.

HOW TO LIVE RENT-FREE IN A MANSION

Accompanying us the day we started for the Old Merchant's House at 29 East 4th Street were two friends, Tom Ellis, a young actor and our Village guide, and Betty Kauffman, Director of Nurses at Bellevue Hospital. "This house we're going to see is said to have been the inspiration for Henry James's novel *Washington Square*," said Helen. "So we're going pretty far afield." But when Betty heard Tom Ellis give the address to our taxi driver, she felt right at home. "East 4th Street!" she exclaimed. "That's where we pick up most of our stab cases."

Which caused Tom to remark, "From today's stab cases to the restrained elegance of Henry James opens up quite a wide social gap."

When we arrived at the handsome front door with its lacy fanlight and Ionic columns, we found a not-so-handsome sign proclaiming that the house was closed for August. Undaunted, Tom rang the bell several times until finally a third-story window opened and a young woman appeared. "The house is closed! Can't you read?" she called down wearily. Tom gestured toward Helen. "But this is Miss Helen Hayes!" The young woman gave a start, cast a brief glance at Helen, and called down, "Don't go 'way. I'll be right with you." She came to the door so quickly that she might have slid down the early American banisters. Trailing her was a pretty little two-year-old girl.

Our cicerone proved to be Mrs. Davis, an actress as yet undiscovered by Broadway. Her husband is a painter, as yet undiscovered by the art world. But the baby, who has already discovered herself, made no problem of expressing her own cute personality. The Davises live there, rent-free, as caretakers. Actually, their home, although shabby, is one of the more elegant abodes in town.

The house was built early in the nineteenth century by a merchant named Seabury Tredwell. His fortune having dwindled by the time he died, in 1865, his descendants were forced to put the house up for auction. It was bid in with its contents by George Chapman, a distant relation of the Tredwells. He presented it to the city as an example of a gracious old New York home and provided a fund to maintain it.

This fund is inadequate to keep the place in order nowadays. The beautiful Brussels carpets are threadbare; the period furniture, some of it designed by Duncan Phyfe, is badly in need of repair; walls and carved woodwork cry out for attention.

"We make out the best we can," said Mrs. Davis, "but there just isn't money enough to do all the things we should."

Helen tried to reassure her. "Just the same, the old place is still here with its original furniture, drapes, and chandeliers. No amount of rust and wear can keep their beauty from shining through." She sat gingerly on a rickety loveseat. "I can almost see Henry James sitting here tête-à-tête with Edith Wharton, sipping tea."

Her daydream about that literary tea party might have gone on interminably, so I urged, "Come along, Helen. The old teacups are cracked now and folks socialize today with a different kind of 'tea.' "

As we left, Helen insisted that we issue a serious message about the Old Merchant's House. "After all," she said, "the Davises have coaxed the garden back into a semblance of its old charm and, with a little financial help, they could give New York City back one of its treasures in pristine order."

LA VIE DE BOHÈME

Tom Ellis, again serving as our Village guide, escorted us to a huge complex of studio apartments which are a far cry from the Old Merchant's House. The project could only have been realized by someone of enormous wealth plus an equal amount of love for art and artists; in short, a person such as Jacob Kaplan.

Westbeth has been converted from an old thirteen-building complex that formerly belonged to the Bell Telephone Laboratories. It is at the juncture of West and Bethune Streets, which gave it its name. It is a haven for artists, who can live in sympathetic surroundings at very low rent.

"Is it only for painters?" Helen asked Tom.

"Painters, poets, composers, designers of every sort, from costume jewelry on up to heroic sculptures." Westbeth is a godsend to sculptors who need an extra-large space for their work.

In front of Westbeth is a broad playground, with scientific equipment for climbing, swinging, and falling off of, and painted in the garish colors beloved of childhood. It was swarming with young fry, dressed in fanciful garments, as the children of artists should be. We had to drag a lot of them away from Helen, she being a classic symbol of motherhood to all youth.

We next had to pull her past the ground-floor studios where, through the windows, we could see exhibits of several painters on display. Sightseeing with Helen is largely a matter of dragging her away from things.

To lead us to the studio of Tom's friend Robert Patrick Sullivan, Tom guided us through the enormous downstairs hallway, where we came upon the first evidence of Westbeth's communal spirit, a wide bulletin board to which were tacked messages from occupants to their neighbors. One of them reported: "Our cat has just had kittens. Any takers?" Another read: "Can someone supply a bed for our weekend guest? He isn't choosy."

We found Mr. Sullivan's quarters to consist of a big white studio. It is longer than it is wide, and has a broad window that reaches high up to the ceiling. Daylight was streaming all over the place. There is a screened-off kitchen area and a smallish bathroom, sufficient for a bachelor's needs.

Patrick Sullivan turned out to be tall, gaunt, handsome, and bronzed. "He looks just like a young Indian chief," Helen said, in an aside. I agreed. But what he *doesn't* look like is a designer of tiny three-dimensional collages, some of their elements being miniature toys from the five-and-dime stores. And they are contained in box frames of Patrick's own manufacture.

Much of his work is done on order, to symbolize the personality of the owner. He had just finished a collage to commemorate his own birthday—"A sort of autobiography told in bits and pieces," he called it. It is colorful and exquisite.

"But," said Helen, "I only wish he had included some Indian wampum."

"Perhaps he couldn't afford it."

After offering us tea, Patrick took us to the rooftop gardens of Westbeth where we saw vegetables that are organically grown by the whole community. Because of a ruling against vegetable beds as being too weighty, the organic spinach, carrots, peas, and even corn are forced to do the best they can in outsized flower pots.

Adjacent to those rooftop vegetables is the largest studio in the entire complex. Its sculptor tenant wasn't home, but peering through his windows we saw a simply enormous statue of an omnisexual nude. "The only other place big enough for it will have to be Mount Rushmore," said Patrick.

"Except," I reminded him, "those other statues might turn their backs on it and cause a landslide."

Before departing that Alice in Wonderland world of modern art, Patrick took us to the first-floor office where Jacob Kaplan's daughter, Joan Kaplan Davidson, holds forth as president. If Westbeth is a product of the present, Mrs. Davidson's quarters belong distinctly to the future. Their décor includes one art work in which the medium is light waves, motivated by electricity.

Mrs. Davidson is a beautifully spare type of aristocrat who resembles Katharine Hepburn and wore her slacks with the same dash. She must take after her father in spirit because she has dedicated her life to being a den mother to his artist protégés.

Helen asked if she had any favorites among all those geniuses. "They're like all people," she said, "some are lovable and some are a great big nuisance. But there are a few who are acclaimed all over the world. There's Muriel Rukeyser, the poet, and Stefan Volpe, the composer. And really great artists, of course, are always lovable."

To Helen it all looked so artistically domestic that, when we went on our way, she enviously asked how one could get into Westbeth. "All one has to do is to produce an income tax record that proves you're broke," said Patrick.

"That should be easy!"

"Maybe," he replied, "but there's a waiting line as long as the building is high."

"I should think the chief requirement for getting into Westbeth," I said, "is a miracle."

So Helen still lives contentedly at Pretty Penny in Nyack.

308

HOME IS WHERE YOU FIND IT

One day while talking on the phone to the young playwright Mart Crowley, I asked him for his home phone number and thought it sounded familiar. Then later, when time came to send out Christmas cards, I found I didn't have Mart's address so I called his number to inquire. An unusually pleasant voice answered, saying, "Algonquin Hotel. May I help you?"

No wonder Mart's number sounded familiar! I asked if Mr. Crowley had checked out yet. "Oh, no," said that pleasant lady. "He lives here permanently, but he's in California for a few days. Sorry!"

"That's all right," I told her, "I only wanted his mailing address."

"With this present mail service your letter may not get here before he does," she commented. "And if I recognize your voice, this is Miss Loos, isn't it?"

"How did you ever guess?" I asked.

"It's a gift," she said as she rang off.

When I told Helen of the incident she asked, "How long is it since that operator heard your voice?" But I couldn't even remember when I'd last phoned someone at the hotel.

And then, misty-minded with nostalgia, Helen said, "Why not go there for lunch, just the two of us, tête-à-tête, as we did in the old days?"

"I don't recall we ever lunched tête-à-tête in the old days, Helen. I didn't have much truck with you at that time."

"I know, darling, but never mind, we can make up for it now."

When Helen phoned the Algonquin for a reservation, *her* voice was accountably recognized. Then, half an hour later, the news of our plan must have filtered through the hotel, for Helen got a call from the company's president, Ben Bodne, who insisted that lunch be on him.

"How yummy!" Helen said when she told me. "That means something special!"

"*And* on the cuff!" I added.

"Yummy again!" said Helen.

The day of our date with Mr. Bodne, the New York weather was at its best, cool but sunny. And that morning, when we left our publisher's office at Third Avenue and 48th, Helen said, "Let's walk to the Algonquin." So we started across 48th Street.

"How well I understand Mart's making his home at the Algonquin!" Helen mused. "All those years when he starved in Hollywood while he was writing *The Boys in the Band*, he must have dreamed of belonging to the New York scene, just as you and I did when *we* were kids!" She sighed. "In those days we rubbed shoulders in the elevator with all three Barrymores and Tallulah and Henry Mencken. And today Mart does the same with Larry Olivier, whenever Larry's in town. And those two French boys when they're here to visit their plays *Cactus Flower* and *Forty Carats*. I always get those boys mixed up. Which is which?"

"Jean Pierre Grédy looks the more ribald of the two, but Pierre Barillet *can* put up a serious front when required."

By this time we had crossed Lexington Avenue and right there on the corner ran smack into another outpost of our past: the pharmacy of Caswell-Massey, the oldest in the United States. We stopped to press our noses against the window where there was a display of the cologne once beloved of George Washington and supplied to him by the selfsame firm. "To freshen up after the Battle of Brandywine!" I suggested.

"*And*," said Helen, "to send a bottle to the Marquise de Lafayette and let her know her husband wasn't in a land of total savages."

In the second window there were little jars of Patwe's Lime Chutney, Brinjal Pickle, and Manley's Ginger Marmalade. Looking at them gluttonously, Helen asked, "D'you think we dare take time . . . ?"

I glanced at my watch. "We'll *take* time and grab a taxi when we leave." So, in we went.

Luck was with us, for Mr. Taylor, the co-owner of the firm, was in attendance, having just come in from a scouting trip to the Near East, rounding up a special kind of attar of roses.

Chatting as we looked about, Helen told him of a recent visit when she bought a present for Alfred Lunt and had asked that it be accompanied by a copy of their catalogue. "When Alfred wrote to thank me," said Helen, "he added a postscript to say, 'Lynn has read the catalogue from cover to cover and says it gives her a great feeling of security to learn that one is still able to purchase bear grease.' "

But there was no whiff of bear grease in the air that day. It was redolent of Devon Violets, Patchouli, and Vetiver.

As I asked who wrote their delectable catalogue, Mr. Taylor himself took the credit. Only a writer truly inspired by his subject could turn out its exotic phrases: "Lavender Water from Yorkshire, prepared according to a 250-year-old formula; Seaweed Soap from Spain for Nature lovers; eggplant pickled with green chillies . . . some combination! Chewing gum that's made—guess where? . . . In *Paris!* Barley sugar drops and old-fashioned razors from the Auvergne district of France."

"Shades of our great-grandmothers!" I heard Helen exclaim. She had found those little booklets of tissue paper impregnated with face powder to carry in one's purse—beg pardon—reticule. The repair job they'd do on a shiny nose would be too minuscule to make any impression on a Max Factor pancake make-up. "They were only allowed in Grandma's day," mused Helen, "provided she shielded her face with her fan while the application went on!"

"How could she have done that with only two hands?" I asked.

Changing the subject, Helen went on reminiscing. "When I was playing Josh Logan's version of *The Cherry Orchard* this store was the only place in New York where I could find beauty spots.

311

They're put up in envelopes with the original old lettering and come in every size and shape: stars, hearts, half-moons and butterflies!"

By now we were due at our lunch date and, when bidding Mr. Taylor good-by, I chided him that I'd heard his shop had gone commercial.

"Don't let that worry you," he stated. "We *are* opening departments in various big stores throughout the country, but only for our main items. The bald-heads of the world will still have to send here for their bear grease."

At the Algonquin Ben Bodne was waiting for us near the door. Studying the lobby as we entered, Helen said, "It all looks so much the same as it did in the old days that we scarcely notice things any more."

"Yes," said Ben, "but it's only the same through colossal effort. Oliver Smith has just done the place over." He gestured toward a love seat. "He was dying to change the upholstery on that," he said, "but I forced him to smother his personality and keep it just as it was when Mary Pickford and Doug Fairbanks sat there and began a love affair that shook up the universe."

On our way to the dining room Ben stopped to point out the frosted globe on one of the lamps. "This design went out of existence in the early Twenties, so today we have them reproduced by hand at an unheard-of expense. We could, of course, substitute a modern globe when one gets broken, but it wouldn't be the same."

We lunched in the small, side dining room where Charlie used to court Helen, away from the leering coterie at the Round Table. The food, being American, is the kind Americans can eat every day and not tire of. In honor of our past, we both had chicken pie.

After lunch Ben took us on a tour which ended in an unoccupied apartment on the top floor. Ben indicated a doorknob of the type in vogue when everything was done by hand and pretty fancy. "We have to keep a stock of these," he told us, "because so many college kids come here on weekends and wrench them off as souvenirs."

The apartment's furnishings, woodwork, and wallpaper were quite chaste and proper. "Your friend Mart occupies a similar suite," Ben told us, "but of course he has a lot of personal photos around."

"Noël Coward?" Helen asked.

"Naturally, and all the other friends Mart's made here."

For all the Algonquin's renown among sophisticates, Ben is perhaps even more proud of the fact that it's as folksy as a New England wayside inn. It is even included in a guidebook devoted to back roads and country taverns—the only metropolitan hotel to attain that wholesome rating.

On our way out we passed a group of Frenchmen holding forth vociferously in the lobby. "They're a contingent from Paris to the New York Film Festival," said Ben. "I felt obliged to warn their leader that they'd be better off staying closer to their headquarters at Lincoln Center than here. So now they're talking it over."

Helen and I stretched our ears and heard their leader say, *"Monsieur Bodne dit qu'ici nous serons bien loin de Lincoln Centre."*

"Mais j'aime cette atmosphère de vieux New York," spoke up another, *"et la cuisine Américaine très . . . intéressante. Ici nous serons . . ."* He groped for a phrase . . . *"Ici nous serons* at home."

Smiling up at our host, Helen said, "An excellent substitute for home in any language is *Algonquin*."

And Ben, whose feelings for his hotel amount to an unadulterated obsession, beamed.

THE GHOST WHO WON'T MOVE OUT

Helen and I approached the historic Jumel Mansion at West 160th Street and Edgecombe Avenue with mixed feelings. On

Helen's side, reverence for our colonial past; on mine, an even keener interest in an alleged murderess who went as a bride to the mansion but whose ghost refuses to move out.

Its spacious lawns and garden cover a high hill and the view takes in the entire city. The house, for all its years, looks almost new. It is painted white, has a portico with four impressive columns; a second-floor balcony sports a decorative wooden grille and the roof is crowned by dormer windows and ornamental railings.

Trudging up the steep path, I stopped Helen in the front yard. "This is where a group of school children were waiting for the museum to open one morning when they heard a woman screaming at them in a cracked voice: 'Stop making that noise! Go away now! *Scat!*' Looking up, the children saw a witchlike old creature in a bright red dress, glowering down on them from the balcony. While they gaped up at her, the old woman suddenly turned and departed by going through a *closed* door—red dress and all."

"Now, Anita, what ghost ever wore a red dress?"

"Wait till you hear the rest! The children asked an attendant about the old woman who lived there. There was no old woman. The house is without any occupant until it opens every day as a museum. What those children saw was the ghost of that murderess!"

Now, Helen had once visited the museum in the distant past and she was skeptical. "Personally, I have my doubts about that famous murder. There wasn't any mention of it in the guidebook I read!"

"Guidebooks are required to be stuffy," I insisted.

So Helen gave in far enough to say, "Well then, when we meet the curator, *you* ask her about it."

We had made an appointment over the phone with the curator, Mrs. LeRoy Campbell, and I had visualized her as a grim caretaker of the spooky type one finds in *Wuthering Heights*. But she proved to be bouncy, attractive, and so normal that I hesitated to mention that ghost.

As Mrs. Campbell showed us around the house, there was plenty to satisfy Helen's appetite for old furniture, paintings, *objets d'art*, knickknacks, gimcracks, and, in a well-stocked playroom, any number of early American toys.

In addition to Americana, the mansion contains a certain quota of Napoleonana. Leading us up to Madame Jumel's bedroom, Mrs. Campbell said, "The lady was an ardent Francophile. She had once journeyed to France and dragged home an enormous amount of loot." She gestured toward an impressive mahogany Empire bed. "That's Napoleon's own bed! Madame bought it in Paris and brought it across the Atlantic in a packet ship."

Another room had been used by George Washington as an office during the Revolution. Admiring its Federal décor, Helen kept saying, "What simplicity! What taste! What purity!" I almost expected her to salute the American flag beside the desk where General Washington made out the payrolls for his army. This was not the moment to bring up the subject of a ghost, so I continued marking time. In the next room were memorabilia of Aaron Burr, during the short time he occupied it as her husband.

Mrs. Campbell next showed us the life-sized portrait of Madame Jumel in the spacious hallway. As pretty as a movie star, she sits benignly between a young niece and a nephew. "How touching!" Helen exclaimed.

That portrait didn't fool me. The artist, Alcide Ercole, must have painted it under instructions from Madame herself, for her expression is too saccharine to be true. It seemed so phony that, in half a glance, I concluded she could have committed murder. I seized this chance to ask about her ghost, and Mrs. Campbell didn't let me down. But first she related the story of the murder.

"Stephen Jumel, who was a lot older than his beautiful wife, fell off a hayrack one morning and burst an artery. Bleeding profusely, he was carried to a third-floor room just at the head of the stairs." (I gaped up toward the room, as did Helen.) "A doctor staunched the blood by binding up his wound, then left the patient in care of his wife. Madame soothed her husband to sleep, and then she proceeded to search through his papers for a will. As she suspected, it cut her off from his fortune of over four million dollars.

"Realizing that should Jumel die intestate, his estate would legally go to her, Madame is said to have tossed the will into a fire. Then she tiptoed to her husband's bedside and ripped off his bandage.

"At daybreak the self-made widow roused her household to inform them tearfully that poor dear Stephen had torn the bandage off his artery in his delirium, and was no more.

"But just the same," Mrs. Campbell continued, "I doubt Madame Jumel's spirit is altogether evil. I've even had evidence that it's trying to compensate for some of her wickedness."

"How?" Helen and I asked simultaneously.

"About two years ago a young man showed up here and asked leave to go to the third floor and remain alone there for a few minutes. It was a strange request," said Mrs. Campbell, "but I was busy, so I told him to go ahead."

"A little later he came down and stopped to thank me. I then had a chance to quiz him. Somewhat reticently, he gave me a cryptic account of a visit he'd made to the museum at the age of eleven. He had wandered alone onto the third floor, where something happened he could never forget.

" 'A bad experience?' I asked him. 'Oh no,' he said, 'it was very pleasant.' And then he explained why he'd come back this day. It seemed he was soon leaving for Vietnam and wanted to find out whether he'd come back alive. 'And did you find out?' 'Oh yes,' he replied with a jubilant smile. 'Everything's going to be all right. I'll be coming home in good shape.' "

Mrs. Campbell was anxious to learn just what had happened to the young man on the third floor. But then the museum was invaded by a group of tourists. When she looked for the young man, he had left.

"Only recently," she continued, "the young veteran of Vietnam came back here, hale and hearty, but he still refused to tell what had happened on the third floor that day.

"And now, if you come to my office, I can even show you a photograph of the ghost."

This was satisfaction beyond my wildest hopes, and by this time even Helen was awed. We followed Mrs. Campbell into her tiny cubbyhole, where she pulled a dim photograph from a stack of documents. The truth is, it took a little imagination to pick out the ghost, but once we did, we couldn't see anything else.

"Do you think we could meet the photographer?" I asked.

"I believe so," said Mrs. Campbell, and she gave me his name and number.

No sooner did I get home than I called Irwin Baeder, who lives on the Grand Concourse. Mr. Baeder was agreeable to paying me a visit, but sounded rather timorous about it. For a man brave enough to snap a ghost that seemed surprising. Was my apartment in a mugging district? he asked, and was relieved to learn that while West 57th Street might possibly be a mug area, it had enough traffic to make it self-protective.

At the time of Mr. Baeder's visit Helen was away, so he had none of her skepticism to contend with. A commercial photographer, he had developed a hobby of photographing the Jumel Mansion's architectural details.

"I can turn my camera in any direction there and find something important to document. Mrs. Campbell is very co-operative. She allows me to work in the museum on quiet days when there are no scheduled groups going through. On the day I took this picture I was focusing on the staircase and naturally thought I was alone."

"You weren't even thinking of the ghost?" I asked.

"Oh no! I was only interested in the balustrade and the newel post. I hadn't even noticed the framed indenture that hangs halfway up the stairs. Then I developed the negative."

Impressively, he handed me a copy of the photo. "The ghost

was apparently standing just above me on the second floor," he explained, "so that her figure was reflected in the glass of the framed indenture on the wall—a woman in a colonial bonnet and a lace jabot."

Staring at the photo of that murderous colonial dame's ghost, I got the most delicious thrill and goose pimples since the last Hitchcock movie I'd seen. And I was glad Helen wasn't present, for with her Catholic skepticism she might have scoffed at my credulity.

CHÂTEAU ON 57TH STREET

"Well, Anita," said Helen, "you of all people must take pleasure in reporting that old-world elegance is alive, well, and flourishing on a New York roof."

She was speaking about the sixteen-room penthouse on top of the building in which I live. It is a replica of an eighteenth-century French château, complete with carved woodwork, chinoiserie, crystal chandeliers, and a lofty white-and-gold ballroom where the murals might have been painted by Fragonard. A row of tall French windows opens on a formal garden with a lawn, flowers, trees, and an ancient stone fountain.

This is the home of Mr. Earl Blackwell, who had been so helpful to us in charting the future of the New York theatre. The staff of Earl's château is presided over by Miss Phoenix, who looks like an eighteenth-century marquise. During our visit she made tea for us because the butler was on a holiday abroad.

Sitting at a table in his solarium, we asked Earl how his career began. "Well," he said, "I had just three hundred dollars and an idea. My capital was sufficient to pay one month's rent on a tiny office in an offbeat area and to order some printed stationery that read 'Celebrity Service.'

"My first interview was with the publicity head of M-G-M's New York office. I tried to sell my services as a go-between to connect M-G-M stars with social, charity, or promotional events that could put their glamour to good use. But M-G-M was very leery of letting such precious assets fall into the wrong hands."

Both Helen and I could understand that. When we two worked at the M-G-M studios on the West Coast, the most elaborate precautions were taken to protect the public images of their stars. I used to think that Howard Strickling, the publicity chieftain, spent more time covering up for stars like Lana Turner and Jean Harlow than he did in publicizing them.

"It took all my persuasiveness," Earl went on, "to get them to understand that I didn't mean their glamour girls any harm. Finally convinced that I was trustworthy, M-G-M became my first client. They agreed to supply me with information on the comings and goings of all their stars. And with this as my only asset I went in search of a customer.

"My first prospect was C.B.S., and after my difficulties with M-G-M I was prepared for a setback. To my amazement C.B.S. simply grabbed at my idea. They were always in need of personalities for guests on radio talk shows, and if I could supply a weekly list of the whereabouts of stars it would save the network infinite time and trouble. 'How much do you charge for your service?' asked C.B.S. And, bad businessman that I was, I settled for ten dollars a month."

"I think you've never been a good businessman," said Helen. "That may account for your success."

This is true. Earl's greatest asset is his genuine adoration of his famous clients. He has never gotten over being a fan and, because nothing succeeds like sincerity, his business has grown by leaps and bounds. He now maintains offices in New York, Los Angeles, London, Paris, and Rome. He publishes *The Celebrity Register*, with biographies of international V.I.P.s, and issues a daily newsletter listing their whereabouts, with addresses and telephone numbers.

Earl's subscribers include shops, business houses, publishing and theatrical firms; every sort of institution that needs to know who's who and where at any given moment. He also gets out an annual containing useful information for New York pleasure seekers, such as diagrams of all theatre seatings.

He is one of the few sophisticates who, these days, keeps a guestbook. Fetching it for us to sign, he opened it to show us a bold, clear entry: the signature of Greta Garbo. "Where did you ever get that?" I asked.

"Right here. Greta came with a few of my friends one day. When they signed this book, Greta watched as the others avoided her in passing it around. Suddenly she blurted out, 'What *is* this? Don't you want *my* signature?' I tried to play it cool and told Greta, 'Please don't sign if it will embarrass you.' 'But I want to,' she said. 'This is fun.' "

Many of Earl's friends make his penthouse their home on a visit to New York. When Noël Coward spent a week there, he asked if Earl would mind his renting a piano. Yes, Earl would mind. For he went right out and bought the Steinway concert grand that now stands in his ballroom.

"I wish I could coddle my guests like that," Helen sighed.

She asked him about the loss of glamour in theatrical celebrities these days. "Remember the party for Gloria Swanson last week in Shubert Alley? The young fry were all in Levi Strausses and only stars of another era had glamour. They took plenty of pictures of us, but at our age to see one's picture in the paper comes as a nasty shock."

"The young people of show business are problems," Earl confessed, "because they've discarded the gentility which should be the basis of all social life. Maybe that's why I've bought an old house in Atlanta with a garden and magnolia trees, a retreat where one can find the gentility that's died out everywhere else."

IF YOU HAVE TO BE

BORN IN A GHETTO . . .

*O*n one of our last forays, Helen and I set off in pursuit of a part of our youth. We were making a return visit, after more than fifty years, to the old Neighborhood Playhouse in a lower East Side slum. The theatre, as we remembered it, was a small colonial-type building which glittered at nighttime like a diamond on a trash heap.

The Playhouse was an adjunct of the Henry Street Settlement, which was dedicated to the relief of poverty and ignorance among the poor, mainly immigrants from Russia, Italy, and Ireland. Largely owing to the schooling provided by the Settlement, the children of those immigrants became almost instant Americans and the smartest of them were soon polished New Yorkers.

The Settlement gave courses in all the arts, and the drama students used to write and act intimate little revues which they produced at the Neighborhood Playhouse. They were done with such wit and élan that uptown Manhattanites used to troop downtown to see them. It was the smart thing to do and worth a long ride into the messy but not yet crime-ridden slums.

The revues, called *The Grand Street Follies*, satirized the hit plays of the Broadway Establishment and poked fun at its most eminent stars.

On our way to the old Playhouse a wellspring of happy memories opened up. "I'll never forget, Anita, when Edith Meiser, then unknown, did a burlesque of Lynn Fontanne as Queen Elizabeth."

Helen, too, had her come-uppance when a little actress named Paula Truman did an impersonation of her that was just too awfully cute. But those satires were done in fun and good taste; they not only had wit but were pretty instructive to their victims. "These days," Helen sighed, "they don't poke fun at the successful. They poke daggers."

I recalled a certain incident in which those brats of the Neighborhood Playhouse came a cropper and lost out, hands down, to the Establishment. It all involved the eminent dramatic star, Emily Stevens. Emily was eccentric and full of quirks, one of which was negligence of her very good looks. In spite of her glorious golden hair, green eyes, and majestic stance, she could only be called, to use a vulgar word, a slob.

Now, Emily had a devoted pal named Nathan Gibson Clarke, a fashionable milliner of that day. One morning Nate was awakened by an alarming phone call. *The Grand Street Follies*, he was informed, would include a skit that night in which Emily Stevens' big, tragic scene in *Fata Morgana* would take a ribbing. Worst of all, she would be played by Albert Carroll, an outrageous young female impersonator wearing a messy wrapper and a tousled fright wig. As usual, all Broadway would be at that premiere. Emily might never be able to live it down.

Determined to save his adored friend, Nate cooked up a plan. It required Emily's co-operation, so he closed shop early, hurried over to her apartment, and explained what he had in mind. The idea tickled Emily and she immediately proceeded with its first step, which was to get into her somewhat neglected bathtub and give herself a good scrubbing. Meanwhile Nate summoned a leading hairdresser, who rushed over to do Emily's hair in a dazzling marcel wave. To finish the project in high style, Nate then borrowed a Paquin gown, an ostrich feather fan, and an ankle-length chinchilla cloak from Mrs. August Belmont.

That night a metamorphosed Emily strode down the aisle of the Playhouse on the arm of Nate. Grinning like a Cheshire kitten, she greeted friends to right and left with a gay flick of her fan. Amazed, people began to ask, "What has Emily Stevens done to herself?" When the skit that lampooned her came on, the audience sensed the stratagem and broke into applause, not for her impersonator but for Emily herself.

"That dear, talented, holy mess of an Emily," exclaimed Helen. "How she shone in an era that was far from drab."

Aside from our happy memories of the old Neighborhood Playhouse, we recalled its grim surroundings: cluttered tenements and sidewalks swarming with derelicts. "If the city's so much worse now, what can the neighborhood look like today?"

"It must be frightening," said Helen.

But when our car turned into Henry Street we got the surprise of our lives. Before us spread a view of about five blocks which, I venture to say, is now one of the most attractive sights in town. The Federal-type houses, recalling a once gracious way of life, had been restored and were shining in the midday sun. A new, red brick housing project for middle-income families harmonizes with the old neighborhood's cozy charm.

Open spaces, though not planted as parks, are immaculately clean and provide ample breathing space. In the near distance looms the old Williamsburg Bridge to Brooklyn. There wasn't a derelict in sight, and children in the streets and playgrounds were tidy, well dressed, and well behaved.

When we had first decided to go down to Henry Street we were advised to contact the director of the Settlement, Mr. Bertram M. Beck, who graciously offered to give us a guided tour of the whole area.

We found that Mr. Beck conforms to the type we've come to recognize as the modern New York executive: spare, rangy, and handsome like our Mayor and Mr. Haack of the New York Stock Exchange.

Mr. Beck informed us, first of all, that the project, which in our youth was simply called the Henry Street Settlement, is now called the Henry Street Settlement Urban Life Center. "The new words carry on the ideals of Lillian Wald, who founded the Settlement nearly eighty years ago," said Mr. Beck. "Only last week I went to her installation into the New York University Hall of Fame. It took a long time, but she made it."

The Settlement got its start when Jacob Schiff purchased for Miss Wald an old house at 265 Henry Street in the heart of a downtown ghetto. As it turned out, her use of it couldn't have been improved on. In the seventy-nine years of its existence, the project has had only two heads preceding Mr. Beck. Following Lillian Wald came Helen Hall, who carried along in the tradition of its founder until Mr. Beck took over five years ago.

He showed us through the executive offices and public rooms which occupy the very house first bought by Jacob Schiff for Lillian Wald. We entered a spacious lobby which at the time was shared by a Puerto Rican receptionist and the telephone exchange. "Most of the people on the staff come from the neighborhood and represent the different ethnic groups that live down here," said Mr. Beck. "This is just one more way of making connections with the community."

Off the lobby is an art gallery where the exhibitions of students' work are held. Across from it is a salesroom for ceramics which are largely done by children. We had no time to shop, but there's a comic cat that I'll acquire as soon as I can get back there.

We went on into an expansive dining room, furnished in Federal antiques which have been gifts to the house. A Duncan Phyfe dining table was set for twenty places and looked formal enough for a banquet.

Mr. Beck told us about a service which is the most far-reaching of any the Urban Center provides. It is a unique course in community planning and methods of communication between different ethnic groups. The students are housed in two different residences, ten to each house, and they join up three times a day for discussions over the dining table.

324

"Do the students do the cooking?" I asked.

"Oh, no. Most of the residents do some kind of volunteer work, but to prepare three meals a day for twenty people we hire a cook."

And on the subject of food, Mr. Beck told us about a Henry Street program which provides about two hundred old people of the neighborhood one nourishing hot meal a day. Most of them are Jewish and Puerto Rican with a sprinkling of blacks. This brings about the dilemma of supplying a diversity of diets: kosher food for the orthodox Jews, native dishes for the Puerto Ricans, and soul food for the blacks. "But our problem was solved by sheer luck," said Mr. Beck. "We happened on a black chef who is an expert in all three styles: kosher, Puerto Rican, and soul. As a matter of fact, our neighborhood abounds in all sorts of ethnic cookery. Not far from here is Bernstein's Chinese-Kosher Restaurant.

"Most of the elderly people in the Henry Street program live on their Social Security checks alone, but they didn't want free meals. They arranged a price to fit their slim purses—sixty cents for lunch. They know it costs more but they don't want anything that smacks of being a 'soup kitchen.'

"Every program at Henry Street is initiated and monitored by the people who use it. Our programs are as diverse, therefore, as human need," Mr. Beck went on. "Volunteers from the neighborhood run a credit union where members of the community can pool their small savings as in a bank. In time of need, loans are available at such a low interest rate that they're offered a real alternative to the loan sharks who used to infest the neighborhood.

"Then we have another program that operates during the hot months, a summer camp at Echo Hill. Every day a different group of a hundred and fifty parents and children leaves here for an hour's free bus trip to a camp where they can breathe invisible air and have a little country relaxation."

We crossed the lobby to the living quarters of Mr. and Mrs.

Beck and their two adorable little girls. Their home is furnished with fine Federal pieces; apparently Mrs. Beck is an expert on that period.

Next door to the executive house stands an ancient building, which was New York's first fire station and is still in service. "Firehouse red!" Helen exclaimed. "Is there any other color half so dramatic?"

A fire engine clanged down Henry Street, returning from a call. The up-to-date engine and firemen entered a station house which could have belonged in a Currier and Ives print.

For no apparent reason its original ornate façade had been embellished with bas-reliefs of tiger heads. "The firehouse was installed by Tammany Boss Tweed," said Mr. Beck. "In his eyes it was Art with a capital A. The old crook so admired those cast-iron tigers that he chose a tiger as the symbol for Tammany Hall."

Turning the corner from Henry Street, we passed a group of children playing hopscotch on the sidewalk. They looked extremely normal and healthy. "I doubt *those* kids provide any problems of crime or dope," I remarked. But Mr. Beck quickly disabused me.

"Of course we have those problems," he said. "They're a part of childhood in every quarter of the city. This is no reflection on New York. It's the same all over the country. And even with the enormous publicity focused on the problem, I doubt that most people realize its awful prevalence.

"In our Youth Development program we involve many young drug users who give up drugs when they join the youth movement. Those with a strong physical addiction are referred to local treatment centers. It's tragic that many young addicts seeking the methadone cure must be placed on waiting lists because, despite public concern about addiction, sufficient facilities aren't provided to cure addicts who want to be cured."

Then there is the Music School, a honeycomb of small studios and practice rooms. It is all in the care of Mr. Frierson, who, besides his duties at the Urban Center, conducts programs of Afro-American music in public schools throughout New York.

That day Mr. Frierson was jubilant over a gift to the school: an electric organ. "It just happens to be one of the few instruments we didn't have," he told us. "It was used in the pit of the Danny Kaye musical, *Two By Two*, and when the show closed, its producer, Dick Rodgers, sent it down to the Urban Center."

The Music School offers instruction in every instrument. (We dropped in on a very young lady wrestling with a flute. "She must make her neighbors happy with *that*," observed Helen.)

On leaving the Music School I asked Mr. Beck, "Are there evidences of extraordinary talent among any of the present pupils?"

"Plenty! I want you to see one of the movies the children have made over at our Film Club."

The film department is in another modern building, and in its hallway hangs a dramatic poster reading, "Film Your Way to Hollywood!"

"Hollywood!" I exclaimed. "Little do they know how much that image has been tarnished."

In the large main studio young film makers in a state of excess energy, if not downright euphoria, were conferring with their teacher, Bruce Spiegel. It was as if those students realized their exceptional luck. For experience in film making is hard to come by. The equipment for any other art requires a small financial outlay, but the cost of raw film is almost prohibitive. And these kids are getting all they need of it, supplied in part by donations and in part purchased with a grant from the New York State Council on the Arts.

Mr. Spiegel ran a film entitled *Crime Is a Hurting Thing*, written, directed, and produced by sixteen-year-old Robert Cuadrado. The actors were even younger. The main character, a boy of about ten, was up to such advanced tricks as mugging, picking a lock by inserting a cellophane strip, and other acts that are eloquent of how much today's youngsters know about crime.

In this movie crime did *not* pay and the little outlaw's career ended in the grip of a big cop. The only adult in the film, he looked as if he were a genuine policeman.

I thought the film very moving because it was naïve and utterly sincere.

"And," said Helen, "because its creators weren't mad at anybody."

Now, at last, we came upon the lodestar that drew us down to the lower East Side in the first place: the Neighborhood Playhouse. In the past the beauty of the old building was obscured by a huddle of shabby shops and tenements. It was a jewel badly set. Now it shines forth in full loveliness on a spacious plaza.

In its spick-and-span white lobby we found a plaque that read:

This Playhouse is a gift to
The Henry Street Settlement
from
Mr. and Mrs. Louis W. Abrons
and
Mr. and Mrs. Herman Gettner

Helen observed, "How much of the beauty and culture of this city comes from our great Jewish philanthropists. Weren't we lucky that most of their antecedents stopped right here after they stumbled ashore at Ellis Island with their bundles and their families! They might have pressed on, and then Peoria or Kalamazoo would have been the center of the world's culture."

Inside, the small theatre is of the same classic proportions as the exterior. It is decorated in restrained elegance which, now that so many fine uptown playhouses have been demolished, makes it unique.

Helen swept the auditorium in a dramatic gesture. "What a waste that this doesn't belong to the professional theatre! Why do we overlook the fact that the actual playhouse is an important part of theatregoing? It makes me sad to think of the ardent young off-Broadway professionals who perform in squalid surroundings when they might be able to strut forth in this lovely place."

Helen was mollified when Mr. Adna Karns, director of the theatre, told us that the Playhouse is in constant use and a center of life in the community, even though its working sections are impractical for professional productions: the stage too shallow, no facilities for modern lighting.

"But just the same," said Helen, "I'll never forget a stunning production of *The Dybbuk* in which a beautiful young girl named Mary Ellis earned stardom way back in the Twenties."

Mr. Beck intervened. "Don't ever think our modest workshop has no impact on the profession today. Last season a group of students put on an original play called *Black Girl*. It was such a hit that it was moved to a major off-Broadway playhouse, the Theatre de Lys, and is having a successful run there. During the coming season *Black Girl* will be sent on a commercial tour by the firm of Needlander. And we plan soon to do a review of the best skits of our old *Grand Street Follies*."

"Save us two seats for the opening!"

"Walter Matthau and Red Buttons began their careers on this stage," Mr. Beck added. "Donald Oenslager, the stage designer, has been helping us to raise money to improve our facilities, and Sammy Cahn, the famous lyricist, has established a scholarship to help other neighborhood youngsters get their start here. Our alumni don't forget us. Only recently Tony Curtis heard that the floor of our stage was wearing thin. So he called me up and said, 'Put in a new floor, Bert, and send me the bill.' "

We left the Urban Center that day with the impression of having visited a model city, equipped with every new convenience and backed by the culture and tradition of the past. Also, we were beginning to suspect that the only *true* underprivileged youth in New York live on Park Avenue.

As we passed Attorney Street, Helen stopped the car for a moment. "This is the very street where Jacob Javits spent his boyhood. He was born down here in the urban counterpart of a log cabin, the janitor's basement in a tenement.

"Jack's father earned the family's rent as a janitor, but to provide food he worked at his trade as a pantsmaker. The mother sold dry goods from a pushcart. It was here that Jacob, as a youth, witnessed the corruption of the Tammany political machine; watched the payoff system in operation, with its bribes to the police and the city's higher-ups."

"Just like today."

"But the city has a Jacob Javits. And even if it still has a certain amount of corruption—what city is without it?—there are men like him who won't allow it to go too far too long. The day of opportunity isn't over in the New York ghettos. Jack's story proves *that*."

Helen's encomium to her friend sent me off to buy a copy of Jack's memoirs, *Order of Battle*, written after he was elected to the U. S. Senate. No tribute to a New York ghetto as a forcing ground for character and achievement can be more poignant than the book's closing paragraph:

"I will always believe that the United States is a unique land touched with that wondrous idea that the least of us, the most faltering of us, has a right to justice under law, liberty, and equal opportunity."

NEW YORK—YES OR NO?

*O*ur adventure was drawing to a close. Time had come, it seemed to me, for a stocktaking of both the good and the bad. For there was no denying that some pretty awful things were happening around town. In some cases Nature was the culprit, but all too often mankind was to blame. Murders, rapes, burglaries, and muggings were daily occurrences.

"Looking back, it seems to me New York has let us down," I said to Helen in a phone talk one morning.

"But, Anita darling, we are, after all, citizens of the Planet Earth and it's a pretty rugged place. Just the same, enough of the best things are right here. And if you let the place exasperate you, at least you've got a lifetime job that's pretty fascinating: trying to make it better."

"What a chance! When outsiders complain that New Yorkers come upon violence in the streets and don't even stop to look, let alone try to help the victims."

"But that isn't particular to New York. If it were, there'd never have been the parable of the Good Samaritan. Oh, I do agree that violence has made us apathetic; it's part of this New York sophistication—the fear of being 'square.' Well, I'm a square and thank heaven for it."

"There's a new cause for you, Helen. Liberate the squares."

"That's just what I hope our book will do."

"Well, in a spirit of fair play, let's talk things over once more before we turn our manuscript in."

Helen came up with a bright suggestion. "Let's go back to Whyte's tomorrow and hold a conference over a delicious sea-food luncheon, just as we did when our project began."

Her suggestion only added to my gloom. "Haven't you heard that Whyte's has closed down?"

Helen was stunned. "It doesn't seem possible—after all these years! Why, the place was blooming when we were last there."

"That doesn't mean a thing in this town. Any building may be torn down to make way for another of those glass menageries you love. And Whyte's isn't the only place we've counted on that's failed us. Last Saturday I went over to the 42nd Street Library and found the doors bolted."

Helen sighed. "I know. I've had a letter from Mrs. Sulzberger's Committee that explained the cutdown in services. And if money doesn't appear from an unexpected source, some departments will have to close for good."

"Well, what about our lunch tomorrow?"

At this point Gladys, who was watering our indoor garden within earshot, spoke up. "Why don't you two go to Whyte's?"

"But it's closed."

"Oh, I don't mean *that* Whyte's. There's a branch in the next block. It's been there for years. And you can eat outdoors in a beautiful garden."

Somewhat chastened over my ignorance of my own neighborhood, I turned back to the phone. "We can still have that fish lunch tomorrow. Gladys says there's a branch of Whyte's nearby."

This was enough to give Helen's downtrodden spirits a lift. "You see! The one thing that will never fail us in New York is surprise."

Our lunch in Whyte's big garden was pretty enchanting, I had to admit. Since the old Fulton Street Market was abolished, our fish came from the Bronx, but it had traveled well.

Those delights, however, didn't prevent me from bringing up some discouraging news. Two of our most irreplaceable citizens had just been forced out of action: Irving Rosenthal, who ran Palisades Park and made life zestful for the poor, and Mainbocher, who gave the rich something worth paying for.

332

"But," said Helen, "you can't pin Main's closing exclusively on New York. Women won't pay for fine handwork any longer. Don't forget that Balenciaga gave up several years ago in Paris."

I had to admit the truth of that.

"What will Main do now?" Helen asked.

"He plans to settle down in Munich where there's a zoo he adores. It's kept immaculately clean, Main said, because people must pay admission. We New Yorkers feel contempt for anything that's free, and so we desecrate our zoos with litter."

That got us back on the subject of Palisades Park, which had been such a clean and happy haven for us all. "It's been sold to a construction corporation from Dallas," I said. "And to let Dallas dismantle that old place is pretty depressing."

"Your friend Irving Rosenthal loves that park. How will he put in his time?"

"When we last talked, Irving said he was going to move it all to a new location."

"*Move?* Move a roller coaster and all that gigantic paraphernalia? Good Lord!" Helen cocked an eye at me. "Mr. Rosenthal isn't so young either, is he?"

"He's young enough to move the whole megillah over to Weehawken."

"Well, there's a New Yorker for you! That's one bit of good news."

"*Good?* What's good about moving to Weehawken?"

Helen warned, "Quiet, Anita! Or I might drag you *there* to find out what's good."

I changed the subject.

"Oh pooh!" said Helen in slang which to her is the last word. "You're just a Gloomy Gus."

"All right! Let me tell you about the visit I had from Christopher Isherwood last week. He was in town from Santa Monica for a few days and he asked, 'Do you feel it's safe to live in New York?' Coming from a lesser mind, I wouldn't have taken the question seriously. But from Chris . . ."

"What did you say to him?"

"Well, I reminded him of a few awful things that happened in his locality. A young man we both knew had been murdered as he was leaving a restaurant on La Cienega Boulevard. A panhandler had approached him for money. Our friend was slow in fumbling for it, so the thug shot him. A life was snuffed out in less time than I'm taking to tell it.

"Of course, I also brought up the Tate murders and the riots in Watts. 'Well,' said Chris, 'maybe we *aren't* any safer out there in God's country.' Even so, we can't overlook the fact that some pretty important New Yorkers have deserted us of their own volition. For instance, S. J. Perelman has settled for good in London."

"Y-e-s," Helen agreed reluctantly. "And how it delighted the *Times* to publish all his nasty reasons." She asked if I had a copy of that article. I had. From the time we'd started to explore New York, our friends had showered us with clippings, brochures, advice, and advertisements. And I'd put them all together in a file.

"After lunch I'd like to go through that file," said Helen, the indefatigable researcher.

So back at my apartment I dragged forth my portable file. Together we started to examine the incriminating evidence.

The first clippings I pulled out were articles by Perelman and two other prominent deserters: Saul Bellow, who had done us the definitive insult of settling in Chicago, and Brooks Atkinson, who had moved to Durham, a rural community upstate.

Helen started to scan the articles for quotes, much as if she were in a bad play and was looking for plugs to put in the Sunday ads. Presently her face brightened. "Here's something cheerful from Perelman." She read: " 'New York may seem a chameleon, volatile city but, deep down, the old values persist.' "

I couldn't believe that such a serious observation came from that reliable old jokesmith. "Did S. J. really say that?"

"Read it yourself, Anita." Then, chuckling, she added, "And

wouldn't it serve Perelman right if he goes through a year of London climate and finds out his biggest laugh is on himself?"

My skepticism returned as I read on. "The rest of this is just pure poison!"

At this gloomy juncture I was summoned to the phone by a young friend, a hard-working Park Avenue debutante who holds down a public-relations job. I cut her short to get back to Helen. "It was Cissy. She only phoned to say she's exhausted. She blames it on the smog."

Oddly enough, Cissy's complaint began to pull me out of the doldrums and I grinned. "Cissy leaves her office at five, goes on to three cocktail parties, a show, supper at a discothèque, and gets to bed at two. Next morning at around eight fifty she hits the sidewalk, at race-track speed, to get to her job at nine. And she claims it's the smog that exhausts her."

"If you ask me," said Helen, "she proves our smog is full of vitamins."

Back at work, we began to dissect an article by Saul Bellow. And there Helen struck pure gold. " 'What is barely hinted in other American cities, is condensed and enlarged in New York. On every street, people are taught what life is like. . . .' "

"Stop!" I cried. "Don't press your luck by reading any more."

But Brooks Atkinson was reassuring: "My day doesn't commence until the New York newspapers arrive. . . . If the day doesn't begin with them, it has no foundation."

"That blessed Brooks!" Helen exclaimed. "He admits he can only stand Durham because New York exists down here, giving him a reason for living."

Feeling heartened, I mentioned another old friend, who had visited our town for the first time last year. An urbane Italian, Gino Degli Innocenti manages the Hotel Pace at Montecatini where Helen and I have luxuriated together in the past. The Pace is the quintessence of splendor, with its own private park and an enormous swimming pool. Inside, the décor is Edwardian at its most opulent: marble columns, crystal chandeliers, Persian rugs; bathrooms of Carrara marble, supplied twice daily with fresh towels in six different sizes. The Pace staff changes uniforms three times a day. The cuisine is superb. Its top floor is generally occupied by some reigning royalty, complete with retinue.

"Gino came over for a convention of hotel managers," I told Helen. "In those dear departed days, the rate of exchange was so much in our favor that it made all Europeans poor. So the conventioneers were assigned to second-rate hotels in the Broadway area.

"Gino brought along his collegiate son, Paolo, to show him the city. One day I went to pick them up for a sightseeing tour and, thinking of their elegant style of life at home, I was appalled by their awful surroundings: an untidy lobby with vulgar noisy guests and all the appurtenances of a razzmatazz environment. I was primed to apologize for that dreadful hotel, when Gino stopped me by bursting out, 'I never dreamed New York could be so marvelous!' "

"Was Gino trying to be polite?"

"That's what I thought until later on, at Fifth Avenue and 59th, we stopped to let his son take an angle snapshot of the General Motors building." (While Paolo focused on GM, passing females focused on Paolo.) "Then Gino told me, 'I'm arranging for the boy to become an American citizen and to live in New York.' "

"Ah!" said Helen. "I think I see what Gino meant by that accolade of his. He was talking about the *spirit* of New York—its vitality. As a native Tuscan he recognizes that another Renaissance is coming into focus here. He wants his son to have a part in it."

It's certainly true that things which might exist calmly elsewhere take on a special kind of drama here. A glance out the window of the very room where Helen and I were talking provides unfailing entertainment. To live across the street from Carnegie Hall is as exciting as living in Disneyland. I shudder to think how close the old Hall came to being battered down by that big iron ball before it was saved by the unlikely combination of the cosmetic queen Elizabeth Arden and Isaac Stern, the violin virtuoso.

And so the entire neighborhood continues to be diverted by the circus that goes on at Carnegie Hall. During June the street in front of it becomes a costume ball. Sometimes five or six graduation exercises take place there in a single day. The sidewalks are blocked by boy and girl graduates, each group of caps and gowns a different color, red, green, yellow, black, white. The majority are graduates of Harlem schools, and watching them mill about 57th Street, I think they could teach the white students how to carry off a graduation robe with high style.

Sometimes, I must admit, I am chilled when I contemplate the young. Recently I looked out my front window late at night and saw two teen-age streetwalkers laughing and chatting with their pimps. How tragic! Then, another midnight I watched a hundred or more hairy teen-agers of both sexes asleep on the sidewalk in the rain, protected by tarpaulins, blankets, and the Sunday *Times*. They were waiting for the box office to open eighteen hours later. "There were just as many of them waiting for that Heifetz concert," I told Helen, "as there'd been for the Beatles."

"The new youth!" she said. "Sleeping all night on the cement in order to hear a classical concert."

"Mrs. Heifetz took pity on the kids and drove up in her limousine around 6:00 A.M. with coffee and doughnuts."

Her optimism soaring, Helen recalled an encounter last summer with a poetry-reading group. "Its sessions are held outdoors on the rickety old Morton Street pier. It's run by Cicero and Janet Codina. There are no rules, no dues, and anyone who wants to be a poet can be."

Cicero told Helen, "We read our own works in Hindi, German, Spanish, Hebrew, and Italian. We have one Yoga poet who recites while standing on his head. Anywhere else he'd have to do it in hiding. New York, you see, understands."

Back at that file of mine, she found an item quoting someone in the know, Dr. Morton Bard, professor of psychology at City University, who had once been a policeman. "These New York cats," said Dr. Bard, "have a kind of internal discipline. So, when external discipline gives out, their innards are there to take over. And it's possible to survive!"

Then Helen pulled from the depths of my cache an item about Police Chief Edward Davis of Los Angeles. He instructed residents of Southern California to "bar your doors, buy a police dog, call on the police whenever they're available. *And pray.*"

"Give me that article to send to Chris Isherwood," I said.

Helen's time was running out and we had to abandon the file. "But never mind, darling, we'll get back to it on Monday."

By Monday morning I'd gone through my file from the point where we'd left off. So when Helen showed up for our *really* final session I was ready.

"Let's go on with the foreign views," I suggested. "Now we know how some Italians feel about us, let's see what the French and British have to say. Here's an interview with Raymundo de Larrain, a distinguished French designer, choreographer, director, and producer, and the man who launched Nureyev after he escaped to the free world. Listen to this:

" 'The French will not be happy with what I have to say, but I happen to know that French designers come to New York for inspiration. They go to Central Park, Greenwich Village, and to private parties and then they depart from New York with a portfolio full of ideas. One hippie in the Village can inspire a whole new trend. . . .

" 'This is the only country in the world with two completely opposite cultures: The Establishment wants to get to the moon; the hippies want to get back to earth. That's why people keep young here. In France we put an age on everybody.' "

Next came a British view sent me by our friend Cathleen Nesbitt. (Cathleen played the beautiful, silver-haired mother of Rex Harrison's Henry Higgins in *My Fair Lady*. With great regret she'd left her long-time home in New York because her family wanted her back with them in London.) Cathleen's contribution was an article by Jean Campbell, titled "New York, We Love You," which said:

"Why do we English exports live in New York? We're told it's dirty, dangerous, disorganized and expensive. Yet we wouldn't trade our uncertain New York lives for all the certain charms of London. Of course it takes a definite kind of nature to love New York, but given that nature, we wither and sicken in our own cities. Most human beings are driven to seek security and comfort. But there is another group that can only thrive on change and the unexpected. Anything that stinks of monotony gives us the willy billies."

Helen grabbed the clipping to scan it herself. "And how about this:

" 'Possibly the career of Alex Phillips supplies the most revealing answer to why foreigners love New York. He left London because the firm he worked for told him he wouldn't be able to go into management; he was too young at twenty-four to be handed responsibility. Alex arrived in New York, enrolled at Columbia Business School, and after two years founded a company for public relations. Today he has a staff of fifteen and he's not yet forty. "In New York," says Alex, "they give the young a chance. They take risks. In London, business has to be the way it was centuries ago.

" ' "Whenever I see New York at night a terrific surge of love comes over me. New York is hope and challenge; good and evil; mystery and change and, most of all, the unexpected. The feeling I have for this city is akin to sexual love. It lies here waiting like a mistress for her demon lover at the very beginning of the affair." ' "

Another testimonial from a Briton, the critic Alan Pryce-Jones, who has lived here many years: "The gutters overflow and nothing ever works but I know now I shall live and die here. Anything I do is all right just as long as I make a go of it. Last night my water pipe burst at 3:00 A.M. I had to figure a way to mend it. And I did!"

Perhaps the most valuable nugget in our whole gold mine is a letter from Deputy Commissioner Malito of the Department of Public Events, enclosing a list of annual parades. This record of events, which sets New Yorkers marching, follows:

March 17	*St. Patrick's Day*
	(Our parade brings people all the way from Ireland who've never seen its like, even in Dublin)
May 2	*Loyalty Day*
May 16	*Armed Forces Day*
May 17	A double feature:
	The Greeks in Manhattan
	The Norwegian-Americans in the Bronx
May 25	*Martin Luther King*
June 1	*Salute to Israel*
June 5	*Brooklyn Sunday Schools*
June 8	*Puerto Ricans*
June 14	*Spanish Christian Children*
Sept. 20	*General von Steuben*
Sept. 21	*Afro-Americans*
Oct. 5	*General Pulaski*
Oct. 11	*Hispanic Day*
Oct. 12	*Columbus Day*
Oct. 19	*Massing of the Colors*
Nov. 11	*Veterans Day*
Nov. 27	*Thanksgiving*

But that list by no means tells the whole story. We have glorious protest parades for special groups: homosexuals march proudly to the Sheep Meadow in Central Park and hold a "gay in"; Liberated Women crash saloons, en masse, and win their inalienable right to plant their ground-grippers on a bar rail. Our half a million Italians hold a parade to protest that they're not Mafiosi. What an adorably childlike demonstration until their leader got shot as a Mafioso; maybe by another, who knows?

"But then," said Helen, "perhaps people's ties are strengthened by this violence: by getting trapped together in traffic snarls or flooded out of subways or jumped on in hallways and overtaxed by the State Government or overcharged by taxis.

"But in spite of it all, New Yorkers get to their jobs, just like your little Cissy, and keep the city running in high gear.

"And just think of the things we've done here that one can't do anywhere else in the world. And most of them for free."

"Well, don't forget we've had pretty special treatment," I reminded her.

"You mean free lunches and guided tours? True. But for the most part we've wandered around by ourselves. We've hardly spent a dime except for bus tokens, taxi fares, and an occasional meal out.

"But the more we've done," Helen added, "the more we've realized how much we were missing. A lifetime isn't long enough to cover New York even once over lightly. It's like trying to shampoo an elephant with a toothbrush!"

But the most positive thing of all is that nobody ever has to be alone in New York. You're alone *with* New York, which makes a whole world of difference. What other companionship could be so varied, stimulating, dramatic, and so available?

For Helen and me the city has widened our lines of vision; no longer are they bound by Broadway, Park Avenue, and 57th Street. We've met characters so unique that we'll never forget them.

Val Wenzel, for one, keeps in touch with us, and asks us to parties on the old South Street dock. We often think of him and all the others. "Hi there, Val!" "Yoo-hoo, Mr. Raguso!" "How's it going, Ophelia, honey?" "Greetings, Your Eminence." "Hello, Charlie Dempsey, what's the score?"

The best quote from all our reading matter we kept for last. It is an accolade to our city by the Welsh author James Morris, the final paragraph of his book *The Great Port*. I handed it to Helen. "Just read this section, won't you?"

"But I've already read it."

"Read it again—out loud. I'd like to hear this paragraph in a Helen Hayes rendition."

A little quizzically she began:

" 'And so in the end I was left, like so many voyagers before me, trapped by the great port. I loathed it like a lover. The questions it asked I resented; the answers it gave I mistrusted; the spell of it, the chivvying of conscience, the temptations, the delight, I felt to be unfair. Damn you, New York! Damn the bright sweep of your spaces, and the ungainly poetry of your names! A curse on all your archipelago, and on those rough fresh winds off your Bay—which, catching me like an embrace as I stepped out of the helicopter, so often ravished my spirits, and made my heart sing!' "

I wish Helen would make a recording of that prose poem for every love-hater of New York to hear. It left me pretty limp.

All the same, my stubborn answer as to whether it's possible to live a good life in New York had to be the same as the answer to every riddle since the Sphinx was built: "Yes *and* no."

"Darling, you're wrong," Helen countered. "The answer lies buried in the minds and hearts of all the people in New York. And if they'd only stop repeating stupid clichés, if they'd dig down through the phony attitude they call 'sophistication,' they'd know the answer is 'Definitely *Yes*!' "

Glad to be contradicted, I gave in.

"Lordy, Anita, what a relief! Now we can relax and I'll be back in my garden the first thing in the morning."

Suddenly her face clouded over.

"What's wrong?"

"Oh, nothing. I just remembered how many places we never got to: those small museums, the restaurants with all the different kinds of native dishes; the little libraries, and hundreds of odd specialty shops. There's a place Sylvia Sidney told me about, a cubbyhole at the wrong end of Madison Avenue that deals in nothing but antique buttons."

"And what about the herb shop we passed on Carmine Street in the Village? Remember the sign over the door that read 'Aphrodisia'? But the place was closed that day."

"So now we'll never know about it, will we?"

"Well, I know something about it because I sent for a catalogue."

This booklet explained that the shop could make no legal claim that its products were aphrodisiacs but then went on to list some erotic-sounding nostrums that set one's brain to whirling. Grains of Paradise, Passion Flower, Devil's Shoestring, Black Cohosh, Buchu Leaves, Fo-Ti-Teng, Mugwort, Szechuan Pepper, Hi-John-the-Conqueror, Skullcap, Tonka Beans, Valerian Root, and Wahoo Bark.

I was mentioning a few of those magic potions when Helen interrupted. "Oh shoot! And to think we never got inside that place."

She looked so dejected that I ventured a suggestion. "After all, it hasn't disappeared, you know. It's still right there on Carmine Street."

Helen was silent, but only for a moment. "How about my picking you up here about noon tomorrow?"

And we were right back where we started.